THE TIME IS
OUT OF JOINT

THE TIME IS
OUT OF JOINT

Skepticism in Shakespeare's England

Benjamin Bertram

DELAWARE

Newark: University of Delaware Press

Associated University Presses
2010 Eastpark Boulevard
Cranbury, NJ 08512

The paper used in this publication meets the requirements of the American National Standard for Permanence of Paper for Printed Library Materials Z39.48-1984.

Library of Congress Cataloging-in-Publication Data

Bertram, Benjamin, 1967–
    The time is out of joint : skepticism in Shakespeare's England / Benjamin Bertram.
        p.   cm.
    Includes bibliographical references and index.
    ISBN 0-87413-885-X (alk. paper)
    1. English literature—Early modern, 1500–1700—History and criticism. 2. Skepticism in literature.   3. Shakespeare, William, 1564–1616—Philosophy.   4. Marlowe, Christopher, 1564–1593—Philosophy.   5. Scot, Reginald, 1538?–1599—Philosophy.   6. Hariot,   Thomas, 1560–1621—Philosophy.   7. Skepticism—History—17th century.   8. Skepticism—History—16th century.   I. Title.
    PR428.S59B47   2004
    820.9′384—dc22   2004011343

For Judy

Contents

Acknowledgments

THE RESEARCH FOR THIS BOOK BEGAN AT THE UNIVERSITY OF CALI-
fornia, San Diego, where I benefited from the intellectual generosity and moral support of many people, especially Louis
Montrose and Don Wayne. Stephanie Jed, Masao Miyoshi, and
Robert Westman were also vital to my growth as a graduate
student at U.C.S.D. I am also indebted to Marcus Hellyer,
Karen Raber, David Kuchta, and other members of the graduate group for the study of the early modern period who gave
thoughtful comments at the dissertation phase. Richard
Abrams, my colleague and friend at the University of Southern
Maine, offered extensive criticism of the entire manuscript and
helped me out of many jams.

Over the years the intellectual stimulation provided by conver-
sations with my friend Andrew Zimmerman has been indispens-
able and the wise counsel of Rabbi Harry Z. Sky guided me
through the final stages of the writing. I owe special thanks to
Elaine Rosen, who has been a great editor and a real mensch. I also
wish to thank my parents, Ed and Alice Bertram, who have never
wavered in their support of my education, hopes, and ambitions.

In the course of writing the book I received a Faculty Senate
Research Grant from the University of Southern Maine that
enabled me to spend a Summer in London working at the British Library. I would also like to express my gratitude to William Sherman and other interlocutors at the Shakespeare
Association of America who listened to my ideas about Christopher Marlowe. In addition, I thank the participants of
GEMCS and NEMLA who raised important questions about
my work on Thomas Harriot and Shakespeare, respectively. I
also profited in important ways from the detailed criticism of
the anonymous readers at the University of Delaware Press.
The support of Donald Mell, the chair of the editorial board at
Delaware, will not be soon forgotten.

Finally, this book is dedicated with love to my wife Judy,
who has been the pattern of all patience.

THE TIME IS
OUT OF JOINT

Introduction

WHEN ELIZABETHAN PLAYGOERS HEARD HAMLET ANNOUNCE THAT "the time is out of joint," they may well have thought about the social and intellectual dislocations that were then troubling their own society. Tumultuous changes brought about by the Reformation, the emergence of capitalism, and state-formation affected most areas of life. Even after Protestantism took a firm hold of the nation during Elizabeth's reign, the Queen's subjects could not have felt very certain about religious doctrines that remained in a state of flux. It is not surprising that they found themselves resistant to such confusing changes. In fact, church authorities often complained, as Richard Greenham did, of the "intractableness, and unteachableness" of churchgoers. One wonders what the church had to say about the spiritual outlook of a man who, on his deathbed, told his minister that "his soul . . . was a great bone in his body; and what should become of his soul after he was dead, that if he had done well he should be put into a pleasant green meadow."[1] Authorities' attempts to propagate notions of social order did little to stabilize the nation, either, as social mobility, riots, and rebellions continued to defy the traditional hierarchical scheme, the Great Chain of Being.

The skepticism of Reginald Scot (1538–99), Thomas Harriot (1560–1621), Christopher Marlowe (1564–93), and William Shakespeare (1564–1616) grew out of these dislocations. Reginald Scot responded to the persecution of witches by taking the bold, virtually unheard-of position that witchcraft was a leftover fiction from Catholicism. Scot was also aware of the economic predicament in English village life that led to most accusations of witchcraft: the poorest members of the community, typically women, were blamed for various misfortunes such as the death of a child, the sickness of an animal, or the destruction of a barn. Thomas Harriot, who was often defamed as a "conjuror" for his religious doubt and scientific experimentation, wrote the finest early English ethnography of the North American Indians. His detailed and receptive cultural analysis suggested that many of the religious and social truths the English authorities struggled to maintain as absolute, permanent, and everywhere the same were in fact relative and contingent.

Shakespeare and Marlowe grappled especially with the economic contradictions that emerged during this time of change: self-advancement and the desire for monetary gain beyond one's position at birth grew more common and acceptable even as the church and state insisted people remain in their God-given position; capital investment became crucial to the livelihood of many even as the Bible informed them of the immorality of usury; and the state responded to the startling rise in numbers of vagabonds and beggars with brutal poor laws that placed them in work houses, punished them inhumanely, or banished them. As we will see, these two dramatists revealed in their work that such economic turbulence was having a deep skeptical impact on both religion and epistemology.

Because *Hamlet* reads almost as a compendium of English culture at the turn of the seventeenth century, it provides an ideal introduction to the social context of skepticism. Hamlet's skepticism fuels much of his well-known irresoluteness. In his third soliloquy—"To be or not to be"—Hamlet borrows a move from classical skepticism, "equipollence," weighing two opposing possibilities and suspending judgment.[2] The soliloquy suggests that even something so fundamental to Christianity as the afterlife could be called into question. By the end of his rumination, death becomes "the undiscover'd country" that "puzzles the will," and this lack of knowledge about hell or damnation leaves Hamlet undecided whether to "take arms against a sea of troubles." He not only questions the idea of punishment in the afterlife, he criticizes specific social practices and institutions—speaking of the "law's delay," or, in the first quarto, "the orphan wronged" and "the widow oppressed."[3] Given such doubts about the hereafter, the "whips and scorns of time" are especially severe to those with little ability to enact social change, those who must regard suffering as a cruel fate that may never be redressed even in the afterlife. Thus the socioeconomic situation fuels much of the uncertainty in the play.

Moreover, despite its many references to the Reformation, *Hamlet* does not adhere to an entirely Protestant worldview. For example, Shakespeare places King Hamlet's ghost in the fires of purgatory, a notion that was rejected by Protestants.[4] The Reformation had not managed entirely to sweep away the debris of older pagan and Catholic practices. Historians remain uncertain about the extent to which the English population had moved beyond the old religion by the end of the sixteenth century. A minority continued openly to practice Catholicism, yet the bigger problem for the Anglican Church was weaning the common people off the old daily rituals and "superstitions." For centuries people had relied on charms, prayers, and blessings to protect themselves from anything ranging from the devil to inclement weather. As we will see in chapter one, Reginald Scot traced the source of ungodly superstition to Catholicism: "these conjurors have gotten them offices in the church of Rome, wherby they have obteined authorite and great estimation."[5] His fellow Protestants would agree that the Catholic church was filled with charlatans, but they would deny that witchcraft was a mere fiction. Such expressions of doubt about fundamental religious truths were inevitable in a society undergoing drastic religious change. If people were torn between different ways of performing daily religious practices, might they not, like Hamlet, come to question something as basic as the punishment of sin in the afterlife? The existence of competing religions and smaller sects could lead some to wonder which path to take for salvation, or if there even was such a path.

Religious doubt takes a number of forms in *Hamlet*, including the curiously unorthodox materialism of the gravediggers and the prince. In act five, the gravediggers point out that Ophelia is given a Christian burial only because she is one of the "great folk," the aristocracy, a charge that is confirmed by the priest. Immediately after these comments on the power of the court, the gravedigger jokes about what happens to human corpses after death. He replaces the eternal laws of salvation posited by Christian dogma with an account of how long it takes for a body to decay: "A tanner will last nine year," the gravedigger tells Hamlet, because "his hide is so tanned with his trade that a will keep out water a great while, and your water is a sore decayer of your whoreson dead body" (5.1.163–

66). Impressed by the gravedigger's wit, Hamlet builds on his materialist outlook, speculating about Alexander the Great's ultimate end: "To what base uses we may return, Horatio! Why, may not imagination trace the noble dust of Alexander till a find it stopping a bung-hole?" (5.1.197–98). We can imagine how significant these skeptical views would have been to an audience accustomed to hearing Elizabethan homilies on the fear of death. Of all the reasons for fearing death, one homily warns, the most important is the legitimate, indeed essential, fear of the "condemnation both of body and soul (without either appellation, or hope of redemption) unto everlasting pains in hell."[6] An audience might well have found refreshing secularity in this alternative to the Christian concern over eternal damnation.[7] Of course, some might also have found it terrifying: if there is no damnation, there is no salvation, either. Skeptical anxieties, as we shall see, tend to recur and build on themselves.

The ghost, one of the central tropes of revenge plays, must have baffled Elizabethans, for whom questions about the afterlife were rather more acute than they are for us today. Audiences would have been especially intrigued by the figure of pathological estrangement pervading Hamlet's Denmark, the "thing" or "perturbed spirit" signaling that the "time is out of joint." The discourse of the supernatural in *Hamlet* contributed to Elizabethan debates on the assumptions behind beliefs in ghosts, demons, and purgatory. The questions raised in the play—what does the ghost signify? what is it? does it really exist or is it just a hallucination?—were pressing outside the confines of the theater. A great many popular practices, including prayers for the dead in purgatory or ceremonies for bringing dead spirits into the world, depended on the answers to these questions.

Horatio's empiricism (he believes in the ghost only when he has actually seen it) is an echo of Reginald Scot's skepticism toward popular beliefs in fairies, ghosts, witches, and demons. After providing detailed descriptions of popular attempts to raise the dead, Scot denounces belief in ghosts not only because there is no ocular proof of their existence, but because they distract the nation from the proper Protestant worship of God. Ghosts, he insists, are mere fictions of "sicke folke, children, women, and cowards," who are fearful and weak in mind and body. Yet he also thanks God that "this wretched and cow-ardlie infidelitie, since the preaching of the gospell, is in part forgotten: and doubtles, the rest of those illusions will in short time (by God's grace) be detected and vanish awaie."[8] More-over, Scot denigrates belief in purgatory, declaring that it serves only to line the pockets of the Catholic church: giving money to the clergy in the hopes of having sins forgiven was widespread. Such skepticism toward ghosts was consistent with Scot's anti-Catholic position. As Keith Thomas has shown, sixteenth-century doubt about ghosts became a "shib-boleth which distinguished Protestant from Catholic almost as effectively as belief in the Mass or the Papal Supremacy."[9] Thus, reactions to *Hamlet* must have been wildly mixed, with some in Shakespeare's audience indulging a poetic fiction, a remainder from pre-Reformation days when ghosts were be-lieved to come from Purgatory,[10] while many others perhaps understood it literally, still believing in ghosts along with other such religious remnants from before the Reformation. The stage ghost clearly had an important place in the shifting sym-bolic meanings and practices of late Elizabethan life. Hence, the questions surrounding the status of the ghost in *Hamlet* re-flect the questions surrounding popular practices that were in flux.

Along with religion, there are many other areas of skeptical uncertainty in *Hamlet*. Commenting on how the wit of the gravedigger approaches his own, the Prince says, "We must speak by the card or equivocation will undo us . . . the age has grown so picked that the toe of the peasant comes so near the heel of the courtier he galls his kibe" (5.1.133–38). As the exist-ing social structure came under increasing stress from social mobility, many began to worry about their status and the very nature of order and degree. "Men of noble birth," Francis Bacon observed, "are noted to be envious towards new men when they rise; for the distance is altered; and it is like a deceit of the eye, that when others come on they think themselves go back."[11] Lawrence Stone points out that these changes "were generally regarded as a dangerously excessive degree of mobil-ity among nearly all groups."[12] Unease about the fluidity of rank was common, and, as historians have pointed out, the ide-ology of order preached in England hardly reflected the na-tion's complex, shifting social conditions. Rather, during this time authorities became more insistent about the traditional scheme of social order precisely because it was constantly under threat.[13]

Hamlet's remark about mobility alludes to the many peasant rebellions that further fomented political disorder throughout the sixteenth century.[14] Juxtaposing his remark about the rising peasant with his riddling language about social hierarchy, we find that the implicit commentary on economic change takes on skeptical meanings. He undermines the hierarchical model of the Great Chain of Being, which fixed all creatures in their God-given place as a model of an ideal, harmonious order. Thus Hamlet's metaphor for the social body of his time is horizontal rather than vertical:

> *Ham.* A man may fish with the worm that hath eat of
> a king, and eat of the fish that hath fed of that worm.
> *King* What dost thou mean by this?
> *Ham.* Nothing but to show you how a king may go a
> progress through the guts of a beggar.
>
> (4.3.27–31)

The grotesque riddle, a heterodox, materialist view of the afterlife, abandons any precise division between human beings and natural processes. The king, who has lived on lavish banquets, is ultimately consumed by the very beggars he has excluded, and the continual chain of feasting levels social differences. With the word "progress," Hamlet alludes to the royal progresses, the rituals of state power that were replacing the festive traditions of the plebeians. On the occasion of a royal procession or "progress," Elizabethans greeted their Queen with bonfires and bells, music and drinking. Such nationalistic celebrations became more common, and many Protestant authorities hoped they would serve as a substitute for the papist festivities held on saints days. By foregrounding the basic needs of the plebeians, Hamlet's materialist vision places a dark cloud over the joys of royal progresses. In fact, the social hardships manifested in the frequent riots of the sixteenth century lie behind Hamlet's carnivalesque version of the royal progress.[15]

John Donne, expressing consternation over the rising tide of doubt, follows Hamlet's lead by relating social dislocation and skepticism. Echoing Hamlet's line, "the time is out of joint," Donne writes in his *Anatomy of the World*: "Then, as mankind, so is the world's whole frame/Quite out of joint, almost created lame" (191–92).[16] But whereas Hamlet further unhinges his community through his "wild and whirling words," Donne longs to return to a time of greater moral certainty, a time when the individual was subsumed by the community:

> All just supply, and all Relation:
> Prince, Subject, Father, Sonne, are things forgot,
> For every man alone thinkes he hath got
> To be a Phoenix, and that there can bee
> None of that kinde, of which he is, but hee.

While Donne's poem, well known for its line "and new Philosophy cals all in doubt," is clearly referring to the new scientific ideas from Copernicus and Kepler, it is equally concerned with the social changes that destroy "cohaerance" and community. Everywhere he looks, Donne finds symptoms of cosmological and moral decay—people's identities have become fragmented, and they "lack conviction"; the bonds that tied people together into a greater collectivity have disintegrated. The poem suggests not that scientific ideas have created social change, but rather that chaos has broken out on all fronts. Donne dramatizes or perhaps overdramatizes the confusion of his society by linking the collapse of cosmic harmony to the death of what he nostalgically believes was once social harmony.

Donne's "new philosophy" refers to classical skepticism as well as to the new science. Richard Popkin's classic *The History of Skepticism* demonstrates that classical skepticism contributed to the debates of the Reformation and to the major intellectual controversies that led to modern philosophy.[17] Although Popkin is primarily interested in the history of ideas rather than social or cultural history, his work reminds us that classical skepticism played an active role in some of the most difficult religious and political transformations, especially the Reformation. The fact that Pyrrhonism, the earliest school of philosophical skepticism, contributed to religious debate and change is ironic, since its main goal was to avoid conflict and pain. For the Pyrrhonists of antiquity, the goal of skepticism was to make a "eunuch of reason": ideally, the devaluation of human reason (particularly of the Aristotelian and Platonic varieties) and the suspension of belief would bring the skeptic to a state of *ataraxia* or unperturbedness.

Popkin touches on the famous debate in the 1520s between Erasmus and Luther on the authority of scripture. Using classical skepticism to attack Luther's idea of a criterion of religious knowledge, Erasmus suggested that Pyrrhonism could develop a political dimension over and above its quietistic and individualistic ends.[18] Skepticism, Popkin explains, especially the notion of equipollence, became an argumentative style or dialectic. With skeptical tools at their disposal, Catholics could dismantle rational claims to the truth of scripture and move toward fideism, grounding religious beliefs on faith rather than reason. Eschewing philosophical and religious dogmatism, Erasmus argued that since there can be no rational means of arriving at the truth of scripture it is better to trust the authority of tradition, in this case the Catholic church. Luther, on the other hand, believed that conscience, assisted by the Holy Ghost, could guide the individual worshipper to scriptural truth; the authority of the Catholic church was merely an obstacle to the individual's understanding of God. When Luther and others argued that they were getting to the truth by turning to the Word itself, the counter-reformers responded that there needed to be some authority to provide the criteria for true belief: who would say which of competing individual views was the correct one? Thus the dialectic of philosophical skepticism appeared on the scene just as fierce ideological battles in religion were beginning to expose the gaps and uncertainties of language and argumentative logic.

Pyrrhonism made its way into England in the late sixteenth century in time to participate in the creation of a world that, as John Donne put it, "Tis all in pieces, all Cohaerance gone."[19] If classical skepticism worked in Erasmus's favor as a means to support religious ideas, it tended to arouse more concern among interested parties in England. Responses to Pyrrhonism ranged from Thomas Nashe's belligerent accusations of atheism in *Christ's Tears Over Jerusalem* to Francis Bacon's measured and philosophical engagement with its scientific implications. Inevitably, classical skepticism evoked religious responses: Pyrrho's relativism and refusal to affirm the power of providence stirred enmity in the orthodox. But it did not only evoke religious ire; classical skepticism itself was evoked by religious instability. As I will argue in chapter three, the socioeconomic and religious conditions provided a context for philosophical skepticism. There was in effect a symbiotic relationship, with skepticism and socioeconomic shifts feeding off each other. Pyrrhonism coincided with feelings of dislocation at a time when competing religious ideologies destroyed older certainties, traditional family ties were severed, social mobility upset the hierarchy of status, and economic contracts replaced feudal bonds.

The work of intellectual historians like Popkin has been essential to the study of skepticism.[20] Since the publication of *The History of Skepticism*, intellectual history has benefited from explorations of the relation of text and context.[21] The work of contextualization, it is often pointed out, requires interpretation, a heightened sensitivity to the role of language in creating our sense of "reality," past and present. Indeed, to a large extent, intellectual history has been subsumed by the "new cultural history" or, as it is called in literary studies, cultural materialism and the new historicism. Cultural historians, influenced by the "linguistic turn" in philosophy and literary theory, emphasize that language and "real" material conditions cannot be seen as independent entities. Distinguishing themselves from social historians of the sixties and seventies, who tended to treat culture as a reflection of material conditions, cultural historians now take a more dialectical approach to linguistic systems and material practices.[22] Material practices, they argue, are intertwined with the discursive system that gives them meaning. For most cultural historians, however, the move away from the positivism of older modes of social history does not entail a complete postmodern rejection of the materialist tradition in favor of Jacques Derrida's notion of "discourse."[23] Language-games have a tremendous power to shape social life, but language is never merely a form of linguistic play entirely divorced from material practices.[24]

My contextualist approach to skepticism will make use of recent advances in cultural history and Marxist or post-Marxist theories of ideology. We credit Marx's notion of ideology (and the innovations since) with critically relating "thought" to material, social practices and laying the groundwork for an understanding of consciousness as irredeemably and irreducibly

social. And we remain indebted to Marx for his model of base
and superstructure, economy and culture. Even Marx's notion
of praxis, which now seems dated, referred not only to physical
production but to a "mode of life" or a "form of activity" sufficiently broad as to encompass more than material production.
Nevertheless, recent theories of language and culture have improved on Marx's realist position by showing how the social
relations of production do not "determine" cultural phenom-
ena and ideology. Instead, our categories of the social or economic are themselves in part the product of language or
culture.

The title of this book is itself a point of entry for theories of
ideology. As twentieth-century theories have taught us, the
image of wholeness supplies a necessary ideological framework for society and the subject. Ernesto Laclau, for example,
argues that ideology is the means a society has for creating a
"fixation of meaning" or "closure." The ideological, he writes,
is the "will to 'totality' of any totalizing discourse."[25] Few theo-
rists think of ideology as false consciousness or an illusion that
can be unmasked in order to arrive at a vision of reality or
truth. I follow Louis Althusser's definition of ideology as "a
representation of the imaginary relationships of individuals to
their real conditions of existence."[26] Althusser, of course, uses
"imaginary" in the Lacanian sense of the "image," not the
"imagination." This definition is particularly valuable in enabling us to grasp the images of wholeness or fragmentation
that pertain to skeptical engagements with pressing social
issues.

Althusser's definition of ideology derives from Jacques Lacan's theory of the mirror-stage, which demonstrates that the
image of a whole, unified self or ego is a necessary form of mis-
recognition. In the first eighteen months or so of development,
a child perceives that its body is unified and in this discovers
an image that enables it to experience a satisfactory sense of
self. The child, "caught up in the lure of spatial identification,"
moves beyond the original "fragmented body-image" to an
image of totality.[27] Lacan also maintains that despite this
image of the ego as a unified whole, the human subject remains
fragmented.

According to Althusser, then, ideology works in a similar
way: like the child misrecognizing its poorly coordinated phys-

ical state, we come to think that society is more coherent and unified than it actually is. Whereas we cannot escape ideology and do not have much control over it, we can critique some of its effects. The formation of an ego depends on the mirror image of wholeness, yet resistant subjects may well strive to reveal that there are alternatives to the dominant order that only *appears* to be complete, unified, and unchanging. Hamlet's "the time is out of joint," for example, is one of many images of fragmentation we find throughout the play that call into question Claudius's ideological image of the whole kingdom "contracted in one brow of woe."

If skepticism surfaces when "the time is out of joint," its ideological position will depend on how a writer chooses, in a specific context, to respond to the disorder of society. For example, Reginald Scot believed not only that witches could not be the agents of disorder but that the responsibility lay with the witchmongers themselves, who added to the misery and despair of villages already besieged by the privations of poverty. Scot's response, however, went beyond persuading witchmongers merely to put aside their mistaken beliefs; he wanted to reinforce the Protestant ideology in particular, by altering the common people's "lived relation to the real," as Althusser calls it. Eliminating traditional rituals of devotion, magical practices of all kinds, and popular beliefs in supernatural forces like fairies and demons would fundamentally transform the social and mental world of large numbers of people.

Other skeptics, like Christopher Marlowe, put their efforts into a full-scale, global challenge to any image of wholeness and unity that would bind society. Depicting the gaps and contradictions of his time, he presented his audience with alienated protagonists who challenged the moral foundations of institutions and the beliefs that organized society. For example, religious doubt can be seen in Marlowe's Tamburlaine, who sees nature as a chaotic war of material forces; there is no universal "natural law" or spiritual unity to which humans can appeal: "Nature that framed us of four elements,/ Warring within our breasts for regiment, /Doth teach us all to have aspiring minds" (I: 2.7. 18–20). The traditional appeal to a Christian moral order carries little weight in *Tamburlaine*. Indeed, the only time divine retribution seems to occur is when Tamburlaine burns the Koran. At that point near the end of the play,

the former Scythian shepard, now a great conqueror at the ap-
otheosis of his career, finds himself "distempered suddenly"
and then on his deathbed.[28] Moreover, Tamburlaine leaves
open the possibility that there is no God at all: after turning
from Mahomet, he looks for the Christian God: "Seek out another godhead to adore, /The God that sits in heaven, *if any
god*,/For he is God alone, and none but He" (my italics)
(II:5.1.198–200). Unlike Donne, Marlowe never looked back to
an idealized time of religious unity, nor did he (like Scot) antic-
ipate a Christian society fully reconciled with itself.

Can "ideology" help us understand religion in the sixteenth
and seventeenth centuries? Should we be wary of such concepts that would have been alien to the religious sensibilities
of that era? It is, of course, impossible to immerse ourselves
fully in the religious imagination of the sixteenth century.
Still, the modern notion of religion as ideology can enhance
our historical understanding of how religion shaped early
modern group identity. Only the most vulgar materialist reading would dismiss religion as a form of ideological masking or
"realpolitik."[29] We simply lack the rationalist, humanist confidence of Marx when he maintained that religion is "the opium
of the people." But once we abandon the idea that we can
somehow stand entirely outside ideology from a lofty position
of scientific neutrality, Marx's dictum that religion is "an expression of real suffering" gains renewed force. Since the Enlightenment, our confidence in reason has weakened; it has
become harder to treat religion as a mere distraction from the
effort to alleviate immediate or, as Marx would say, "real" material conditions.

The texts we will examine each tell us a great deal about the
social and religious context of skepticism in Shakespeare's England. In Reginald Scot's case, our primary focus will be on the
source of his skeptical thinking, which I will argue was not so
much his scientific objectivism as it was his anti-Catholicism
and the social changes of the Reformation. Scot's empiricism
cannot be separated from his ideological outlook. Challenging
the authority of the *Malleus Maleficarum* and other powerful
Catholic texts, Scot's *Discoverie of Witchcraft* (1584) denies
the very possibility of witchcraft and thus distances itself from
more orthodox positions within Elizabethan Protestantism.
Nevertheless, Scot's logic is rooted in the widespread anti-

Catholic ideology of the 1580s. Scot responded to the social disruption and misery caused by witchcraft persecutions by advocating greater religious unity. The first chapter looks at how he sought social as well as religious reform in order to transform a society that was (in Claudius's terms) "disjoint and out of frame."

Focusing next on Thomas Harriot and his scientific circle, the second chapter extends the discussion of popular witchcraft and magic to the problem of religious doubt in an elite circle of state power. Widely recognized as holding heterodox views throughout his life, Harriot put his religious skepticism to work in an analysis of the religious and social customs of the Algonquin Indians. Stephen Greenblatt's essay "Invisible Bullets" argues that the "subversive" ideas in Harriot's *Briefe and True Report of the New Found Land of Virginia* (1588) are "contained" by Protestant ideology. Now that Greenblatt himself has abandoned the subversion/containment model, it is time to take another look at the ideological tensions that Harriot was unwilling or unable to smooth over. Examining the New World context of Harriot's skepticism, I suggest that his ethnographic receptivity points to the serious limitations of evangelical colonialism.

Many of the distressing changes that were taking place in Tudor England found their way into Marlowe's drama and the scandalous charges against him. The third chapter builds on the discussion of religious controversy and social change in the previous chapters; it also emphasizes the importance of economic dislocation in Shakespeare's England. While Reginald Scot supported the anti-Catholic ideology of the 1580s, Marlowe responded quite differently to the newly established authority of the Protestant Church. Religious dissent was widespread, but Marlowe delved deeper than most critics into the core assumptions of both Protestantism and Catholicism. The historical source of skepticism in *Doctor Faustus*, I demonstrate, is the unstable transition from Catholicism to Protestantism. The final portion of this chapter suggests that economic upheavel was an important source of the religious skepticism of Marlowe's *The Jew of Malta*.

The tropes of classical skepticism are powerfully explored by Shakespeare in *King Lear*: the problematic role of sense-perception in obtaining knowledge, the questionable existence of the gods, the role of custom in determining morality and adjudicating truth-claims, the nature of one's identity, and the devaluation of reason. The fourth chapter argues that such concerns about knowledge are deeply rooted in the economic turmoil of the *Lear* world, and that we can trace the intractable disputes of this skeptical world to economic struggles in Shakespeare's England.

I have selected these historical topics—witchcraft debates, the discovery of the New World, economic struggle, and religious reformation—in order to show the diverse contexts in which skepticism appeared and the many contributions skepticism made to a nation undergoing radical change, a nation in the process of rethinking many of its basic assumptions from centuries past. It is commonly assumed that religious and philosophical skeptics are so marginalized that they have a limited impact on social and intellectual life. Mary Douglas, for example, argues that religious and philosophical doubt has flourished mainly among intellectuals who lack power and authority in society. Skepticism, she claims, is the product of specific social and institutional situations; in particular, it is a form of "non-attachment," a quietistic withdrawal from genuine political engagement: "Sustained scepticism is a feasible stance for those who do not expect to command or unify society, but stand apart from it. Belief/scepticism patterns have much to do with the claims of power and revolt against its claims."[30] Douglas maintains that skepticism thrives in a sector of the elite, educated class that is marginalized and virtually powerless. Unable or unwilling to effect genuine change, skeptics prefer to stand on the margins of society, entertaining abstruse ideas that could never be effective in political life. If we look at Diogenes Laertius's account of the life of the first philosophical skeptic, we find that Douglas could easily use Pyrrho as an example.[31] In his account of Pyrrho's encounter with Anaxarchus, Diogenes appears almost to be parodying his brand of skepticism. Upon finding his friend Anaxarchus stuck in a swamp, Pyrrho shows indifference to his colleague's plight. Most onlookers are outraged, but Anaxarchus, still caught in the swamp, praises Pyrrho's sang-froid. Another pithy narrative describes Pyrrho's reaction to the sinking of a ship and his unnerved fellow-passengers: Pyrrho points to a pig and tells them that that is "the unperturbed state [in which] the wise man should keep himself."[32]

But the skeptics in Shakespeare's England, while alienated in many ways from their society, still found themselves engaging the minds of their readers or audiences and fomenting much debate and disagreement. Sir Walter Ralegh, who fused the *vita activa* and the *vita contemplativa*, developed a reputation as a skeptic, even as an "atheist." The charge of atheism may have been unjustified, yet it derived from more than Jesuit propaganda: rarely satisfied with the assumed pieties of his day, Ralegh so alarmed Ralph Ironside in a debate on God and the soul that a government investigation was begun. The commission at Cerne Abbas in 1594 sought information about anyone who had doubts about the existence of God, the immortality of the soul, divine providence, heaven and hell, or the truth of the scriptures. Depositions from a number of witnesses accused Ralegh and his tutor Thomas Harriot of calling into question the immortality of the soul. Indeed, in the debate with Ironside, Ralegh demonstrated that the former, caught in his circular reasoning, did not have a valid explanation for the composition of the soul or the existence of God.[33]

Ralegh also took a serious interest in classical skepticism, at least enough to translate much of Sextus Empiricus into English. "Sir Walter Ralegh's Skeptic" makes a point not unlike Hamlet's "There is nothing either good or bad but thinking makes it so." Ralegh's translation of Sextus Empiricus reads: "these Men then, may tell how these things seem to them good, or bad; but what they are in their own Nature they cannot tell." The opening line of the text offers a central tenet of classical skepticism, the notion of equipollence: "The Sceptick doth neither affirm, neither denie any Position: but doubteth of is, and opposeth his Reasons against that which is affirmed, or denied, to justify his not Consenting."[34] Such relativism does not, of course, characterize Ralegh's own theological or philosophical outlook; nevertheless, Ralegh engaged intellectual and political life with a questioning and receptive, yet also forceful and active, frame of mind, countering Douglas's notion that skepticism is a kind of quietism. Ralegh and the skeptics selected in this book provide a window onto the difficult choices—social, religious, and intellectual—that confronted people in many areas of life in Shakespeare's England.

1

"The spirit of blindness and error dooth seduce them": The Skepticism of Reginald Scot

THE WITCH PERSECUTIONS OF THE SIXTEENTH CENTURY HAVE always presented a significant challenge to modern, historically-minded scholars. Searching for anyone who did not succumb to the hysteria, scholars are often too quick to portray skeptics anachronistically, condemning the witch persecutions in terms that would be alien to the political and religious norms of the period. The skeptical tradition might seem to offer a glimmer of hope amid the gruesome witch hunts; we might expect to find an outspoken critic of demonological dogma, someone who applied a rigorous scientific method to contemporaneous witch trials. The thinker often taken to be the most likely candidate for heroic standing is not one of the great Renaissance skeptics such as Montaigne or Ralegh but a country gentleman from Kent: Reginald Scot. But, I will argue, Scot's skepticism was fueled not so much by a modernistic scientific drive as by religious anxieties, in particular a strong anti-Catholic sentiment. Indeed, we look in vain for someone who anticipated modernist hostility to demonology.

Throughout the late twentieth century, scholars have regarded Scot as a proto-Enlightenment purveyor of commonsense. The pre-industrial age, they tell us, was stuck in a quagmire of superstition, but it managed to produce a few enlightened minds. Scot is often viewed as a participant in a cosmic relay race; he is labeled a pragmatist who raced ahead of the superstitious claims of his day, handing the baton of modernity to later English philosophers and scientists. His argument that devils can take no corporeal form and that so-called witches are merely deluded old women supports modern assessments of him as a levelheaded man with logical, naturalistic views. Robert West, for example, argues that Scot was "ahead of his time," informing us that devils and witches "existed in the public imagination as generally and threateningly as, say, the dangers of nuclear power generation do in ours."[1] Such a comparison, which exemplifies the common strategical use of the idea of "superstition" for particular ideological ends, is symptomatic of attempts to celebrate sixteenth-century texts by uncomprehending modernization of them. Writes another historian, Brian Easlea, "For the modern reader Scot's work shines like a beacon. One wants almost to embrace him."[2]

The most important essay on Scot to date is by Sydney Anglo, who champions Scot's empiricism: "He was neither a theologian, philosopher, nor magus. He was a learned, independent-minded country gentleman used to making decisions on his own initiative, and in evaluating what he read against what he observed."[3] An empiricist worldview, as Anglo observes, can be seen throughout *The Discoverie of Witchcraft* (1584): Scot repeatedly dismisses miracles (except those performed by Christ) because they cannot be verified; he argues that all magic is merely deceit that can be uncovered through diligent observation. Stories of demons and spirits, he insists, have no basis in human experience. Most important, Scot denounces the Catholic Church for performing rituals like the Eucharist and exorcism that he claims are as fraudulent as the legerdemain of conjurors.

As Anglo suggests, such skepticism was radical in the sixteenth century, when the majority of people believed in the corporeality of demons and spirits. But Anglo downplays the importance of Scot's religious convictions in order to celebrate his "commonsense" or "positivist" thinking. He states, "were it not for his leap of faith in proclaiming an unshakeable acceptance of the Word of God on the very basis of the miracles contained therein, his philosophical position might aptly, if anachronistically, be described as thoroughly positivist."[4] Here we are told that all that bars Scot from a modern worldview is his religious faith, implying, in effect, that his empiricism stood outside ideology. I will instead focus on Scot's Protestant ideology as an integral, rather than incidental, part of his skepticism toward witchcraft. As Scot himself put it, Christ "is the substance and groundworke of truth it selfe."

For Protestants like Reginald Scot, who saw witchcraft and magic as vestiges of Catholicism, the time had come for sweeping reform. Indeed, his opposition to the witch trials rested on the premise that the very belief in witchcraft ought to be thrown in the ashcan of history along with all related papist practices.[5] Scot's doubt toward witchcraft, I hope to show, is impossible to separate from his challenge to the authority of the Catholic religion and its cultural presence in England. His hostility toward witchcraft was the outcome not of a positivistic bent but of trenchant anxieties about Catholicism that permeated the political atmosphere of the 1580s, the decade in which Elizabeth's policies directed at recusants, priests, and Jesuits grew more severe.[6] Rejecting the authority of the Catholic Church, Scot circumscribed all social practices and beliefs that smacked of transubstantiation, and, in the process, he denounced all beliefs that did not "set foorth the glorie of God, and be many waies beneficiall to the commonwealth."[7]

Like other Protestants, Scot valued conscience, divine providence, repentance, and prayer over the "magical" solutions offered by the Catholic church and its remnants in English culture. He believed the formal rituals of the church to be much less important to one's salvation than one's own inner conscience, which, once properly guided by scripture and reason, would reveal to worshippers the truth.[8] In his zeal to rid England of Catholicism and the social practices influenced by it, Scot could no longer tolerate rituals that compared in any way to papist culture, and this extended to the practices of witchcraft, divination, and charming. Thus he distanced himself from his fellow Protestant reformers in one key respect: he took the spiritualization of religion so far that he wound up standing virtually alone in his skepticism toward witchcraft. Protestant reformers typically focused on conscience and providence rather than the particular details of how witchcraft was performed.[9] Unlike many of the parishioners involved in witch accusations, reformers tended not to take much interest in the specific rituals involved in conjuring devils. Instead, believing in the efficacy of witchcraft, they warned people to engage in a *spiritual* battle against the temptations of the devil. Scot took this line of thought a step further: he believed that the focus ought to be shifted from what he regarded as the false, "papist" belief in the physical efficacy of witchcraft to the spiritual dimensions of the true, that is, Protestant, religious experience. To this end he paid a good deal of attention to the details of witchcraft practices as a means to dismantling their alleged efficacy altogether.

The first section of this chapter will focus on the anti-Catholic source of Scot's skepticism while also examining his goal of reforming popular culture. The second section will discuss another source of his skepticism: a patriarchal understanding of gender hierarchy common in post-Reformation England. I conclude the chapter by looking at the social context of witchcraft accusations, comparing Scot's response to conditions of poverty to that of Dekker, Ford, and Rowley in their play *The Witch of Edmonton.*

I

Scot's *Discoverie* contributed to the ideological project—so important to English nationhood—of rooting out any papist and unchristian practices. Scot spoke out in favor of a more rigorous intervention by the Church of England to reform large segments of the population that seemed hardly to be following the new religious practices. Throughout the Elizabethan period, authorities found that despite the new laws suppressing the "superstition" of Catholicism, the task of taking down altars and removing Roods and images seemed endless, since many parishes were reluctant, if not adamantly unwilling, to change. Scot made his contribution to this push for religious conformity by "discovering" the fraudulent, papist practices of witches and witchmongers throughout England. He made use of rationalistic ideas, as shown in his pithy line "nihil est tam occultam quod non sit detegendum"—nothing is so secret that it cannot be revealed—to support his quest to expose and extirpate the deep, Catholic roots of superstition.

Although Scot did not agree with the state's method of handling witches (interrogation, torture, and imprisonment), his hostility to witchcraft was, to a great extent, encouraged by the formation of a National Church. In the 1530s, Henry VIII provided a foundation for the union of Protestantism and nationalism that would grow much stronger in the latter part of the century. Richard Hooker, in his *Laws of Ecclesiastical Pol-*

ity (1593), expressed the new, but quickly spreading notion that church and state are inseparable: "We hold that . . . there is not any man of the Church of England but the same man is also a member of the commonwealth; nor any man a member of the commonwealth that is not also of the Church of England."[10] Thus Protestantism, in England at least, was hard to separate from nationalism. Spreading the proper practices of religion, Scot believed, would strengthen the Church of England as well as the English nation.

As Christina Larner points out, this drive for religious conformity contributed to the development of nation-states throughout Europe. She draws a parallel between the "evangelisation of the populace" and the building of nation-states:

> Nation-states could not depend on the old ties to bind their people to them. Like all new regimes they demanded both ideological conformity and moral cleansing. Ideological conformity in the sixteenth century meant overt adherence to the form of Christianity preferred within the regime concerned.[11]

The new witchcraft statutes of 1543 and 1563, which made witchcraft, magic, and sorcery a crime against church and state, were part of this movement toward "ideological conformity"; and when debates on witchcraft reached a fevered pitch in the 1580s, anti-Catholicism played an important role in widespread attempts to rid England of unchristian practices. Of course, the evangelization Larner describes was only partially successful, and reformers like Scot would remain disappointed at the large numbers of people who led their entire lives without ever fully abandoning their "papist" practices.

Historian Jean Delumeau draws a similar conclusion about the effect of the trend toward universalization and ideological conformity by both Reformation and Counter-Reformation groups. Although he does not concern himself with the rise of the nation-state, he shows how ecclesiastical institutions increased their surveillance over rural parishes. Since the Middle Ages were never precisely Christian, he maintains, the Christian spirit was awakened—not reawakened—in the fourteenth and fifteenth centuries. Demonstrating that "the religion of the mass of people in the west has been confused with the religion of a clerical elite,"[12] Delumeau points out that it was not until the end of the Middle Ages that serious attempts were finally made to educate the lower clergy and to offer more rigorous guidance about the meaning of Catholic rituals. Luther, then, was only an extreme case of a great pressure for moral cleansing that was already being enacted by the Catholic church. Delumeau writes that on the eve of the Reformation

> the average westerner was but superficially christianized. In this context the two Reformations, Luther's and Rome's were two processes, which apparently competed but in actual fact converged, by which the masses were christianized and religion spiritualized.[13]

The English Reformation provides a fine example of Delumeau's point. As authorities visited parishes across the country they found, to their horror, not only that people maintained Catholic practices but also that animistic and pagan ways of thinking continued to thrive. Indeed, until the Reformation the animistic rites of magic and the rituals of the church overlapped. For large numbers of people, the precise doctrines of Christianity were less important than the daily magical rituals that gave them greater confidence in their ability to control agricultural productivity, human fertility, and disease.[14] Magic, sorcery, and other practices that were predicated on the vital forces of nature always bore an ambiguous relation to Christianity; it was not until the Reformation, however, that magic and Christianity became so polarized as enemy camps.

Scot's *Discoverie* arrived after the Reformation had made great gains in England and anti-Catholicism had captured the imagination of large numbers of people. His anti-Catholicism is most apparent in his discussion of the Eucharist. He puts the Eucharist in the same category as the practice of witchcraft, since he sees both as unnatural and impossible. Bound by a strict Catholic/Protestant binary, Scot does not say anything about the various ways in which the Eucharist might legitimately be performed. Modern readers of the *Discoverie* might easily come to believe that all Protestants shared Scot's position on the practice of communion, that it was akin to sorcery. But this was not the case. In fact, Elizabeth's *Book of Common Prayer*, which followed her Act of Uniformity in 1559, kept some of the older language of transubstantiation intact while maintaining that the real presence of Christ was spiritual rather than material: "The body of our lord Jesus Christ, which was given for thee, preserve thy body and soul into everlasting life: and take and eat this, in remembrance that Christ died for thee, and feed on him in thy heart by faith, with thanksgiving."[15] Thus there was much vagueness regarding acceptable religious practice that Scot did not acknowledge. At a time when many people were torn between the old ways and the new, Scot put forth a seamless Protestant ideology that did not recognize the debate and dissension among reformers themselves.

Furthermore, Scot's position on the material presence of spirits is more radical than Luther's and Calvin's, since they never abandoned their belief in devils and spirits. Protestants frequently objected to the notion that the utterance of Latin words might alter the material qualities of bread and wine, but Scot took the objections much further than most. While Luther and Calvin objected to the magical qualities of the Catholic mass, they did not make the connection between the carnality of demons and the body of Christ. Luther, in fact, was reluctant to embrace the symbolic as a substitute for the material; the Eucharist still suggested to him that things were present in words. Scot, on the other hand, sees the Eucharist as a feast of cannibals; in the absence of deification, there is, in keeping with empiricism, only defecation:

> And to make their tyrannie the more apparent, they are not contented to have killed him once, but dailie and hourelie torment him with new deaths; yea they are not ashamed to sweare, that with their carnall hands they reare his humane substance, breaking it into small gobbets; and with their external teeth chew his flesh and bones, contraire to divine or humane nature; and contraire to the prophesie, which saith; There shall not a bone of him be broken. Finallie, in the end of their sacrifice (as they say) they eate him up rawe, and swallow downe into their guts everie member and parcell of him: and last of all, that they conveie him into the place where they bestowe the residue of all that which they have devoured that daie. (109)

This satirical attack on the Eucharist is crucial to Scot's argument "that divels assaults are spiritual and not temporall." He reminds his readers, for example, that since "a spirit hath no flesh," the stories of witches kissing the "bare buttocks" of the

Witches kissing the devil's buttocks, from Francesco Guazzo, *Compendium Maleficarum* **(1608)**

devil must be false. Just as the blood and the body of Christ have no real presence in the Eucharist, demonic spirits can take no temporal or carnal form. In both cases, Scot points out, we simply have no empirical evidence that spiritual entities have taken material form. In fact, the only difference between conjurors and Catholic priests, he maintains, is that the former perform their rites in private while the latter shamelessly execute them in public. "Conjurors are no small fooles," he tells us; whereas witches are "poore and needie," "these conjurors have gotten them offices in the church of Rome, wherby they have obtained authoritie and great estimation" (262).

Thus Scot's writings, while filled with what seems like logical, scientific rhetoric, are colored throughout by his anti-Catholicism. He quotes more than once, "The will of a sound mind, is the desire for a possible thing" (33). One of his favorite lines runs, "And whatsoever is contrarie to nature faileth in his principle, and therefore is naturallie impossible" (39). Transubstantiation became his model for practices, especially witchcraft and Catholicism, that were contrary to the operations of nature. The loaded word "transubstantiate" appears repeatedly in his debunking of witchcraft. For example, he recounts the confessions of witches: "And as they sometimes confesse impossibilities, as that they flie in the aire, transubstantiate themselves, raise tempests, transfer or remoove corne"; and, in a chapter dismissing Catholic miracles and witchcraft, he states, "Som saie they can transubstantiate themselves and other, and take the forms and shapes of asses, woolves, ferrets, cowes, apes, horsses, dogs" (28, 6). In this context, the word "transubstantiate" forges a link between the fraud of witches, who believe they can change form, and Catholic priests, who believe they can change wine and bread into the blood and body of Christ. In such passages we see Scot's anti-Catholicism driving his skepticism toward witchcraft.

Once we eliminate the material, bodily force of the Catholic Christ, Scot insists, we can turn to a more abstract, moral force that will teach us to distinguish between the "spirit of error" and its antithesis—the "good spirit of God." Without the presence of this divine authority, the mind is "alienated"; it is detached from the objective truth of his presence. True Christians, then, should judge others on the basis of their rational understanding of God rather than on the way they perform material rituals. Since there are no corporeal spirits in the world, belief in such spirits only distracts us from the proper, that is, Protestant worship of God. This empiricist outlook is also evident in the supplementary section of the *Discoverie*, *A Discourse Upon Divels and Spirits*. Scot tells us that spirit, an abstract force that generates proper judgment,

> dooth signifie a secret force and power, wherewith our minds are mooved and directed; if unto holie things, then it is the motion of the holie spirit, of the spirit of Christ and of God: if unto evil things, then it is the suggestion of the wicked spirit, of the divell, and of satan.[16]

Note here that Scot does believe that the devil plays an active role in human affairs, but the latter does not appear in corporeal form. Christians, then, should turn inward in order to reflect on their relation to God and avoid practices like exorcism, divination, or conjuration, which position Satan in the material rather than spiritual realm. Thus he insists that those minds that through "credulitie addict themselves to divine oracles, or the voice of angels breakeing through the clouds," are not inhabited by Satan, but that

> the spirit of blindness and error dooth seduce them; so that it is no mervell if in the alienation of their minds they take falsehood for truth, shadowes for substances, fansies for verities, &c: for it is likelie that the good spirit of God hath forsaken them or at leastwise absented it selfe from them: else would they detest these divelish devises of men, which consist of nothing but delusions and vaine practises, whereof (I suppose) this my booke to be a sufficient discoverie. (Scot, *Discourse*, 460)

Throughout this work, Scot complains that people across England have been seduced by two inextricably linked forms of error: the practices of witchcraft and Catholicism. The above passage, placed in the context of his anti-Catholic rhetoric, implies that those who have not left behind the errors of the old religion, along with the witchmongers, are alienated from the "good spirit of God." In other words, both groups "go awhoring after strange gods."

Scot's skepticism extended to other forms of popular culture he perceived as remnants of Catholic superstition. Belief in ghosts and fairies came under heavy fire, as did practices like fortune-telling, astrology, and divination. Indeed, the *Discoverie* provided a compendium of popular magical beliefs and practices for writers like William Shakespeare who, ironically enough, appropriated Scot's text and perpetuated some of the very beliefs the reformer wanted to dispel. The mischievous fairy Robin Goodfellow, for example, who appears throughout the *Discoverie* as a representative of popular superstition, became one of Shakespeare's most memorable characters. Had Scot found himself in the audience of *A Midsummer Night's Dream*, he no doubt would have sided with the skeptical Duke Theseus, who dismissed such "antic fables" and "fairy toys."

Scot was, of course, not alone in his desire to reform popular culture. One might easily read his work alongside a contemporary like Phillip Stubbes, who, in a tirade against the theater, denounced festive practices and popular sports. Plays lead not

A woodcut depicting Robin Good-Fellow, from the title page of *Robin Good-Fellow, His Mad Pranks* (1639)

to the "Godly recreation of the mind" but to "idleness, unthriftines, whoredome, wantonness, and drunkeness."[17] Peter Burke notes how from 1500 to 1650, both Catholics and Protestants—and most vehemently the latter—attempted to replace diverse forms of popular culture. The reformers, Burke says, objected to "actors, ballads, bear-beating, bull-fights, cards, chap-books, charivaris, charlatans, dancing, dicing, divining, fairs, folktales, fortune-telling, magic, masks, minstrels, puppets, taverns and witchcraft."[18] Scot assails many items on this list, while remaining focused on Catholicism as the root cause of all superstition.

English reformers like Scot and Stubbes had a lot of work

cut out for them, since large numbers of people in England maintained at least some of the older Catholic practices. After the Act of Uniformity in 1559, the Anglican Church made every effort to transform the religious and social practices of the nation, and to further the reform begun much earlier in the days of Henry VIII. The state abolished Mass, introduced a new prayer book, banned the cult of the Saints, dismantled Roods, and outlawed Corpus Christi plays. But as Eamon Duffy, Christopher Haigh, and others have pointed out, reforms were not always carried out willingly. In many cases, people were merely being reluctantly obedient to state authority. As Duffy puts it, "Dislike of change, Catholic instincts, hope for a speedy restoration of the old ways, and Tudor thrift, combined to struggle against the instinctive obedience of well-schooled subjects, in a conflict not strong enough for resistance, but which ensured widespread inertia and concealment."[19]

Scot's frustration with beliefs in witchcraft took place in this context of the Reformation. His complaints about popery were commonplace in the 1580s; preachers often criticized the ignorance of the laity who refused to let go of older practices. Hence, when Scot spoke out against popular culture or what he called the beliefs of the "common people," his anti-Catholicism was never far behind. In fact, his anti-Catholicism was far more a driving force than his scientific methodology. For example, he points out that Robin Goodfellow, also known as Puck, "ceseth now to be much feared, and popery is sufficiently discovered." He thanks God for the death of Puck: "Well, thanks be to God this wretched and cowardlie infidelitie, since the preaching of the gospell, is in part forgoten: and doubtles, the rest of those illusions will in short time (by Gods grace) be detected and vanish awaie" (123). The cataloging of magical practices in the *Discoverie*, far from representing modern, scientific rationalism, is instead one compelling example of how Protestants tried to reform the Catholic culture.[20]

We can see that Scot's anti-Catholicism is the main source of his skepticism by examining how he argues against witchcraft. An important strategy for Scot is to link beliefs in witchcraft to the practices of the Roman Church and other popular superstitions in England. For example, in a series of bawdy stories, he attacks priests who participate in and perpetuate magical practices. Priests, he tells us, have concocted cures for be-

witched love that include making "a jakes of the lovers shooe."
Even more defamatory is his story of a priest who told a
woman she was bewitched and that in order to release the
charm he would need to "sing a masse upon hir bellie." Once
she consented, he had her "laie naked on the alter . . . to the
satisfieng of his lust, but not to the release of hir greefe" (46).
Catholics would also try to cure those "bewitched in their pri-
vie members" through a series of "ceremoniall trumperies"
such as Ave Marias, crossings, and the sprinkling of holy water.
Scot tells many stories of lewd priests who have sexual exploits
with their clients. One of these satirical, anti-clerical stories
describes "exceeding bawdie and lecherous" holy persons—
monks and abbots—who had to have their "stones" removed by
angels in order to remain chaste (46). In addition, Scot insists
on (without proving) the papist origins of popular English beliefs in auguries such as cocks that don't crow on time, owls
screeching in the night, strange cats walking in the house, or
hens falling from the rooftop. Throughout the *Discoverie*, Scot
treats Catholicism as a form of witchcraft, and thus condemns
both.

But reforming popular superstition entailed reforming many
social practices. The practices Scot objected to were part of the
daily lives of many people. He linked the practice of divination
to the "cousening tricks of oracling priests and monkes" and
objected to these and other practices of village wizards, often
referred to as "cunning folk" or "wise" men and women. Offering magical and non-magical services, local wizards assisted
people in finding missing persons, locating buried treasure, in-
terpreting dreams, and countering the effects of witchcraft.
Cunning folk were skilled at probing the character or mindset of their clients, listening attentively, and connecting their
physical illnesses to their social problems. Yet this practice was
made possible only by the charisma of particular practitioners,
whose power relied on their clients' unwavering faith in their
abilities. The skeptical George Gifford admitted that "out of
the question they be innumerable which receive helpe by going
to the cunning men."[21] Gifford's ultimate aim, like Scot's, was
to eliminate all practices of sorcery, "good" as well as "bad"
witches. The Puritan William Perkins put the matter forcefully
when he said that all good Christians had to "abhorre the wizard, as the most pernicious enemy of our salvation . . . as the

greatest enemie of Gods name, worship, and glorie, that is in the world, next to Satan himselfe."[22]

Although Scot argued that the practices of cunning folk needed to be eliminated, he was clearly fascinated by such work. For example, he took great pains to describe how helpful spirits can allegedly be conjured up into crystals. Mirrors or other reflective surfaces can be made that present the faces of whomever one wishes to see: "You may have glasses so made, as what image of favour soever you print in your imagination, you shall thinke you see the same therein" (179). But he adds that these are merely optical illusions: "non est in speculo res quae speculatur in eo." Having expressed his appreciation for the perspective glass—an entertaining house of mirrors—he makes it clear that the visions of things in the mirror are not the things themselves. Such admiration for optical chicanery is ultimately superseded by his contempt for the cunning men who produce these images. Comparing their practices to the legerdemain of priests, Scot makes the skeptical point that once we know how such papist practices are performed, we are no longer enthralled by them. Furthermore, his empiricism serves his ideological interests: after debunking the practices of cunning men, he further insists that such unchristian practices ought to be dismissed altogether.

Scot also objects to the practice of astrology, arguing that it does not recognize the omnipotence of God: "The providence of God is denied, and the miracles of christ are diminished, when these powers of the heavens and their influencies are in such sort advanced." He links astrology to other superstitions, including witchcraft: "we are so fond, mistrustfull & credulous, that we feare more the fables of Robin good fellow; astrologers, & witches, & believe more things that are not, than the things that are" (121). Scot's religious objection to astrology is similar to his objections to other popular practices. As Bernard Capp points out, "Astrology thus appeared as the rival of Christianity, leading men away from God, and serving the Devil. There was a sustained attempt to link astrology with witchcraft, sorcery and demonism."[23]

Scot's ethnographic distance from popular culture provides a useful test of the acculturation thesis put forth by historians of witchcraft. Robert Muchembled, for example, argues that much of the witch persecution in Europe was the result of the desire of the elite to reform popular unchristian practices. The superstitious practices that had existed in rural life for centuries became criminalized as the elite made witchcraft a crime against God and the state. In England, this process was crucial, even if it was not nearly as pernicious as in the regions identified by Muchembled.[24] Scot's discourse of discovery was merely one logical step ahead of those Protestants who still believed in superstitious practices and wanted to see witches punished. While the courts and ecclesiastical authorities probed England for unchristian wizards and witches in order to reform or eliminate them, Scot dismissed their credibility entirely as a means of purifying the religion of the commonwealth, a drive based more in anti-Catholic fervor than in a rational skepticism.

II

Another important source of Scot's skepticism can be found in his implicit patriarchal assumptions. One of his major objections to the belief in witchcraft is that it gives too much power to women, who were, in the majority of cases, the ones accused. In this section I will examine why Scot objected to witchcraft on these grounds and suggest that some of his criticisms of Catholicism were also closely connected with his ideas of gender.

Scholars have often linked witchcraft persecutions to male anxiety concerning disorderly or powerful women. The curses of witches were, in fact, a means for women to imagine revenge upon people in the community. Cursing was perceived as a dangerous form of "disorderly" behavior, akin to the language of shrewish women. As Frances Dolan puts it, "some [witchcraft suspects] believed themselves to be the agents of an anger that blew apart their socially constructed subject-positions as dependent, subordinate, and submissive, an anger that upset social order by overturning its distributions of power."[25] Forceful, disobedient, or disorderly women preoccupied male writers in the sixteenth century. Advice manuals for marriage and household management fluorished at a time when women came under fire for an assortment of crimes, including witchcraft, infanticide, and verbal abuse. Although there was no consensus about gender roles, an orthodox position did emerge amid the many prescriptions for proper female and male behavior. For example, *An Homily of the State of Matrimony*, read every week in English churches, declared the widespread doctrine of wifely obedience. The homily condemns the violent behavior of "the common sort of man," advocating a gentler form of discipline.

> Now as concerning the wife's duty. What shall become her? Shall she abuse the gentleness and humanity of her husband and at her pleasure turn all things upside down? No surely, for that is far repugnant against God's commandment. For thus doth St. Peter preach to them: Ye wives, be ye in subjection to obey your own husband.[26]

Advice manuals offered a similar ideology: men should use the power of language to control their wives; physical force was not as effective as "gentleness and humanity." William Perkins, for example, insisted that while the wife is "subject to her husband," and "yieldeth obedience unto him," the husband "may not chastise her either with stripes or strokes."[27] Underlying all these doctrines is an analogy between the husband or father and God. The man carried the "image of God"; in fact, the patriarchy in the family reflected the patriarchy in the heavens.

Although the Protestant Reformation opened new paths for women by increasing literacy and giving more spiritual authority to women in the home, it also closed off other opportunities. Lawrence Stone argues that the Reformation caused women to lose some of the control they formerly held in several areas. For example, they no longer organized the household rituals they once performed in the Catholic religion, and avenues outside the confines of the patriarchal family vanished: Protestant reformers were hostile to unmarried women and nunneries no longer presented an alternative to marriage.[28] Most important, notions of order in society as a whole placed a tremendous emphasis on the husband's control over his wife. Indeed, the family became a metaphor for the state: just as the king was the father to the people, the father was the king of the household.

Increasingly concerned about the proper role of women in

the household, Protestants created images of the good woman as submissive, silent, chaste, and obedient. The women accused of witchcraft often had the opposite qualities: they were often widows, scolds, shrews, or sexual deviants. Witches, like disorderly women in general, might, as the homily on matrimony states, "turn all things upside down."

In accordance with the patriarchal mindset of Reformation England, Scot devoted a significant portion of the *Discoverie* to delimiting the powers of women. How could women, who were by nature weaker than men in virtually every psychological and intellectual quality, compete with God's power by raising storms and casting spells? In Scot's thinking, the very fact that most accusations were directed at women made the practice of witchcraft highly suspect. How could such creatures take on the powers of their Creator?

Scot launches extensive complaints about how, aspiring to be witches, women attempt to usurp the power of God. He quotes Galen's line, "Incantamenta sunt muliercularum figmenta" (enchantments are the delusions of foolish women), when he insists that the hubristic powers of woman must be held in check. The problem with these women, he argues, is that they take on powers which, in his cosmology, can be attributed only to God:

> They take upon them to be the mightie power of god, and to doo that which is the onelie work of him, seducing the people, and blaspheming the name of God, who will not give his glorie to anie creature, being himselfe the King of glorie and omnipotencie. (65)

We can see in such lines, repeated *ad nauseum*, how Scot wants to maintain boundaries in religion that reinforce social hierarchy. God is the "King of glorie," and women could not possibly perform magical feats that resemble his "omnipotencie." In the conduct literature of the period, as we have seen, women were told repeatedly that their husbands were in the image of God and that their obedience to them should flow from their obedience to the monarch and to God. The oft quoted line from Paul, for example, stated, "Wives, submit your selves unto your husbands, as unto the Lord. For the husband is the wives head, even as Christ is the head of the Church."[29] Scot follows a similar line of thought in his complaint that women who believe they are witches are, in effect, challenging the power of God, the "King of Glorie and omnipotencie." Like the disobedient wife, the witch is essentially acting out of her place in society. Rather than challenge her husband's power (although that too could be the case), the witch presents a fundamental challenge to an even greater patriarchal authority—God.

In his chapters on miracles, Scot compares the false notion that mere women can perform miracles as Christ did with the false claims of the Catholic church, and we find his misogynistic tendencies intertwined with his anti-Catholic bias. On female witches, he throws down the glove in defiance: "And I challenge them all (even upon the adventure of my life) to shew one peece of a miracle, such as Christ did trulie" (86). He finds it particularly upsetting that the female sex should lay claim to such power. Women, he tells us, especially those who are superstitious papists with "drowsie minds," have no potential for making contact with the supernatural or creating miracles in Christ-like fashion. All such interaction would be a form of popery and thus an offense to God.

Scot here takes the opportunity to rail against the Catholic church for its belief that miracles continued after the early days of Christianity. Adopting the standard Protestant view that "miracles have ceased," he says it is scandalous not only that Protestants continue to believe women can perform miracles but also that Catholics continue to perpetuate such false beliefs: "our faith is alredie confirmed, and our church established by miracles; so as now to seek for them, is a point of infidelitie. Which the papists (if you note it) are greatlie touched withall, as in their lieng legends appeareth. But in truth, our miracles are knaveries most commonlie, and speciallie of priests, whereof I could cite a thousand" (86). Moreover, Scot points out that the witchmongers, in particular Catholics, who go along with such popular superstitions, are themselves "effeminate," and thus lacking the power of reason. For example, in a discussion of divination, he says "Amongst us there be manie women, and effeminat men (marie papists alwaies, as by their superstition may appeere) that make great divinations" (116). Here we can see the importance of gender in Scot's skeptical outlook: he associates reason and empiricism with the masculine mind. The feminine mind, on the other hand, lacks the ability to see through superstitious beliefs, and is thus more likely to take an interest in divination.

Sixteenth-century patriarchal norms relied heavily on theories of women's biological inferiority. Scot was particularly impressed by the work of his continental, skeptical counterpart, Johann Weyer, the doctor who proclaimed that all witches were melancholics. Weyer based his medical diagnoses on misogyny:

> Le diable ennemi fin, ruzé & cauteleux, induit volontiers le sexe feminin, lequel est inconstant à raison de sa complexion, de legere croyance, malicieux, impatient, melancholique pour ne pouvoir commander à ses affections: & principalement les vieiles debiles, stupides, & d'esprit chancelant.[30]

In chapters on the melancholy of witches, Scot also draws on classical sources for this notion of women's biological inferiority, relying on the medical works of Weyer, Galen, Aristotle, and Erastus, which describe women's bodies as unclean and their minds as passive and rationally deficient due in part to "cold humours." The melancholic humor, which is "the cause of all their strange, impossible, and incredible confessions," torments the minds of such women (33). Medical theory suggests to him that the woman's body is naturally more susceptible to the elements' vagaries. Because the women charged with witchcraft are so often "poore, sullen, superstitious, and papists; or such as know no religion," whenever "mischeefe, mischance, calamitie, or slaughter is brought to passe, they are easilie persuaded the same is doone by themselves; imprinting in their minds an earnest and constant imagination hereof"(4). They are "easilie persuaded" because they are "destitute of reason." It might seem that his skeptical outlook leads Scot to pursue a biological rather than supernatural explanation for women's belief in witchcraft. Of course, he hardly arrives at a greater truth as a result, since the medical theories he draws on are not themselves based on empirical methods. What is driving his skepticism here is more misogyny than a modern scientific worldview.

Scot also declares that priests who believe in certain outlandish wonders or miracles are afflicted with melancholy. Recounting the story of a priest who was convinced he saw a fellow member of the clergy transported to another country by air, Scot notes that this vision was not caused by witchcraft, as people believed, but claims rather that the "imagination shall abuse such as are subject unto melancholie." Catholic priests, like witches, are vulnerable to the power of the imagination and the disease of "melancholy." Again, we see that the source of what might seem to be Scot's rational skepticism is in fact a mix of prejudice against women and the Catholic church. Patriarchal authority, of course, occupied the minds of the witch-mongers. For sixteenth-century demonologists, the inferiority of women was self-evident and, by suppressing witches, they believed they were creating greater social control. In fact, on the topic of women, Scot has distinct similarities with many of the witch-hunters he deplores. We might consider, for example, his attack on Brian Darcey, the justice of the peace who was extremely active in the assize trials at St. Osyth in 1582.

Darcey's record, like that of Matthew Hopkins, the witch-finder general of the mid-seventeenth century, is noteworthy for its inquisitorial nature. In one of his pamphlets, Darcey, revealing a web of relations between many women and all their familiars, argues that the women use devilish spirits to revenge the local "collector appointed for the poor," who has deprived them of beef and bread. Darcey and others convince numerous women that they are using familiars to enact revenge on those who have refused them charity. Scot spends a great deal of time refuting jurors like Darcey who assume in their arguments the power of the devil and the capacity of women to make enchantments, reminding us once again that to attribute such agency to women is misguided:

> She, being called before a Justice, by due examination of the circumstances is driven to see her imprecations and desires, and her neighbours' harms and losses to concur, and as it were, to take effect; and so confesseth that she, as a goddess, hath brought such things to pass. Wherein not only she, but the accuser and also the Justice are foully deceived and abused, as being through her confession and other circumstances persuaded, to the injury of God's glory, that she hath done or can do that which is proper only to God himself . . . (5)

Scot and Darcy clearly part ways in their assessment of which acts women are truly capable of performing. Nevertheless, their views converge on one key element of this debate: both want to strengthen the force of God by reducing the "glory" of any woman who acts like a "goddess." Darcey writes,

> . . . all the imaginations, all the consultations, all the conferences, all the experiments, finally, all the attempts, proceedings and conclusions of sorcerers, witches and the rest of that hellish livery, are mere blasphemers against the person of the most high God.[31]

Scot agrees that these "imaginations" and "experiments" are a form of blasphemy against God, even if he doesn't believe they are truly effective in the world. Writing at a time when the persecution of Catholics was intensifying, Darcey and Scot turned their attention to the eradication of practices that challenged the "Glorie of God" and the Protestant religion. They also felt the need to control the practices of women who deemed themselves "goddesses" and thus crossed over the patriarchal boundaries so clearly laid out by the Protestant authorities of the day.

Although he states unequivocally that he wants to debunk the myths propagated by the misogynistic fifteenth-century witch-hunting guide, Sprenger and Kramer's *Malleus Maleficarum*, Scot still utilizes much of its propaganda. In particular, he incorporates Sprenger and Kramer's declaration that women are more "impressionable" and "more feeble in mind and spirit" than men. Devoted in part to what we now call, after Lacan, the possession of the phallus, the *Malleus Maleficarum* attempts to uncover the evil nature of female subjectivity, to show how women's power is linked to the power of the devil. Women, lacking a phallus, can obtain power only by using the devil's phallus. Sprenger and Kramer (and their many followers) announced the possibility that witches "may work some Prestidigitory illusion so that the Male Organ appears to be entirely removed and separate from the body."[32] Another claim was that devils used female agents—succubi—to copulate with males in their sleep in order to withdraw the semen that would then be implanted in the woman by the devil in the form of incubi.[33] Moreover, since women's bodies and minds are weaker than men's, this text informs us, they are more susceptible to the workings of the devil. *The Discoverie* and the *Malleus Maleficarum* share a similar contempt for the minds and bodies of women.

After arguing that women lack the capacity to usurp God's rule, Scot further circumscribes the powers of all human beings who attempt to perform his duties. Social practices and philosophical pursuits—from Neoplatonism to treasure seeking—are associated with the irrational female mind. Since to compete with God's power is impossible, any attempt to do so is the product of a weak, feminine, or effeminate mind; Scot thereby effectively disavows the idea that women can have autonomous magical power of their own. Thus, with a skepticism powered by misogyny more than objective scientific method, he dismisses the beliefs of cabalists, talmudists, and magi. By putting his rhetoric of reform in gendered terms—by claiming that only "effeminate" men "go ahoring after strange gods"—Scot is better able to envision religious uniformity in England.

III

Advocating greater mercy for the poor and seeking the reformation of beggars, Scot was alert to some of the most significant social changes in Elizabethan life. Although he was aware of the conditions of poverty that surrounded witchcraft charges, he did not propose any socioeconomic changes that might alleviate the problem. Instead, he believed that casting aside the Catholic religion would ultimately dissolve the charges of witchcraft and thereby reform the social conditions. My concluding section will contrast Scot's religious response to these social ills with the social protest we find in Dekker, Ford, and Rowley's *The Witch of Edmonton*.

Scot was a Justice of the Peace for a short time, but his skepticism of witches was not shared by other representatives of the state; moreover, he was unhappy with the state's treatment of old, impoverished widows. In the opening epistle to the *Discoverie* (1651 edition), he expresses his desires to Sir Roger Manwood, an exchequer:

I know you spend more time and travell in the conversion and reformation, than in the subversion and confusion of offenders, as being well pleased to augment your own private pains, to the end you may diminish their public smart. For in truth, that commonwealth remaineth in wofull state, where fetters and halters bear more sway than mercy and due compassion.[34]

Scot hoped that the courts would treat charges of witchcraft with more skepticism and show greater mercy toward the victims of these accusations. Courts should work toward the "conversion" and "reformation" of offenders. His empiricism is particularly impressive in a series of chapters that look at the way inquisitors gathered evidence: they extracted confessions from old, poor, women through torture and imprisonment; they allowed "infants, wicked servants, and runnawaies" to make accusations. No one had actually seen the accused women flying through the air or copulating with the devil, but that made no difference to the inquisitors or judges throughout Europe, who lacked Scot's skeptical temperament.

Scot also observed the process by which women in English villages were charged with witchcraft. A woman would, out of necessity, beg for charity. Her hopes would be dashed, however, as neighbors refused to help and instead chastised her for "lewdnesse." After time had passed and the woman "waxeth odious and tedious to hir neighbors," she cursed everyone and everything in a household: the master, his wife, children, cattle, and the "little pig that lieth in the stie" (5). Inevitably, some misfortune came to pass: parents died, children fell ill, cattle perished. In the end, the woman would be called before a judge and forced to confess that she had used witchcraft to bring about such misfortunes.

The scenario described by Scot is remarkably similar to that provided by twentieth-century historians as a model for most witchcraft accusations in sixteenth-century England. As Alan MacFarlane, Keith Thomas, and Robin Briggs have shown, the act of begging was crucial to virtually all charges of *maleficium* in England.[35] In contrast with continental practice, English witch trials contained few wild narratives about witches' Sabbaths, orgies, or the Walpurgisnacht. The majority of trials were based on accusations of damage to health or property along the lines of one generic scenario of begging: First, an impecunious member of the community asks for charity, which is evaded. Second, those who have refused to offer charity suffer misfortune (illness, property damage, or the like). Third, the destitute person, usually an elderly woman, is identified as a "witch" who has cursed those who have incurred misfortune and thereby has caused the damage.[36]

The plight of such witches, then, resembled that of vagabonds, beggars, and other poor people who had the misfortune of living at a time of major structural upheaval. Throughout the sixteenth century, population increased steadily while food supplies and employment could not keep up. The dissolution of the monasteries during the Henrician Reformation did away with one of the primary means of assisting the poor. To alleviate the disorder wrought by enclosures, population growth, and the breakdown of manorial estates, the state provided more centralized institutional controls of "masterless men." Poor Law, for example, unlike manorial or feudal poor relief, criminalized poverty while regulating the lives of those trapped in this newly formed underclass. Severe punishments for the poor seeking assistance included, J. Thomas Kelly tells us, "the stocks, pillory . . . ear-boring, ear-cutting, branding . . . houses of correction, and workhouses."[37]

Thus a significant portion of the population in sixteenth-century England shared in the misery experienced by witches. Uprooted and seeking new forms of charity from the state, many suffered from the increasingly wide gap between the rich and poor; consequently, the poor would be regarded as the "quintessential other,"[38] and older, Franciscan attitudes toward poverty and charity gave way to intense fear, condemnation, and persecution.[39] Often the product of prevalent tensions concerning poverty, witchcraft charges led Scot to hope that the state would alleviate much of this disorder and misery. *The Discoverie*, one of many publications bemoaning disorder and superstition, demonstrated by comparison a great deal of perspicuity in its observation that it was mainly beggars who were being charged with witchcraft.

Yet while Scot recognized the problem of poverty, he turned toward religious uniformity as the solution to social ills. His primary concern, as we have seen, was that witches and witchmongers "go awhoring after strange gods" and thereby damage the glory of God. When he does address the treatment of the poor, his attention quickly turns to the "papist" mentalities of those involved in witch trials. In a review of the habits of Catholic witchmongers, for example, he describes judges wearing "conjured salt, palme, herbes" and other items approved by the

Catholic Church for protection against witches in court. Interrogating witches in prison, inquisitors hang crosses around the witches' necks and place relics of saints around their naked bodies. Having exposed similar superstitions in Protestant England, Scot hopes that they will soon be eradicated. At no point, however, does he offer potential solutions to the socioeconomic problems that plagued England at the time.

Several decades later we find a remarkable play that probed more deeply into the social context of witch accusations. Thomas Dekker, John Ford, and William Rowley's Jacobean play *The Witch of Edmonton* (1621) offered one of the most powerful protests against the labeling and scapegoating of the poor as "witches." Based on actual events that had been sensationalized in ballads and moralistic pamphlets, the play allows the witch to reply to her persecutors and perhaps even gain the ear of a sympathetic Jacobean audience.

Early in the play we find Elizabeth Sawyer gathering sticks on her neighbor's property. After Old Banks, the cruel neighbor, beats her, Sawyer curses him, and the scenario outlined by Scot and recent historians runs its course. There is, however, one important addition to the typical scenario: Sawyer displays an extraordinary awareness of the social process that has shaped her consciousness.

> And why on me? Why should the envious world
> Throw all their scandalous malice upon me?
> 'Cause I am poor, deformed and ignorant,
> And like a bow buckled and bent together
> By some more strong in mischiefs than myself,
> Must I for that be made a common sink
> For all the filth and rubbish of men's tongues
> To fall and run into? Some call me witch,
> And, being ignorant of myself, they go
> About to teach me how to be one, urging
> That my bad tongue, by their bad usage made so,
> Forspeaks their cattle, doth bewitch their corn,
> Themselves, their servants and their babes at nurse.
>
> (2.1.1–13)[40]

The real Elizabeth Sawyer may have been less astute than this fictive version, who recognizes her identity of "witch" as a social construct. In this version, Sawyer may be a victim, but at least she is fully aware of the process that has led to her downfall: she has been singled out for being poor, uneducated, and "deformed"; uninterested in witchcraft, she has nevertheless been taught by her accusers how to be a witch.

Who better to illustrate Scot's argument that witches are usually poor, lame women? Although *The Witch of Edmonton* does not deny the reality of witchcraft, it does expose the violent process used to construct a "witch." In fact, the playwrights' protest stems from a striking understanding of the psychological and social factors behind the victimization of the poor. Sawyer illuminates a psychological process we moderns have become more familiar with: interpellation. She has been, to use Althusser's term, "hailed" as a witch. She has internalized a role imposed on her by her malicious neighbors. Perhaps most striking in the speech is Sawyer's high level of self-consciousness and social awareness about the way in which she has been interpellated by the discourse on witchcraft.

Dekker, Ford, and Rowley liberated the story of Elizabeth Sawyer from the hands of the inquisitorial Henry Goodcole. The source for the play, a pamphlet written by Goodcole, a minister who visited Elizabeth Sawyer in prison, outlines the process whereby a figure of authority makes a woman come to believe she is a witch. Goodcole describes Sawyer with what he calls "Truth's authority":

> That tongue which by cursing, swearing, blaspheming, and imprecating, as afterward she confessed, was the occasioning cause of the Devil's access unto her, even at that time, and to claim her thereby as his own, by it discovered her lying, swearing, and blaspheming as also evident proofs produced against her, to stop her mouth with Truth's authority.

The minister says that the "public and private marks on her body" provide the ocular proof of her criminal nature: "Her body was crooked and deformed, even bending together which so happened but a little before her apprehension."[41] According to the minister, Sawyer's blasphemous language made her vulnerable to the Devil and gave him "access" to her. Throughout the pamphlet, Goodcole acts as a kind of ventriloquist, putting words on the page for Sawyer that clearly fit his moral agenda.

It is particularly striking how the authors of *The Witch of Edmonton* invert the minister's misogynistic hostility to the "tongue" of Sawyer (a standard complaint about shrewish, witch-like women) by supplying her with the language of social protest. Indeed, Sawyer speaks out against the filth and rubbish of her male accusers' tongues.[42]

In the fourth act of the play, Sawyer's critique moves beyond the confines of village life. She points out that "witch" is a "universal name" that might easily describe "painted things in princes' courts,/ Upon whose eyelids lust sits, blowing fires/ To burn men's souls in sensual hot desires" (4.1.118–20). She also describes "men-witches" who "can, without the fangs of law/ Drawing once one drop of blood, put counterfeit pieces/Away for true gold" (4.1.157–59). Confronting the judge who will condemn her to death, Sawyer denounces the corrupt mores of those at the top of the social hierarchy: "Men in gay clothes,/ Whose backs are laden with titles and honours,/Are within far more crooked than I am,/And if I be a witch, more witchlike" (4.1.88–91). Sawyer unmasks the corrupt operations of the law and the decadence of life at court with the forceful language of avengers like Hieronimo, Vindice, or Hamlet. Indeed, while the *Witch of Edmonton* does not qualify as a revenge play, the authors were clearly influenced by the frustrations with the law and the complaints about court life commonly found in that genre.[43]

Rather than focus on the metaphysical, demonic pact (as theologians were wont to do), Sawyer directs the audience's attention to the social ills of the time. As Richard Grinnel points out, "Dekker, Rowley, and Ford continue to link the financial world with the demonic, and now place the blame for witchcraft on society and the economy. Poverty and social intolerance, the play seems to argue, make witches."[44] The reality of witchcraft is never fully disputed, however, since Sawyer's desire for revenge does in fact alert the devil. As in Christopher Marlowe's *Doctor Faustus*, devils appear when, as Mephistopheles puts it, "we hear one rack the name of God, Abjure the Scriptures, and his saviour christ,/We fly in hope to get his glorious soul" (3.3.48–49). Sawyer says she will "Abjure all goodness, be at hate with prayer,/And study curses, imprecations, / Blasphemous speeches . . ." (2.1.119–21).

For much of the play, Sawyer is accompanied by Tom, her

canine familiar who does have supernatural power. Nevertheless, the dog adds more pathos to Sawyer's character by estab-
lishing her loneliness and desperation. The audience is
reminded that her isolation is ultimately the fault of a callous
community rather than her evil nature. Thus, while the "supernatural" is surely present, the play leads us to believe that the
discourse on witchcraft is, for the most part, a product of a
time out of joint—when neighborliness has vanished and the
community turns against those most in need of help.

The plight of Sawyer runs parallel to the economic struggle
in the main plot. Frank Thorney, the son of a gentleman, must
work as a servant after his family fortunes fall precipitously.
His master, Sir Arthur Clarington, tricks Thorney into marry-
ing one of his pregnant servants, Winnifride, who also happens
to be Sir Arthur's longtime mistress. But after Thorney marries
Winnifride and the duplicitous Sir Arthur withdraws the financial support he promised his two servants, Thorney's father
insists that he marry Susan Carter, the daughter of a well-to-
do yeoman. Frank complies, and his sin of bigamy leads ultimately to his murder of Susan and, consequently, to his execution. In both plots, then, "unnatural acts" do not result from
some inherent "evil" but rather from social pressures and the
cruel actions of Banks and Sir Arthur. The two plots are neatly
joined by Sawyer's indictment of people like Sir Arthur: "Dare
any swear I ever tempted maiden,/With golden hooks flung at
her chastity,/To come and lose her honour, and being lost,/To
pay not a denier for't?" (4.1.153–56).[45]

The *Witch of Edmonton*, like Scot's *Discoverie,* pokes fun at
popular "superstitions." Kathleen McLuskie points out that
the play would "entertain an urbane audience with scenes
from country life."[46] Indeed, several passages are indebted to
the skeptic George Gifford, who found that many witchcraft
beliefs were based on laughable notions. For example, the
playwrights include a story recycled from Gifford's *Dialogue
Concerning Witches and Witchcrafts*, which reports that "a
third man came in, and he said she [a witch] was once angry
with him, he had a dun cow which was tied up in a house, for
it was winter, he feared that some evil would follow, and for
his life he could not come in where she was, but he must needs
take up her tail and kiss under it."[47] Yet while the play reflects

an urbane skepticism toward such narratives, it does not follow Scot in abandoning belief in witchcraft altogether.

While such links between *The Witch of Edmonton* and Scot's *Discovery* are significant, we should also acknowledge important differences. In particular, Scot does not make such a radical leap toward socioeconomic explanations for human behavior. As Larry Champion points out in his study of Jacobean drama, such tragedies "emerge from the growing spiritual uncertainties of an analytical age no longer prone to accept without question either a universe informed by transcendent and inscrutable reasons or human conduct predicated fundamentally on traditional religio-social values."[48] Scot's skepticism is an entirely different animal: his empiricism, his doubt toward witchcraft practices and beliefs, served to strengthen his faith in the divine providence of the Protestant God.

According to Scot, the mistreatment of women like Elizabeth Sawyer would simply disappear with greater religious order; the solution to social dislocation, in other words, lay not in improving material conditions but in altering religious ideas. He confronted the social dislocations of sixteenth-century England by calling for a more complete extirpation of the roots of the old religion. Scot believed that the Reformation had shed light on the world, and that the truth of God's word had been taken from the wicked hands of priests and witch-mongers: "Now the Word of God being more free, open and knowne, those conceipts and illusions are made more manifest and apparent" (269). The ideological meaning of "discovery" is powerfully expressed in these lines: Scot may have wanted to alleviate the suffering of witches, but he also wanted to expose the deceit of the Catholics, whom he saw as the worst deviants in the world. Driven by this *idée-fixe*, anti-Catholicism, Scot had no idea how to solve the social problems of a time out of joint and instead focused on his ideological goal of spreading the word of the Protestant faith to those who stubbornly persisted in the old religious ways.

As we have seen in this chapter, it is somewhat of a mistake to see in Scot the precursor to the rational, scientific worldview. Although empiricism does play a role in his skepticism toward witchcraft, we must also consider the pivotal roles played by his anti-Catholicism and patriarchal views on women.

In the next chapter we will look at the skepticism of Thomas Harriot, the Elizabethan scientist who took part in England's early attempts to colonize North America. The evangelical goals of English colonialism overlapped to some extent with the goals of reformers like Scot. Scot hoped that the true religion would be spread throughout England, while colonial planners hoped they would be able to eliminate pagan superstition by extending Protestantism overseas. Richard Hakluyt, for example, gave first priority to England's missionary goal of "increasing the force of the Christians," and bringing the "glory of God" to the "infidels." Scot set his sights closer to home, yet he also extended his "discovery" of witchcraft to places outside Europe, thus connecting the superstitious beliefs around the world with those at home. For example, he exposed, or shall we say, re-exposed the errors of the naked gymnosophists of India, who "like apes imitate Esaie."[49] He also compared witchcraft beliefs in Africa and Europe:

> Many great and grave authors write, and manie fond writers also affirme, that there are certeine families in Aphrica which with their voices bewitch whatsoever they praise . . . This mysterie of witchcraft is not unknowne or neglected of our witchmongers, and superstitious fooles heere in Europa. (281)

The disclosure of superstition on the European continent and around the globe assists his identification of internal enemies—papists, witchmongers, and heretics—who remain in England, a country he presents as infested with superstition.

Thomas Harriot was in an ideal position to strengthen the Protestant nation by spreading its culture and beliefs to people overseas. But Harriot, as we will see, did not share Scot's zeal for reform, nor did he share the evangelical enthusiasm of Richard Hakluyt and other colonial planners.

2

"The Mayster of all essentiall and true knowledge": Thomas Harriot in the New World

THE VOYAGES TO AMERICA IN THE 1580S WERE AN OFFSHOOT OF emerging social conditions in England: the establishment of a mercantile class, the growth of the city of London, the concentration of power in the hands of the monarch, and the fusion of church and state. As George Chapman noted, the new mercantile class could accumulate wealth and enhance the power of the monarch through overseas adventures. He asked England's "patrician spirits" to "lift your eies for guidance to the starres,/ That live not for your selves, but to possesse/Your honour'd countrey of a general store."[1] Another socioeconomic motive for travel to the New World was the increasing unemployment and overpopulation in London. Immigrants from the provinces flocked to the city, swelling its population with apprentices, merchants, and others hoping to increase their fortunes. One solution proposed for handling the resulting overcrowding and unemployment was to encourage Londoners to emigrate to potential colonies in the New World. Finally, colonization was seen as an opportunity for the growing nation to spread its religious ideology abroad while consolidating it at home. After all, England was God's nation and he expected it to spread his Word.

The new mercantile class, often blamed for fostering acquisitive or "covetous" behavior, played a central role in the development of the nation even as it exacerbated moral and social uncertainty. The growth of London, as Ian Archer points out, generated much anxiety because the city muddled moral categories and undermined social boundaries.[2] The fusion of church and state, the sine qua non of the new national culture, also fostered much doubt: because unity in religion was essential to political stability, the climate of religious dissonance intensified the political upheavel.

Moreover, many people feared that contact with foreign lands might further upset a time already out of joint. Debates about the value of travel abounded. In Thomas Nashe's *Unfortunate Traveller*, a fictive earl discourages the picaresque English adventurer Jack Wilton from remaining in Italy: "If it bee languages, thou maist learne them at home; nought but lasciviousness is to bee learned here."[3] And vicious criticisms were made of travelers like Thomas Harriot who learned the language of alien cultures. Indeed, the English feared much more than foreign languages, as contact with foreign cultures inspired probing questions about cultural identity: could it be that English social and religious truths were not absolute, permanent, and universal? Such inevitable questions threatened the nation's cultural identity, an identity whose stability was already weakened by internal stresses.

Thus the English, as Karen Kupperman, Jeffrey Knapp, and others have argued, were profoundly ambivalent about the expansion of trade and plans for new colonies. On the one hand, they wanted to assert themselves on the world stage and prove their superiority to other nations. On the other hand, they feared that mingling with foreign cultures might further erode their own national identity. As Knapp observes, England's early colonial failures accentuated the instability of the nation's identity: "England's troubled colonialism . . . seems only to complete a larger picture of National isolation."[4] This sense of isolation, we might add, also reflects the self-doubt of a nation in turmoil.

Hence the arrogance of Queen Elizabeth, who called for the abolition of ignorance, error, and superstition in her dominions in Europe and in the New World, belied deep-seated anxieties. With so much religious discord at home, the English never felt entirely confident about their evangelical colonialism. A skeptic like Thomas Harriot, caught in such controversy over the one true religion, gives us a window onto this struggle.

Long admired by scholars for his contributions to ethnography, mathematics, atomism, and optics, Thomas Harriot became a household name among period scholars only after the publication of Stephen Greenblatt's "Invisible Bullets." That essay, hotly contested in literary debates of the 1980s and early 1990s, is most famous today for its notorious and largely discredited theory of "subversion/containment." Now that this theory no longer seems adequate for our understanding of Harriot's *A Briefe and True Report of the New Found Land of Virginia* (1588), it is time to reconsider this important document in the history of skepticism.

Greenblatt argues that the explicitly Protestant and nationalist goals of Harriot's report manage to "contain" the "subversive" ideas within it. Its appearance of objectivity notwithstanding, the skepticism of the text, he tells us, in fact serves to strengthen the project of evangelic colonialism, since there is a "powerful logic" governing the relation of orthodoxy and subversion.[5] The subversive idea Greenblatt refers to is Harriot's "Machiavellian hypothesis," the notion that religion is merely a form of coercion and control. According to Greenblatt, appearances to the contrary, this heterodox thinking in the *Report* ultimately works to further the English goal of spreading Protestantism and gaining political control of the New World. The English colony relied on Christianity to maintain political and economic control over the natives, and Harriot, Greenblatt says, responded accordingly with the full force of evangelical colonialism. The claim is that whether or not Harriot himself held deeply skeptical views is unimportant; the ultimate effect of his practice is what mattered, and that effect was that religion was used as a means of keeping the Algonquins in awe of English power.

Greenblatt also applies the containment model to the very nature of Harriot's description: "The recording of alien voices, their preservation in Harriot's text, is part of the process whereby Indian culture is constituted as a culture and thus brought into the light for study, discipline, correction, and transformation."[6] Is Harriot's remarkable description simply an ideological means of absorbing, altering, and controlling Algonquin culture? It is clear that the goal of the English was to gain hegemony for a future colony, but is there really an insidious logic of domination behind each and every aspect of Harriot's narrative? Greenblatt's model accounts for the pernicious aspects of this ethnographic description—its goal of controlling and transforming an alien culture—without explaining how it also strives to grasp genuine cultural differences.

In this chapter I will make two interrelated arguments: first, Harriot's evangelical colonialism is not as straightforward as Greenblatt suggests, since Harriot often calls the entire practice into question. Indeed, he rejects the evangelical mindset we find in most travel narratives from the Elizabethan and Jacobean periods. Second, I will argue that the *Briefe and True Report* displays an extraordinary ethnographic receptivity, a willingness to engage cultural difference by occasionally suspending—though not, of course, ignoring—European cultural norms. Putting aside Greenblatt's model of subversion/containment (which others have already deconstructed), I would like to give more emphasis to Harriot's skepticism.

The first section of the chapter will argue that Harriot was indeed a skeptic; the second will show how his skepticism is revealed in his ethnographic receptivity and in the way his report on Virginia complicates the evangelical goals of colonialism. The third section looks at the report's unstable binary of savagism and civility as further evidence of his ethnographic receptivity. The final section, which examines Chapman's poetry about Harriot and other "patrician spirits" in the New World, focuses on the nonevangelical, economic, and scientific interests behind Harriot's voyage.

I

Harriot's reputation for impiety, specifically for denying salvation, the immortality of the soul, and creation *ex nihilo*, began in the early stages of his career and survives to the present. Although these charges were not entirely without evidence, it is impossible to discern the extent of his unorthodox beliefs when we have only fragments, traces, and rumors of Harriot's personal beliefs on theological matters. We will never unlock the heart of his mystery. Why, then, is Harriot often called a "skeptic"? While he may not have followed a philosophical system of doubt or explicitly called the existence of God into question, he did seem to entertain ideas that were threatening to the prescribed beliefs of Protestant England. Harriot was an eclectic thinker who, in the course of experimenting with the diverse religious and intellectual traditions of the Renaissance, appears to have been inclined toward heresy.

Aware of his reputation as a conjurer and atheist, Harriot made a meticulous list of published references to himself and his work.[7] The list includes items that did not refer to Harriot by name, and it would appear he recognized himself in such titles as "mathematician" and "navigator." He also identified himself in some of these works as the unnamed subject of vituperative attacks on atheists.[8] He had reason at this point in his life to worry about how he was perceived by others. In a sense, then, the search for Harriot that continues today was initially assisted by Harriot himself.

It is not surprising that Harriot developed a reputation for heterodoxy, since critics often feared that science neglected religious and spiritual matters. Scientists, the critics argued, often shed light on the material world while leaving the spirit and salvation in darkness. Reason, of course, might be used to support religion; but it might also lead the scientist to focus on matter at the expense of spirit. An anonymous manuscript from 1594, examined recently by Stephen Clucas, describes Harriot's skeptical reasoning as going so far as to question the basic tenets of Christianity. The manuscript raises a series of questions about the Christian God, including the notion that he is the "first cause" and the creator of miracles. Clucas, who argues that the manuscript provides an authentic glimpse at Harriot, ends his lecture on this text dramatically: "But for all the open-mindedness and subtle interrogations, these notes do seem to be evidence of a man who has '[established] reason as his God' and has closed his mind to the truisms of conventional theology."[9] Christian supporters of science often argued that it could be a handmaid of theology: according to this manuscript, however, Harriot replaced religion with science.[10]

Harriot's religious views were often debated by those who worried that he adhered to not only the scientific but also the ethical arguments of atomism.[11] Harriot believed that atoms constitute the smallest, indivisible units of matter. In his manuscripts, he challenged the Aristotelian idea that matter is infinitely divisible:

Nothing comes out of nothing; nothing further comes out of one; a third thing cannot come out of two; from a trinity comes what you please. A plenum cannot come from a plenum; a hand from a hand. Two bodies cannot be in the same place; there is nothing without movement; there is no movement without mass; therefore nothing comes from nothing.[12]

One item stands out for its religious significance: "from a trinity comes what you please." He might have said, following the logical progression, that four things cannot come out of three. Instead, this line seems to mock the idea of the holy trinity with the words "what you please," which suggest a certain randomness or arbitrariness in the doctrine, if not a *reductio ad absurdum* of it. The other lines may be heretical as well, since, when applied to the story of creation in the Bible, they call into doubt the existence of a divine creator. How could he have created something out of nothing?

We know that Harriot pursued this scientific side of atomism; we cannot be certain, however, that he accepted the ethical side of atomism as propounded by the Roman materialist Lucretius, whose religious views clashed with orthodox Christian thought. In Lucretius' *De Rerum Natura*, the ethical and spiritual implications of atomism are clear: when we die, the conglomeration of matter that constitutes individual identity disperses. There is no spiritual afterlife, only atoms moving in the void. The afterlife is mere superstition, and, more important, a source of pain, misery, and much of the violence of humanity. Thus the atomic theory of matter was also a major threat to one of the most crucial doctrines of Christianity, that of the punishment of sin in the afterlife.[13]

Lucretius believed he had unmasked the religious dogma that prevents worshipers from experiencing *ataraxia*, the tranquil state of the mind one reaches by fully accepting one's fate. Over the course of two thousand years, only a happy few seem to have gained solace from his most famous dictum: "Nil igitur mors est ad nos neque pertinet hilum, / quandoquidem natura animi mortalis habetur" (Since the nature of the soul is considered mortal, death matters not in the least to us). Far from providing consolation, the view was more often seen as heretical. Thus, despite the importance of atomist theory for the new science in the seventeenth century, the ethical aspects of such materialism were typically denounced.

Harriot may have simply been uninterested in pursuing the

philosophical aspects of atomism; his main concern appears to have been in the movement of particles of light. Whether or not Harriot was a Lucretian atheist, he must have been aware that his scientific practice was not entirely compatible with the orthodox providentialism of Christianity. The Epicurean/Lucretian doctrine *ex nihilo nihil fit* calls into doubt the notion of decay in Christian theology as well as the moral views of sin and divine retribution. Francis Bacon engaged ancient atomism in his early work, but effaced its radical atheistic stance by arguing that such "infinite small portions" need a "divine marshall."[14] Scientific thinkers were by no means the only ones interested in this Epicurean, materialist doctrine: in Marlowe's *The Jew of Malta*, Barabas says, "Of nought is nothing made"; Shakespeare's King Lear says "nothing will come from nothing." As we will see in chapter four, in the latter play, the word "nothing," which appears over and over again, contributes to an intense and pervasive skepticism. Clearly, this heretical notion was widely in circulation and it appeared from time to time in the context of highly skeptical thinking.

So what did Harriot really think of atomism? Other thinkers of his day claimed he accepted its atheistic side, but what evidence is there for such a claim? John Aubrey, moralizing on Harriot's death from what we now know to have been cancer, tells us that Harriot finally encountered the wrath of God and was put in his place by the providential order he was believed to have called into question when he studied atomism: "a *nihilum* killed him at last: for in the top of his nose came a little red speck (exceeding small), which grew bigger and bigger, and at last killed him."[15] We may never know, however, whether Harriot accepted the ethical ramifications of Lucretian atomism. Still, it is important to note that Harriot's silence on the ethical implications of his atomism may have had a lot to do with his fear of meeting a fate like that of Giordano Bruno. Throughout his life Harriot was on the defensive. In 1605 he wrote to the privy council from jail: "I was never any busy medler in matters of state . . . I was never ambitious for preferments. But contented with a private life for the love of learning that I might study freely."[16] Not all heterodox thinkers were so private about their work. Bruno, for example, publicly professed his passion for an alternative to Catholicism based on an older, Egyptian magic found in the *Corpus Hermeticum*.

When the Roman inquisition burned him at the stake in 1600, it may well have been concerned about his theological interests as well as his belief in the infinity and plurality of worlds. I am inclined to think that Harriot, who had a lot in common with Bruno, did not bring the beliefs of his "private life" out into the public because he wanted to avoid persecution and continue his experiments in peace. Any skeptical leanings would be kept implicit or entirely hidden, perhaps revealed only by clues in his work.

And in fact, Harriot's heterodoxy, as we will soon see in more detail, is indeed further revealed in his report on Virginia. His research on the history of the Algonquins seems to have raised questions others did not want to hear. Richard Baines's scandalous report on Christopher Marlowe to the Privy Council in 1593, for example, accused Marlowe of saying "That the indians and many Authors of antiquity have assuredly written of above 16 thousand yeares agone whereas Adam is proved to have lived within 6 thowsand yeares."[17] This challenge to biblical chronology, also made by Giordano Bruno, was known as the pre-Adamic heresy.[18] Did Harriot's study of the Indians suggest to him that biblical chronology was wrong? He would have been well known as an authority on the religion of the Indians, since his report was already popular by the date of the Baines note (1593). Thomas Nashe's diatribe against atheism makes this connection even more plausible. He insists that such atheists in England "followe the Pironicks, whose position and opinion it is, that there is no Hel or misery but opinion. Impudently they persist in it, that the late discovered Indians, are able to shew antiquities, thousands before Adam."[19] We do, in fact, have evidence from his manuscripts that Harriot was familiar with the Pyrrhonist tradition.[20] We may never know who exactly these "Pironicks" were that Nashe referred to, but who could fit this description better than an authority on the Indians with a reputation for atheistic thinking?

Harriot's detractors saw his ethnographic receptivity as a threat to orthodox Christianity, and thus his reputation for atheism intensified after the widespread publication of the *Briefe and True Report*. Even if Baines and Nashe were merely trying to damage Harriot's reputation, they picked up on an important truth about him: the heterodox ideas in his ethnography raised difficult questions about religion and the process of conversion. It is not surprising, then, that he was widely read in works of pagan humanism, heretical religious doctrines, Patristic texts, and Catholic texts, actively pursuing a comparativist approach to religion throughout his life.[21] In the next section I will demonstrate that Harriot's *Briefe and True Report* does indeed exhibit the kind of heterodoxy that made him notorious.

II

Travel narratives in Elizabethan and Jacobean England generally denounced unchristian practices in no uncertain terms and adopted a particularly harsh tone on native religion. In these texts, we find no hint, as we do in Harriot's work, that there might be a legitimate alternative to the Christian religion. Richard Hakluyt, one of the most important supporters of exploration and colonization in the 1580s, made it clear that evangelism was absolutely crucial to the project; indeed, it was part of God's plan to bring pagans to the faith of Christ. In an attachment to John Brereton's *A Briefe and True Relation of the Discoverie of the North Part of Virginia*, Richard Hakluyt's "Inducements for the liking of the voyage intended towards Virginia" lists the priorities of voyages to Virginia. The first is "the glory of God by planting of religion among those infidels" and the second "the increase of the force of the Christians." Other "inducements" include the enlarging of the Queen's dominions and the expansion of trade.[22] Harriot, whose report on Virginia was included in Hakluyt's *Principal Navigations*, did not prioritize religion in this way.

In fact, in most travel narratives on Virginia, it is hard to find anything remotely akin to Harriot's ethnographic receptivity, and the rhetoric of conversion tends to be much stronger and unyielding than his.[23] Ralph Hamor's *A True Discourse of the Present Estate of Virginia* (1614), for example, cries out for the need to bring the Indians the gospel of Christ: "when these poore Heathens shall be brought to entertaine the honour of the name, and glory of the Gospell of our blessed Saviour, when they shall testifie of the true and everliving God, and Jesus Christ to be their Salvation, their knowledge so inlarged and sanctified that without him they confesse their eternal death."[24] At no point did Harriot write with such evangelical enthusiasm, and indeed he often expressed doubt as to whether or not the English could successfully convert the Algonquins to Christianity.[25]

Typical narratives on Virginia also make repeated and un-equivocal claims to divine providence and support. Hamor's *True Discourse* attributes the cause of most natural events—the fecundity of animals, men's personal safety—to "the provi-dence of God." The Puritan minister Alexander Whitaker, who converted Pocahontas, is even more insistent on the power of God in directing the English in every aspect of their coloniza-tion: "I have shut up many things in few words, and have al-leadged this onely to prove unto us, that the finger of God hath been the onely true worker here; that God first shewed us the place, God first called us hither, and here God by his speciall providence hath maintained us"[26]. As we might expect, Whi-taker, a minister, sees spreading the word of God as the most important factor in the entire colonial endeavor. Conversely, Harriot hardly mentions the power of God, and when he does, the point is overshadowed by his pessimism about the possibil-ity of converting the natives. As we will see, his effort to spread the "true" religion seems halfhearted if not disingenuous.

There is no doubt, of course, that Harriot's report in some sense represents the interests of Protestant England. The in-digenous population, he hopes, will come to "feare and love" the English: "If means of good government bee used, that they may in short time be brought to civilitie, and the imbracing of true religion."[27] These goals are in line with those set forth in Queen Elizabeth's 1584 patent to Ralegh (Harriot's patron in his voyage to North America) "touching the discoverie and in-habiting of certeyn Foreyne Landes and Cuntries":

Whereas the Queenes most exelent Maiestie of her most gracious disposicion to the Benyfite and proffite of her Realme of Englande emongeste sondrie other the singuler frewtes of her goodnes tow-ardes the same Hath by all good meanes endeavored, that the gos-pell of our saviour Jesus Christe might be trewlye and syncerelie sette forth, And Ignorauce error and supersticion Abolished within her Maiesties Domynions, And is also desirous that the knowledge of god and trewe religion might by her heighness Labors be propa-gatyed Amongeste foreign Nacions . . .[28]

Directed at England as well as the "foreign Nacions," the Queen's imperative to abolish "ignoraunce error and supersticion" was one of the most important ideologies of sixteenth and seventeenth-century exploration. The Protestant gospel had several purposes: it would aid in the fight against Spain and other "foreign nations"; it would consolidate the power of church and state within England; and it would propagate "trewe religion" in the New World.

But although Harriot's text includes a similar missionary goal, the *Brief and True Report* ultimately departs from the patent's ideology by making it harder to sustain the binaries of self and other, truth and error, religion and superstition. Indeed, the report leads us to suspect that Harriot's stated goal of converting the natives was merely a kind of lip service, there to appease the more evangelical supporters of colonialism. Throughout the *Report*, the explicit goal of having the Algonquin natives embrace the true religion points to two implicit questions: what, exactly, is the true religion, and how will the English coax, if not coerce, the Algonquins to convert?

Consider first the question of what is the true religion. Is it obvious from his work that Harriot thought Protestantism was the true religion? His interactions with the Algonquins suggest otherwise. At times, Harriot seems quite interested in learning Algonquin religious customs himself, leaving the task of converting them behind. For example, in the first section, he describes the pleasure of partaking in the Algonquin ritual of smoking tobacco: "We ourselves during the time we were there used to suck it after their maner, as also since our returne, & have found maine rare and wonderful experiments of the vertues thereof" (345–46). After describing the Algonquins throwing powdered Uppowoc (tobacco) into the air to delight and pacify the gods, Harriot praises tobacco as a "marchantable commodity" and expresses a sense of wonder at the ritualistic, religious practice.

It is possible that this description is the source of Richard Baines's notorious charge against Christopher Marlowe: "That if Christ would have instituted the sacrament with more Ceremoniall Reverence it would have bin had in more admiration, that it would have bin much better being administered in a Tobacco pipe."[29] Baines goes on in his report to mention Harriot outright, insisting that, according to Marlowe, "Moyses was but a Jugler & that one Heriots being Sir W Raleighs man Can do more than he." While Harriot's participant-observation does not lead him to advocate such a blasphemous cultural relativism, it does contribute to an ethnographic exchange of know-how, a desire to learn about native religious practices and even perform them "after their maner." Significantly, he never moralizes against the religious practice of smoking tobacco. Given such tolerance of the Algonquin rituals, Harriot cannot be said to display here a firm belief that Protestantism or even Christianity should be considered the one true religion.

Consider now the second question posed above: was Harriot ultimately interested in converting the Algonquins? Again, his curiosity and receptivity to Algonquin religious practices make it seem that he was willing to diverge from his official evangelical goal to some real extent. Many travel narratives argued that the Indians would go to hell if they were not converted to Christianity. In Harriot's work, however, we find a detailed account of many native religious beliefs and practices, and, while he does not state they are on a par with those of Christianity, he does not consistently put them in a negative light. For example, he recognizes that they have their own beliefs about the afterlife, beliefs that would surely be considered heretical, and yet he does not place the Algonquins clearly within the Christian framework of divine rewards or punishments:

> They believe that there are many Gods which they call Montoac, but of different sortes and degrees; one onely chiefe and great God, which hath bene from all eternitie. Who as they affirme when hee purposed to make the worlde, made first other goddes of a principall order to bee as meanes and instruments to be used in the creation and government to follow. (372)

Such descriptions are given with an ethnographic detachment unusual in the sixteenth and early seventeenth centuries. In addition, Harriot's description of an Algonquin mortuary for chief lords includes the following statement about the common people kneeling in prayer: "These poore souls are thus instructed by nature to reverence their princes even after their death" (Dover, 72). The line would seem to comment implicitly on the oppressive nature of religion among the Algonquins, and the word "princes" might have raised some eyebrows as readers would have made a connection to monarchs in Europe as well.

Harriot's heterodox fascination with occult practices also places in doubt his evangelical impulses.[30] Scholars have had, as we might expect, very different things to say about this intellectual background, but there is no doubt that Harriot devoted considerable time and thought to alchemy and Hermeticism.[31] Although his chemical experiments may not have begun until around 1599, he was drawn to Hermetic knowledge much earlier. Such experimentation with the occult might explain why Harriot displays a special interest in the Algonquin shaman. If he had followed the pattern of thought in Queen Elizabeth's patent to Ralegh, he would have denounced the Algonquin shaman as superstitious, ignorant, or in error. While projecting the English word "conjuror" onto the shaman, he nevertheless eschews a moralizing Christian perspective:

Engraving of an Algonquin *conjurer*, from Theodore de Bry, *A Briefe and True Report* (1590)

They have comonlye conjurers or juglers which use strange gestures, and often contrarie to nature in their enchantments: For
they be verye familiar with devils, of whome they enquier what
their enemys doe, or other suche thinges. . . . The Inhabitants give
great credit unto their speeche, which oftentymes they finde to bee
true.[32]

Note that Harriot's description effaces the Shamanistic role
and replaces it with conjuring, a concept more familiar to the
English and all too familiar to Harriot's career. The Jesuit Robert Parsons added to Harriot's own reputation as a conjuror in
his attack against Sir Walter Ralegh: "Of Sir Walter Rawley's
Schoole of Atheisme by the waye, and of the Coniurer that is
M. thereof, and of the diligence used to get young gentlemen to
this scholle, where in both Moyses, and our sauior . . . are jested
at."[33] Although the Baines and Parsons libels did not appear
until the 1590s, Harriot's choice of the words "conjuror" and
"juggler" indicates a personal investment, since he was already
aware of his heterodox reputation by the time he wrote on Virginia.[34]

Thus Harriot's self-proclaimed role as deliverer of English
Protestantism is qualified by his own heterodox practices, and
the central binaries of colonization (self/other, truth/error, re-
ligion/superstition) become harder to uphold in an analysis of
his *Report*. The minister Alexander Whitaker's *Good News
from Virginia* (1612), by comparison, provides a more typical
look at Virginian religion:

They acknowledge that there is a great good God, but know him
not, having the eyes of their understanding as yet blinded: where-
fore they serve the divell for feare, after a most base manner, sacri-
ficing sometimes (as I have heere heard their owne Children to
him). Their Priests . . . are no other but such as our English Witches
are. . . . If this bee their life, what thinke you shall become of them
after death?[35]

Harriot's description, we have seen, reveals a much more sympathetic ethnographic perspective: he does not question the
fact that the inhabitants find the shaman credible and truthful.
Whitaker, on the other hand, projects English religious fears of
witches, the devil, and damnation onto the Algonquins. As we
saw earlier in Hamor's narrative, there is no attempt here on

the writer's part to understand a set of unfamiliar religious practices. It would, of course, be impossible for any European entirely to put aside preconceived notions about the world and "reality," but Harriot is undeniably more receptive to the Algonquin religion than his fellow colonialists. Although he projects the English word "conjuror" onto the shaman, he maintains a comparatively impressive degree of distance from the cultural and religious framework that might have blinded him entirely.

Moreover, Harriot was the first European to learn the Algonquin language, and his knowledge in this area almost certainly would have also put his religious orthodoxy in question. A note by John Aubrey reveals the kind of suspicion bred by Harriot's interaction with such a foreign culture: "Dr. Pell tells me that he finds amongst his papers, an alphabet that he contrived for the American language, like Devills."[36] The word "devills" here has a crucial ambiguity—it could refer to the culture of the Algonquins in Virginia, Harriot's occult research (he was charged with necromancy), or both. In Shakespeare's *Henry IV*, part one, Hotspur has a similar reaction to the exotic Welsh spoken by Glendower, a magician whose claim that he "can call spirits from the vasty deep" (3.1.51) makes the English Hotspur hostile to the language of magic and the Welsh language: "Now I perceive the devil understands Welsh" (3.1.225).[37] Two issues most likely inspired Aubrey's anecdote, making Harriot look like an exotic Glendower: first, Harriot made bold attempts to learn a great deal about Algonquin language and culture. He not only put together an alphabet, he became familiar with differences in dialect from town to town: "The language of every government is different from any other, and the further they are distant the greater is the difference" (370). Second, Harriot experimented with occult practices, which marked him publicly as someone who might be raising spirits or devils. Aubrey's note is ambiguous, but given Harriot's reputation as a "conjuror," it is not surprising that learning the language of the Algonquins in detail and working through the language of the occult placed him well outside the boundaries of orthodoxy.

Furthermore, Harriot's knowledge of the Algonquin language made him aware of fundamental difficulties with the missionary project. Acknowledging the disjunction between the two languages, Harriot calls into question the transmission of the Word of God, thus suggesting that English cultural expansion may be a kind of hubris. He notes that:

> They were not so sure grounded, nor gave such credite to their traditions and stories but through conversing with us they were brought into great doubts of their owne, and no small admiration of ours, with earnest desire in many, to learne more than we had meanes for want of perfect utterance in their language to expresse. (375)

English imperialism generally expressed the need to "vent the treasure of our tongue," as Samuel Daniel wrote in *Musophilus*.[38] In most travel narratives of the time, Europeans do not recognize the intersubjective dimension of the encounter. Harriot, on the other hand, shows sensitivity to the way in which the two cultures interact. Thus he notes occasions when language is insufficient for cross-cultural communication or the English comprehension of the natural environment. Of course, he hardly undermines the ideological project of English colonization merely by allowing for mutual error and linguistic confusion, since despite the linguistic limits (or perhaps because of them) the natives had come to admire English traditions and stories more than their own. However, by continually trying to understand the way the Algonquins perceive the world, Harriot maintains a receptive, analytical viewpoint that problematizes any construal of him as self-assured in his possession of cultural truth.

In addition, Harriot's scientific pursuits and interests, as shown in his dealings with the Algonquins, do not reveal a strong evangelical mindset. We can examine, first of all, the rationalism that is particularly prominent in his startling description of how the English subjugated the native population with displays of technological prowess. It is the mysterious objects designed by the godlike Harriot himself, rather than the true word of God (or even any religion), that would enable the English to subjugate the natives. By inspiring awe in the natives, European technology strengthened the colonial enterprise. "Most thinges they sawe with us," he writes,

> as Mathematicall instruments, sea compasses, the vertue of the loadstone in drawing iron, a perspective glasse whereby was

shewed manie strange sightes, burning glasses, wildefire woorkes, gunnes, bookes, writing and reading, spring clocks that seeme to goe of themselves, and manie other thinges that wee had, were so strange unto them, and so farre exceeded their capacities to comprehend the reason and meanes how they should be made and done, that they thought they were rather the works of gods then of men, or at the leastwise they had bin given and taught us of the gods. Which made manie of them to have such opinion of us, as that if they knew not the trueth of god and religion already, it was rather to be had from us, whom God so specially loved then from a people that were so simple, as they found themselves to be in comparison of us. Whereupon greater credite was given unto that we spake of concerning such matters. (376)

With the crucial word "if," Harriot implies that the natives might already know the truth of god and religion. The display of techne may or may not lead them to interrogate their own beliefs. More important, the notion that superior English techne is a sign of divine support is ambiguous, since the passage joins a Machiavellian political logic with a Christian logic of providence, God's support of the English nation. The result of this convergence in Harriot's text is not a form of orthodoxy that balances the charges of atheism against him elsewhere, as some have claimed. Rather, the blend of Machiavellian and Providential reasoning reveals a skeptical mind that tests multiple ways of explaining and describing events. Even as this passage confidently asserts the technological power of the English, it also suggests that religious "truths" are inconsistent and ambivalent.

In the Baines report to the Privy Council, Christopher Marlowe values Harriot even above Moses, who merely puts on a cynical religious performance to keep people under his control: "Moses was but a Juggler, and that one Heriots being Sir W Raleighs man Can do more than he." In the *Briefe and True Report*, Harriot gains authority through the mystification of a technological display.[39] The notion of God as the maker and the English as his chosen few must compete with the more modern notion of *homo faber* and its Machiavellian potential for demystifying providentialism. In other words, Harriot portrays himself as a godlike maker who, far from relying on a divine plan already set in motion, actively shapes the fortunes and perceptions of those around him.[40]

Note that Harriot's display of technology in America closely resembles the displays of royal festivals in the old world: scientific discoveries were often presented, to great interest, in Renaissance courts in the form of political propaganda.[41] Harriot's fireworks evoke the spectacles provided by Elizabeth, Charles I, and others in awe-inspiring royal celebrations of power. Robert Laneham describes the fireworks exhibit for Queen Elizabeth at Kenilworth in 1575 as "blazes of burning darts, flying to and fro, . . . streams and hail of fiery sparks, lightnings of wildfire, . . . thunderbolts, all with such terror . . . that the heavens thundered, the waters surged, the earth shook . . ."[42] Thus Harriot's technological spectacle, believed to make the observers more likely to be in awe of those in authority, had a strong pedigree by the end of the sixteenth century.

To better understand Harriot's use of technology with the Algonquins, we must consider his scientific pursuits before and after his ethnographic description of America. He made major advances in lunar observation, algebra, navigation, map projections, and the trajectory of ordinance. In the area of ballistics, Harriot's mathematics taught Ralegh and other seamen how to stack cannon balls more efficiently and how to make projectile calculations for shooting.[43] Harriot's unorthodox, rationalistic privileging of human as opposed to divine power was indebted to the work of men in his circle. One key figure was Sir Humphrey Gilbert, the visionary explorer who wanted to set up a school called "Queen Elizabeth's Academy" that would train men in letters and science while advancing the imperialist program. Leaving a clear place for Harriot, he says there will be two mathematicians: one employed to work on "imbattleinges, fortificacions, and matters of warre, with the practiz of artillery" while teaching arithmetic and geometry; the other to teach cosmography, astronomy, and the art of navigation.[44] Gilbert also envisions a schoolmaster who will teach Latin and Greek grammar, oration, and philosophy. The point of this academy is to train an elite group of humanists in areas necessary for nation-building, from the art of eloquence to military engineering. Although the academy never materialized, similar schools like Gresham College did. Harriot taught mathematics and cosmography there as a means of educating the men who might help in English efforts at sea. Gilbert clearly saw the academy as an educational alternative to benefit the state, an opportunity to enhance the "gentlemanlike qualitie" gained from more than "schole learninges." The men "shall study matters of accion meet for present practize, both of peace and warre. And if they will not dispose themselves to letters, yet they may learne languages, or martiall activities for the service of their countrey."[45] Harriot would have been an exemplary figure for the academy since he had practical knowledge as well as a traditional humanist education from Oxford. The work envisioned by Gilbert enabled Harriot to think in unorthodox, rationalistic terms on both scientific and religious matters. But he ultimately prioritized and concerned himself with technological mastery or *homo faber*.

One might argue that here is evidence that Harriot was at heart an evangelist, given that he participated in Gilbert's plans for nation-building, which included spreading the "true religion." Here we see that he clearly did intend to contribute to the nationalist project of conquering the New World. But note that this need not entail that he accepted orthodox Protestantism or that he had evangelist motivations. His mention of the "true religion" can be plausibly contrued as mere lip service, given the abundance of other instances where he downplays the authority of Christianity and displays tolerance for the religious practice of the Algonquins. In sum, for Harriot, contributing to this nationalist project did not entail accepting the orthodox Protestantism associated with it.

The *Report*, we have seen, foregrounds the difficulties of converting the natives when there is an extreme language gap. Since Harriot did in fact have the ability to communicate in the Algonquin language, this awareness is all the more impressive. Harriot discovered that while he could not convey the meaning of scripture, he could use religious rituals, as well as technology, as a tool of civic discipline. Religion, he believes, will make the natives come to "fear, love, and obey" the English. Similar language can be found in the "Bond of Association For the Defense of Queen Elizabeth": "all subjects should love, fear, and obey their sovereign princes, being kings or queens. . . ."[46] By framing religion in instrumental terms, Harriot takes such language in a rationalistic direction. In presenting the contents of the Bible, he treats miracles skeptically, as he offers the natives "manie particularities of Miracles and chiefe poyntes of religion."

For when as wee kneeled downe on our knees to make our prayers unto god, they went about to imitate us, and when they saw we moved our lipps, they also dyd the like. Wherfore that is verye like that they might easelye be brought to the knowledge of the gospel. God of his mercie grant them this grace. (Dover, 71)

Instead of explaining the moral lessons of the Bible, as he would if he were moved by evangelical absolutism, Harriot turns religion into a disciplinary exercise in which repetition and practice clear the way for the transmission of knowledge and belief. This activity brings to mind Pascal, who, in trying to find a path toward belief and away from doubt, suggests that repeated prayer can lead the skeptic toward faith: "Proofs only convince the mind; habit provides the strongest proofs and those that are most believed. It includes the automaton, which leads the mind unconsciously along with it."[47] Harriot finds a similar means of getting the Algonquins to internalize religious belief. But unlike Pascal, who portrays repetition as the road toward genuine faith, Harriot is interested in the political obedience created by the act of prayer. Indeed, recognizing the extreme language gap between the two cultures, he literally makes a mockery of Protestant religion.[48] Moreover, this empty ceremony is not unlike the worship of technological objects we saw earlier. Both forms of worship resemble what Protestants would call the idolatry of the Latin mass: the laity need not know the content; they just need to follow the form.

In fact, at the point in the text where Harriot's evangelical perspective is most clearly stated, he makes the act of conversion appear absurd. Perhaps successful at keeping people in awe of technological power, the English nevertheless are seen to fail in their attempts to teach the natives the content of the Protestant religion:

Manie times and in every towne where I came, according as I was able, I made declaration of the contentes of the Bible; that therein was set foorth the true and onelie God, and his mightie woorkes, that therein was contayned the true doctrine of salvation through Christ, with manie particularities of Miracles and chiefe pointes of religion, as I was able then to utter, and thought fit for the time. And although I told them the booke materially & of it self was not of anie such vertue, as I thought they did conceive, but onely the doctrine therein contained; yet would many be glad to touch it, to

embrace it, to kisse it, to hold it to their brests and heads, and
stroke over all their bodie with it; to shew their hungrie desire of
that knowledge which was spoken of. (377)

In Harriot's encounter with the Algonquins, there is no way to
convey the Word adequately, since, as he freely admits, language presents an insurmountable barrier. He claims that he
provided the indigenous population with "the chiefe pointes of
religion, *as I was then able to utter*" (my italics). What, exactly,
was he able to utter in their language? The comic passage exposes the weaknesses of evangelical colonialism, its inability to
fully interpellate the New World inhabitants. Thus the final
line of the paragraph on the fetish is equivocal: the Algonquins
do in fact show "their hungrie desire of that knowledge" by
embracing the Bible, kissing it, and rubbing against it. Their
practice suggests that the physical gratification of feeling the
Bible does provide an important experience for them. Indeed,
the seriousness of the beginning of the passage makes for a
comic contrast with the description of how the Algonquins
actually respond to the "true and onelie God" of the Bible.
Repeatedly raising doubts about the English ability to communicate the truth, Harriot implicitly calls into question whether
the evangelical goals touted in documents like Elizabeth's patent to Ralegh are at all realistic.

Moreover, Harriot's description of the Indians' attraction to
the material book raises questions about how religion might be
practiced at home as well as abroad. Note that the Algonquins
confront an extreme version of a common Protestant dilemma:
how should religious faith be internalized and spiritualized?
Richard Mulcaster's account of Queen Elizabeth holding a
Bible reveals that even Protestants could gain physical gratification from their religion:

> For when her grace had learned that the Bible in English should
> there be offered, she thanked the City therefore, promised the
> reading thereof most diligently, and incontinent commanded that
> it should be brought. At the receipt whereof, how reverently did
> she with both her hands take it, kiss it, and lay it upon her breast,
> to the great comfort of the lookers-on![49]

Elizabeth's sensual pleasure in touching the Bible shows her
appreciation for its contents. She might not fetishize the Bible

in the Algonquin manner, but she does display a kind of "hungrie desire" for it. Elizabeth demonstrates a healthy enjoyment of the physical book itself. At the same time, however, Protestants were deeply troubled by their desire for religious cathexis. Unable entirely to eschew such desire, they sought substitutes for the material pleasures offered by the Catholic Eucharist and other forbidden practices. Even as Protestants believed that they were getting closer to the truth of God through the Word, schisms formed over how far to go in getting rid of papist or pagan forms of ceremony and ritual that smacked of fetishism.[50]

One might again argue, given that Harriot clearly states that religion will contribute to his plan for making the natives come to "fear, love, and obey" the English, that surely he was motivated by evangelism. Here he is pointing to religion as the very thing that will in fact transform the Indians. Nevertheless, he is relying on a Machiavellian view of religion, according to which it is merely a tool for domination. This view contrasts sharply with the claim that Protestantism (or any religion) is the one true religion. Harriot's Machiavellianism dramatically complicates his role in the Protestant mission to eliminate superstition, error, and ignorance.[51] Machiavelli was widely read in England and Harriot clearly found his political wisdom of great importance. While many Elizabethans found the Florentine's secular understanding of politics disturbing, it was increasingly possible for thinkers on the cutting edge to see politics as an autonomous activity, independent of divine intervention or providence.[52] Harriot, like his patron Ralegh, experimented with the new science of politics and thus contributed to the rethinking of traditional ideological concepts in a time of rapid social and political change.[53]

Concerned that the Church of Rome had failed to keep Italy united, Machiavelli believed that religion, especially the performance of miracles, could be used to strengthen the state. His *Discourses on Livy* tells us about the importance of miracles for Roman politics:

Such was, in fact, the practice observed by sagacious men; which has given rise to the belief in the miracles that are celebrated in religions, however false they may be. For the sagacious rulers have given these miracles increased importance, no matter whence or

how they originated; and their authority afterwards gave them cre-
dence with the people.[54]

Harriot echoes Machiavelli when he says that the Algonquins,
who can be brought to "the trueth" through "discreet dealing"
and "government," will "honour, obey, feare, and love" the English. He also behaves like one of Machiavelli's "sagacious
men" when he uses English technology as a substitute for genuine miracles in order to awe the Algonquins into obedience.
Algonquin priests, with whom Harriot has "special familiarity," are portrayed as cunning Machiavellians who manipulate
the religious belief of the "common sort." The stories of the afterlife benefit the governors (the Wiroances and Priests) whose
"subtilty" Harriot greatly admires. Thus we are left with the
suggestion that the Christian account of the immortality of the
soul is itself merely a fiction used to control the "simple sort":

> What subtilty soever be in the Wiroances and Priestes, this opinion
> worketh so much in manie of the common and simple sort of people
> that it maketh them have great respect to their Governours, and
> also great care what they do, to avoid torment after death, and to
> enjoy blisse; although notwithstanding there is punishment or-
> dained for malefactours, as stealers, whoremoongers, and other
> sortes of wicked doers; some punished with death, some with for-
> feitures, some with beating, according to the greatnes of the factes.
> (374–75)

This passage raises the question: would Harriot also characterize Catholic priests and other religious authorities, including
Protestant ones, as "subtle"? Does he see religion in general
merely as a form of political domination? If so, both Christianity and the Algonquin religion become, in certain respects, stories told to awe people into submission. Leaving it open that he
might apply the same notion to the princes of Europe, Harriot
reveals a significant ideological gap that is hardly contained,
as Greenblatt would have it, by evangelic colonialism. The
narrative at least raises the possibility that Harriot himself
does not firmly accept the truth of Christian religion. Greenblatt thinks that Harriot's silence on this matter should be interpreted as an affirmation of the truth of Protestantism and a
negation of the religious truths of the Algonquins. But this
reading is by no means forced on us. Why not allow the ambi-

guity of passage to remain? Besides, we know from one of his letters to Kepler that Harriot often felt compelled to keep many of his ideas secret. He informed Kepler that he could not "philosophize freely" on the nature of a vacuum, because in England "we are still stuck in the mud."[55] So his silence can be easily interpreted as reticence rather than acquiescence to Protestantism.

The language of deceit in Harriot's text echoes Machiavelli's advice in *The Prince* that "there is nothing so important as to seem to have this last quality [religion]. Men in general judge by their eyes rather than by their hands . . . Everyone sees what you appear to be, few experience what you really are."[56] Religion will increase the Prince's power if it is performed properly, a principle Harriot puts into action by witnessing how his display of technological mastery grants him the ability to put the natives in awe.

There are further instances of Harriot's Machiavellianism. When a large number in various towns begin to die from diseases brought by the English, the Wiroans observe that the inhabitants in many of these towns were enemies of the English. Doubting the explanation of divine providence offered by the English, the chiefs suggest that such speeches are mere "dissembling," since in their observations, the English clearly have the power to influence God and aid them against their enemies. The word "dissembling" suggests that Harriot was projecting his own Machiavellian thinking onto the chiefs, attributing to the chiefs a familiarity with the language of cunning political deceit.

During this disaster Harriot also portrays the Algonquin physicians as Machiavellians. Some Algonquins believe that people are dying from "invisible bullets" shot by incorporal supporters of the English who float in the air firing upon them. In the discussion of the disease that spreads throughout the population, Harriot tells us that "To confirm this opinion their phisitions to excuse their ignorance in curing the disease, would not be ashamed to say, but earnestly make the simple people beleve, that the strings of blood that they sucked out of the sicke bodies, were the strings wherewithal the invisible bullets were tied and cast" (380). In this case, it is the physicians rather than the priests who deceive the "simple people."

Moreover, Harriot's reflections on signs from heaven and re-

lations of cause and effect further point to a skeptical, Machiavellian perspective on miracles and divine providence. He
doubts that an eclipse or a comet had anything to do with the
spread of the disease spread among the natives, and he equivo-
cates about the role of the "speciall woorke of God" in supporting the English: "some said that it was the speciall woorke of
God for our sakes, as wee our selves have cause in some sorte
to thinke no lesse." This statement is hardly definitive about
the role of divine providence—he has only "cause in some sort"
to believe that God had anything to do with it. Keenly interested in natural philosophy, Harriot considers several different
explanations for diseases that wiped out so many of the natives. He could stand on the stable ground of Christian belief,
as he would were he a "true believer" with evangelist motivations, but he instead seems as baffled as the Algonquins. Having no knowledge himself of how infectious diseases spread, he
entertains multiple explanations without arriving at certainty:
"But to conclude them from being the speciall causes of so speciall an accident, there are farther reasons then I thinke fit at
this present to be alleadged" (381). Harriot opts to defer the
quest for truth when he could just as easily perpetuate the
stronger ideological explanation of divine providence. The
most likely explanation of this, I suggest, is that he was not in
fact motivated by evangelism.

III

Harriot's ethnographic receptivity in the *Report* is further il-
luminated by a look at his treatment of civility. For writers like
Whitaker or Hamor there is little ambiguity in the relation of
civilization and savagery. In Harriot's usage, however, the
word "savage" is not demarcated by clear cultural boundaries:
once he tries to understand the natives' social and cultural
practices, the word begins to crack under the weight of its Eurocentric meaning. In fact, when describing the Algonquins,
Harriot often uses terms like "natural inhabitants" rather than
"heathen" or "savage," as if to suggest that he may not be entirely comfortable with the pervasive English belief in their
own cultural and religious superiority.

The term "savage" was ubiquitous in the literature of coloni-

zation, where it functioned as an inversion of the term "civil."
Civility was associated with religious morality, political order,
legal authority, and particular social arrangements such as
marriage.[57] Since the Algonquins, in the English view, lacked
these things, how could the English explain the great social
successes they did find? On the one hand, the Algonquins appeared savage because—as the etymology of the word, from
Latin selva (forest) suggests—they were closer to a "state of nature" in which human artifice remains underdeveloped. On the
other hand, Harriot's writings show that he found this simplistic characterization inadequate, since the inhabitants had social and technological skills that made the English look almost
inferior. In fact, as we will see, their social arrangements inspired Harriot and others to criticize European practices.

Enmeshed in the paradoxical topos of the golden age, savagism portrayed New World inhabitants as children whose inno-
cent condition might be envied in a condescending fashion,
while nevertheless implicitly despised for its barbarism. At the
same time, the topos enabled writers to challenge the norms of
European civilization by demonstrating the distinct advan-
tages of a less civilized way of living. Montaigne's "Of Cannibals," for example, argues that the Brazilians are closer to
"their original naturalness"; they do not have the vices of European artifice, nor do they have the techne (literacy, tools,
etc.) to exploit nature. The practice of cannibalism may be barbaric, he says, but in a more fundamental way the natives are
not as barbaric as the Europeans: "So we may well call these
people barbarians, in respect to the rules of reason, but not in
respect to ourselves, who surpass them in every kind of barbar-
ity."[58] Montaigne's Pyrrhonism leads him to suspect the ratio-
nality (including the techne) of the Europeans and to take a
perspectival, relativistic view of their social practices and customs.[59]

The golden age paradox had been discussed so often by the
seventeenth century that Shakespeare, alluding to Montaigne,
turned it into comedy in The Tempest, a play that resonates
with the English experience in Virginia. Gonzalo, who would
be "king" of his own island utopia, will not allow "traffic,"
"letters," "riches," "metal," "bound of land," or work of any
kind (2.1.140–62). In a less playful context, Peter Martyr's Dec-

ades of the New World also inverts norms of European civilization:

> It is proven that amongst them the land belongs to everybody, just as does the sun or the water. They know no difference between *meum* and *tuum*, that source of all evils. It requires so little to satisfy them, that in that vast region there is always more land to cultivate than is needed. It is indeed a golden age, neither ditches, nor hedges, nor walls to enclose their domains; they live in gardens open to all, without laws and without judges. . . .[60]

With no private property, laws, books, or judges, the natives live in a savage yet golden age. Harriot, too, offers his own adaptation of this self-flattering Eurocentric model: "Doubtless it is a pleasant sighte to see the people, somtymes wadinge, and goinge sometimes sailinge in those Rivers, which are shallowe and not deepe, free from all care of heapinge opp Riches for their posterite, content with their state" (Dover, 56). The notorious rapaciousness of the Europeans is nowhere to be found in Algonquin society. Harriot praises the natives for their lack of the desire for "heapinge opp Riches for their posterite" and for their ability to enjoy the fruits of nature without exploiting others. Moreover, even in this Edenic state they have a know-how that is, in many respects, equal if not superior to that of the Europeans: Harriot notes that they have a "cunning" way of fishing unknown to the English, and that they "make do" without iron. The "hollowe tayle of a certain fishe" serves as a fishhook. Consequently, they appear to live in a time before the Iron Age.

Harriot extracts what he needs from the golden age motif—namely, a means of criticizing European culture. But in keeping with his ethnographic receptivity, he does not stick to the motif, which all too often in other writers becomes yet another obstacle to learning about non-European ways of living. In contrast, Arthur Barlowe idealizes the land and its people without providing much detail: "We found the people most gentle, loving and faithful, void of all guile and treason, and such as live after the manner of the golden age."[61] Harriot, on the other hand, does not distance the Algonquins from the Europeans by idealizing them, nor does he draw a clear cultural boundary between civility and savagism. In telling us, for example, that the technological wit of the Algonquins is not obviously inferior to that of the Europeans since the former can create so much without possessing iron, he recognizes a complexity in their way of life that he could not were he merely idealizing them.

Harriot may be quick to point out that the Algonquins lack advanced technology, but he is also an admirer of their economical organization of work and consumption. His description of "the manner of makinge their boates" tells us that although they lack iron, they make their boats "handsomely and fish like we do." He concludes by saying that "this god indueth these savage people with sufficient reason to make thinges necessarie to serve their turnes" (Dover, 55). Even without the technological advances of the English, they live quite well; indeed, their harmonious relationship with nature is enough to make the Europeans envious. His description of how they eat meat becomes an implicit criticism of European behavior: "They are verye sober in their eatinge and drinkinge, and consequently verye longe lived because they doe not oppress nature" (61). Harriot goes on here to moralize explicitly on English consumption habits: the English should follow the example of Algonquin moderation, "for wee should bee free from many kinds of diseases which wee fall into by sumptuous and unseasonable banquets" (Dover, 60). Excessive consumption of rich sauces and an insatiable appetite have led to the plethora of English afflictions. The Flemish publisher Theodor De Bry echoes Harriot's admiration of Algonquin moderation in his address to the reader of the *Report*: "For although they have noe true knowledge of God nor of his holye worde and are destituted of all learninge, Yet they passe us in many thinges, as in Sober feedinge and Dexteritye of witte, in makinge without any instrument of mettall thinges so neate and so fine, as a man would scarsclye beleve the same . . ." (Dover, 41). Harriot and De Bry recognize the power of Algonquin moderation, since the Algonquins are superior to the Europeans in their "sober feedinge" and "dexter
itye of wit."[62] The Algonquins are portrayed as not obviously on the "savage" side of the savage/civil binary.

In another section of the 1590 edition, De Bry describes the Picts of ancient Britain who "show how that the Inhabitants of the great Bretannie have bin in times past as savvage as those of Virginia." If religion creates a sense of difference from the inhabitants of Virginia, the history of technology creates a sense of identity: the two groups can be plotted in a single developmental chronology [63] This sense of identity adds a new dimension to the discussion of wit: the Algonquins are superior in their grasp of reason because they started from a position of inferiority—a lack of iron—and made remarkable achievements with what they had.[64] Again, cultural boundaries become hard to delineate clearly, since the English are not separated from the New World inhabitants by a superior God-given nature but simply by the effects of time.

Harriot's view of the Algonquins was not a simplistic, idealizing one, according to which they would be seen as happy natives; nor was it one that construed them as barbaric savages. His receptivity to foreign customs instead allowed him to see them as members of a complex and radically different culture.

IV

We have seen that it is highly unlikely that Harriot was motivated by evangelism in his interactions with the Algonquins; his naturalistic attitudes and his ambivalence about religious truth show that he could not have been primarily guided by a desire to convert them to Protestantism. What, then, was the true motivation underlying his exchanges with the Algonquins? I will argue that it was twofold: one, a genuine scientific curiosity, and two, an economic opportunism.

While Harriot was setting the new trend of mercantile interests in the New World, his scientific experimentation and exploration were being portrayed in a heroic, imperialist, and epic rhetorical mode. George Chapman, once believed by some to be a friend of Harriot's in an atheistic "school of night," described him as a brilliant, noble, and heroic scientist more interested in alchemical knowledge and New World plunder than the Christian religion.[65] His poems concerning Harriot rarely use religious signifiers. The word "heaven," for example, completes an alchemical metaphor glorifying human reason rather than the religious goals of colonialism. Thus Chapman adds another dimension to our picture of Harriot's heterodoxy: the search for commodities, framed in heroic, aristocratic language, subordinates religion to reason, the work of God to the power of *homo faber*. His poetry points to the fact that there were many nonevangelical motivations for colonizing the New World, and whereas we do not receive precise information about Harriot's views, the poems present a picture of the scientific and economic interests that defined his experience in North America.

In a dedicatory poem attached to *Achilles Shield*, his translation of Homer's *Illiad*, Chapman celebrates Harriot's accomplishments in an aristocratic rather than mercantile code.[66] Chapman describes Harriot as "the Mayster of all essentiall and true knowledge" and praises his use of reason:

> To you whose depth of soule measures the height,
> And all dimensions of all workes of weight,
> Reason being ground, structure and ornament,
> To all inventions, grave and permanent,
> And your cleare eyes the Spheres where Reason moves . . .
>
> (1–5)[67]

These lines resonate with the anonymous text mentioned earlier that, according to Clucas, tells us that Harriot "made Reason his God." Yet Chapman's poem does not make it clear what specific forms of knowledge count as "essentiall" and "true." Later in the poem he refers to Harriot as a "rich mine of knowledge" and claims that his lofty scientific projects will aid in the extraction of wealth: "vertue must wait on wealth; we must make friends/Of the unrighteous Mammon." The clear eyes of reason are not clouded by the desire for filthy lucre. Oscillating between Platonic and pragmatic models of science, Chapman celebrates the contemplative power of Reason as well as its practical, economic benefits.

Chapman does not establish a clear connection to English voyages to Virginia, but Harriot would certainly appear to be one of the "patrician spirits" mentioned in another poem, "De Guiana, Carmen Epicum." Celebrating these men for helping England find "Riches, and Conquest, and Renowne" in the New World, Chapman's dedication to Harriot never portrays reason or "true knowledge" as economically disinterested: the "clear eyes" that are "Spheres where *Reason* moves" look for commodities. Harriot's reason, the gift that impresses Chapman the most, makes him "noble" despite his plebeian origins. Chapman's alchemical metaphors also provide important evidence that Harriot was seen as a heterodox, occult thinker, a member of a circle of men who experimented with Hermetic knowledge. It is also significant that these metaphors, which substitute for spiritual Christian ones, focus on extracting wealth from the New World.

"De Guiana, Carmen Epicum" was attached to Lawrence Keymis's "relation of the second voyage to Guiana," printed in 1596. The poem celebrates the travels of Keymis and Harriot's patron Ralegh while alluding to the work of Harriot as well. Like the dedication to Harriot, the poem stresses the importance of making a profit for the English nation. Although his references to Mammon come from Luke 16, which advocates Christian charity, Chapman suggests that expropriation, not charity, is necessary in a world of corrupt bodies. Thus he reminds us that the new possibilities of mercantilism were forcing people to rethink the role of Christianity in worldly affairs. Even as Christian moralists denounced covetousness and usury, many Elizabethans, who saw the material gains of the Spanish in the New World, could not help but worship at the altar of Mammon.

"De Guiana" also represents conquest as service to Elizabeth and England. Chapman sees Elizabeth as God-like, the *dominus mundi*:

> Then most admired Soveraigne, let your breath
> Goe foorth upon the water, and create
> A golden worlde in this our iron age,
> And be the prosperous forewind to a Fleet,
> That seconding your last, may goe before it
> In all successe of profite and renowme:
> Doubt not but your election was divine . . .
>
> (30–36)[68]

As the divinely elected, in the English imperialist effort at sea, Elizabeth must lead her pure, noble, and brave patricians in the acquisition of gold and the conquest of Guiana and Spain:

> But you Patrician Spirites that refine
> Your flesh to fire, and issue like a flame

On Brave endevours, knowing that in them
The tract of heaven in morne-like glorie opens

(86–89)

Guiana, whose feet are "mines of golde," is rendered as a female who makes "every signe of all submission" to Elizabeth
and "standes on her tip-toes at faire England looking,/kissing
her hand."[69] The sea is a womb that threatens like "avarice" to
"swallow all." Like the alchemical metaphor of refining "flesh
to fire,"the acquisition of wealth is portrayed as a pure pursuit
of the Platonic soul:

> Your Bodies through, to profit and renowne,
> And skorne to let your bodies chooke your soules,
> In the rude breath and prisoned life of beastes:
> You that heerein renounce the course of earth,
> And lift your eies for guidance to the starres,
> That live not for your selves, but to possesse
> Your honour'd countrey of a general store;
> In pitie of the spoyle rude self-love makes,
> Of them whose lives and yours one aire doth feede,
> One soile doeth nourish, and one strength combine;
> You that are blest with sence of all things noble
> In this attempt your compleat woorthes redouble.
>
> (105–16)

Guided by the stars in the search for gold, pure souls will be
drained of earthly pollution, bestial life will be defeated, and
the nobility will come together on "one soile," breathing "one
aire." Elizabeth will bring back the golden age, and her "patrician spirits," including Harriot, will give her a more commanding presence on the map, making her look like the *dominus
mundi* of the Ditchley portrait. In another poem by Chapman,
the "Hymnus in Cynthiam," Elizabeth is implored to replenish
her aging body with the gold from Guiana: "Great Cynthia,
rise out of thy Latmian pallace,/With thy bright bodie, in th'
Atlanticke streames,/Put on those robes that are most rich in
beames" (10–12).[70] Once again, Chapman conveys that baseness can be transformed into nobility by a powerful alliance of
patrician spirits and monarchical power.[71]

As a plebeian devoted to furthering scientific knowledge and
social practice, Harriot did not really live up to the aristocratic

ideology of Chapman's poetry. Harriot had a great deal of contact with the middling sort like Captain John Davis, who praised the new "mechanicall practices drawne from the Artes Mathematick." Insisting that "speculative" and mechanical practices "shall receive favourable place in the honourable opinion of nobilitie," Davis offers particular praise to Dee, Digges, and Harriot as contributors to the power of the English nation.[72] Although Harriot is at one point called an "artisan," a term that fits Harriot given the nature of his hands-on scientific experimentation, Chapman, following his interest in *ratio*, classifies him in the terms set by the Platonist tradition. Nevertheless, this poetry on travel and conquest reconfigures the nature of nobility to include people like Harriot who started life as plebeians. Insisting on friendship with "unrighteous Mammon," Chapman glorifies Harriot as a "rich mine of knowledge" while still lamenting the corruption brought by the body and its need for nourishment.

While Chapman's poem acknowledges the friendship with Mammon, it does not precisely recognize the rise of artisanal work and its importance to an emergent mercantile interest in the New World: his "patrician spirits" look like part of the epic fiction he translated from Homer. Unable to see Harriot as a true artisan, he places him in the context of epic, heroic adventure. Nevertheless, the quest for gold is not only one for "patrician spirits," and Chapman's description of Harriot as "blest with sence of all things noble" was one of many attempts to rethink the meaning of "nobility" and "gentility" in an age of scientific and socioeconomic change.[73]

Chapman's poetry reminds us of the economic goals that guided Harriot's *Brief and True Report*. Indeed, as we have seen, religious conversion is not presented as a serious goal in the *Report*, and Harriot is drawn to other interests: surveying the land for potential commodities and analyzing cultural practices with a rationalistic distance from the shibboleths of evangelical colonialism. In his attempt to classify the natural objects of America as commodities for English consumption, Harriot conveys an experience of scientific wonder at the Algonquins' practices, such as their religious ritual of smoking tobacco. In fact, expressions of amazement in the section on commodities are an outgrowth of the economic and propagandistic goals of the report: the English want to show that the

Algonquins will be good trade partners, or at least a valuable source of material goods.

Harriot's economic bent stands out even more if we consider that the long-standing tradition of such narratives, exemplified by Ralegh's *Discoverie of Guiana* (1595), had been to include stories with no empirical basis. Recalling such "fables" (mainly drawn from *Mandeville's Travels*), Ralegh writes that he hears tales in Guiana of people with "their eyes in their shoulders, and their mouth in the middle of their breasts." Even though he has never actually seen them himself, he confidently asserts: "Such a nation was written of by Mandevile, whose reports were holden for fables many yeeres, and yet since the east Indies were discovered, we find his relations true of such things as heretofore were held incredible."[74] Harriot's narrative, unlike Ralegh's, has been drained of the legends from older authorities.[75] Free of the myths and stories handed down over the centuries, the *Report* describes, catalogs, and praises the plentiful goods on the land. Abandoning the tradition of plugging in fantastic topoi—the anthropophagi or ama-

Sebastian Munster's *Cosmographia* (1572) depicts a few of the monstrous figures often described in travel narratives. Courtesy of Richard Abrams.

zons—Harriot produces a disenchanted narrative that looks
more like a careful survey of potential commodities than a
form of storytelling. Natural goods are reified as potential objects of English consumption: for example, cedar "a very sweet
wood & fine timber" will "yeeld profite" after it is transformed
into "fine bedsteads, tables, deskes, lutes, virginalles & many
things else" (329). Thus Harriot casts an empirical eye on potential commodities and the customs of the people.[76]

De Bry's frontispiece in the 1590 edition of the *Report* depicts the New World as a land of plenty and displays the Algonquins themselves as commodities: fruit is draped in a
symmetrical pattern over classical architecture; the idol Ki-
wasa sits atop the structure with other statuesque "natural inhabitants" below; the conjuror and the priest look up in an
obeisant pose at the idol; and the "cheiff Ladye of Pomeiooc"
stands with her "gourd of pleasant liquor" on one side with a
"cheiff Lorde of Roanoac" on the other. The inhabitants are
thus placed amid the commanding architectural artifice like
items in cabinets of curiosity, the collections of marvels so
popular during the Renaissance. Indeed, during voyages of the
1580s, natives of Virginia were brought back to England and
put on display, as alluded to in *The Tempest* when Trinculo
says, "When they will not give a doit to relieve a lame beggar,
they will lay out ten to see a dead Indian" (2.2.31–32).[77]

The frontispiece advertises the cornucopia of the natural
land and its people together as an attractive picture of colonial
expansion. For the English to acquire the desired goods in this
Edenic New World, the natives must be made to "fear, love,
and obey" the English. What could better frame such obedience than a classical architectural model in which they are fro-
zen in time, positioned as the objects of utopian desire? The
classical architecture—two Doric columns framing the description of the book—reminds us of the contribution made by
humanistic learning to the conquest of America. Indeed, the
inhabitants of the New World are enframed and represented by
this learning throughout the text.

Like the report itself, the frontispiece marks a departure
from older expressions of wonder at the foreign. The inhabitants do not appear alongside fantastic monsters and bizarre
creatures; instead, they are examined with great care along
with the flora and fauna soon to be exported back to England.

A briefe and true report
of the new found land of Virginia.
of the commodities and of the nature and man
ners of the naturall inhabitants. Discouered by
the English Colony there seated by Sir Richard
Greinuile Knight In the yeere 1585. Which Rema
=ined Vnder the gouernement of twelue monethes,
At the speciall charge and direction of the Honou=
rable SIR WALTER RALEIGH Knight lord Warden
of the stanneries Who therein hath beene fauoured
and authorised by her MAIESTIE
and her letters patents:
This fore booke Is made in English
By Thomas Hariot seruantt to the abouenamed
Sir WALTER, a member of the Colony, and there
imployed in discouering

CVM GRATIA ET PRIVILEGIO CÆS.MA^{TIS} SPECIA.^{LI}

FRANCOFORTI AD MOENVM
TYPIS IOANNIS WECHELI, SVMTIBVS VERO THEODORI
DE BRY ANNO CD ID XC.
VENALES REPERIVNTVR IN OFFICINA SIGISMVNDI FEIRABENDII

Title page of *A Briefe and True Report* (1590)

The natives, along with the fruit and vegetables roped around the edifice of the frontispiece, represent the economic might of Elizabeth's England, the newfound mercantile power that now stretched over the Atlantic. Even before Francis Bacon revolutionized the study of nature,[78] the experience of wonder had changed remarkably from the Middle Ages: the secular, rational, empiricist narrative had disposed of older myths while compiling lists of commodities and notes of customs.[79] Thus De Bry, like Harriot, recognizes the power of a utopian desire that would bring more wealth to the English, although it would make Virginia a paradise lost for the Algonquins.

In this chapter, we have seen that Harriot was a skeptical thinker with regard to Protestantism and Christianity. His skepticism was such an integral part of his worldview, in fact, that it was not, as Greenblatt once argued, ultimately contained by the nominally evangelical goal of his interactions with the Algonquins. In fact, we have seen that far from being an evangelist, Harriot was quite receptive to the religious customs of the Indians, exhibiting a respect for their views that is missing from other contemporaries' writing. Instead, what guided Harriot's ethnographic approach was just what it seemed: a genuine interest in foreign customs as well as an economic opportunism.

3

"Religion hides many things from suspicion": Christopher Marlowe's Skepticism

In the two decades before christopher marlowe and william Shakespeare were born, England experienced three shifts in the state religion. Edward VI pushed Protestantism forward in 1547, Mary Tudor took England back to Catholicism in 1553, and Elizabeth reinstated Protestantism as the official state religion in 1558. During this period of flux it was never entirely certain which religion would ultimately prevail. But by the late 1580s, when Marlowe's plays were first performed, anti-Catholicism had reached a feverish pitch. Indeed, the execution of Mary Stuart, war in the Spanish Netherlands, and the Spanish Armada strengthened the bond between Protestantism and nationalism, a bond that had been forged in the days of Henry VIII. While Protestantism gained an increasingly firm hold on society, Marlowe's generation still had the formidable task of determining what shape this religion would ultimately take. As Francis Bacon observed, "It is but ignorance if any man find it strange that the state of religion (especially in the days of peace) should be exercised and troubled with controversies."[1]

By 1587, the year Marlowe's first play was performed, authorities had recognized that religion could provide the glue with which to bind together the nation-state. Indeed, it was clear to many that the Protestant religion could be a valuable tool for maintaining civil order. Having abandoned papal authority, England turned to Protestantism as a means of enforcing obedience to a central authority. Thus Marlowe's generation also had to respond to a new political ideology that linked church and state. This ideology was most clearly articulated in the "Homily on Obedience," a text read from the pulpits that declared that all acts of civil disobedience would constitute rebellion against God: "Forasmuch as God hath created and dysposed all thinges in a comelye ordre . . . concerning good ordre and obedience, that we also ought in all commonwelthes, to observe and kepe a dewe ordre, and to be obedient to the powers, their ordinaunces and lawes, and that all rulers are appointed of god, for a godlye ordre to bee kept in the worlde."[2]

Marlowe's work appeared at this important juncture in English history. His plays offer a vivid picture of the ideological instabilities that remained after the authority of the Protestant nation-state had been firmly established. This chapter will demonstrate that Marlowe responded to these instabilities by raising challenging skeptical questions about the practices of Christianity. Thus Marlowe's thinking differed in extraordinary ways from that of Puritans, Catholics, and other religious critics during this contentious period, in that he seemed to take religious skepticism further than most. If he had focused his energies on eliminating the papist elements of the reformed religion (as Scot did) or, alternatively, conserving fragments of the old religion, his dissidence would have fit more comfortably into the religious debates of the period. Instead, Marlowe forged his own path by creating tragic heroes who challenge religious piety and conventional morality. In addition, his own skepticism gave him a reputation so notorious that Thomas Beard would declare that his violent death was a "manifest sign of God's judgment."

The first section of this chapter will present some of the biographical evidence for Marlowe's religious skepticism, and sections two and three will show how this skepticism is played out in *Doctor Faustus* and *The Jew of Malta*, respectively.

I

Many of Marlowe's activities from the time he arrived to study at Cambridge until the day he died remain enigmatic. His religious beliefs, like those of Harriot, are still surrounded by controversy. The information we have about his life outside the theater world is sketchy and often unreliable. Nevertheless, most scholars today argue that we lose too much information pertinent to our interpretation of his plays when we ignore biographical details simply because they involve a certain amount of speculation.[3] I do not wish to argue for an exact correspondence between Marlowe's biography and his plays, but I do believe that the charges of atheism offer us valuable, if incomplete, information on religious doubt in his work.

During the course of his short life—he died at the age of twenty-nine—Marlowe was infamous for the incendiary views he expounded. As one description put it, he had a "wit sent from heaven but vices sent from hell."[4] The "vices" included homosexuality, brawling, coining, and heresy against the church and state. The charges of heresy came from many sources at different times and places, yet their content overlaps in significant ways, giving us a portrait of a dissident who took great risks in making his views well known. In contrast with Harriot, Marlowe did not seem to care much what opinion others had of him and his work. His fellow playwright and roommate Thomas Kyd, suspected of atheism himself, revealed (under torture) that "It was [Marlowe's] custom . . . to jest at the divine scriptures, jibe at prayers, and strive in argument to frustrate and confute what hath been spoke and writ by prophets."[5] Was Kyd pressured into fabricating this by the authorities? He may have been forced to reveal this description of Marlowe's blasphemy, but it is highly unlikely he fabricated it entirely, since we have on record a plethora of charges not generated under duress that make similar claims about Marlowe's heresies.

Although Marlowe, like his magician Faustus, was born of parents "base of stock," his education gave him the means to leave his hometown of Canterbury and eventually come in contact with people near the center of political power. After his humanistic education at King's School, Canterbury, he moved on to Corpus Christi College at Cambridge University on a scholarship from the Archbishop Matthew Parker to study theology and obtain holy orders. Of course, this was not necessarily indicative of any genuine religious leaning. As Constance Kuriyama points out, although the intention of the scholarship was to direct students into religious vocations, many likely did not pursue such a path.[6] Marlowe, in fact, was likely writing his irreverent, iconoclastic plays while he studied religion at Cambridge.

In fact, much more than academic life occupied Marlowe's time at Corpus Christi. He was often absent from college, owing apparently to his involvement in government business, namely espionage. The Elizabethan secret service was focused on discovering real or imagined Catholic threats to the state, from recusancy to larger plots like those surrounding Mary Stuart.[7] The most important piece of evidence we have that Marlowe worked in this capacity is a Privy Council letter to Cambridge defending him against the charge that he intended to go to Rheims, a site of Catholic dissidence: "in all his accions he had behaved him selfe orderlie and discreetlie, wherebie he had done here Majestie good service and deserved to be rewarded for his faithfull dealinge." The Privy Council overruled the authorities at Cambridge, who were trying to withhold his degree. The letter from the Privy Council doesn't specify what he actually did in "good service" for the Queen, nor does it account for all the absences from Cambridge that distracted him from his studies. Nevertheless, his connection to a network of spies, including Francis Walsingham, Elizabeth's spymaster, suggests that he was engaged in anti-Catholic espionage during much of his time as a student at Cambridge.[8] Still, the contradictory information provided by Cambridge and the Privy Council is indicative of the mysteries surrounding Marlowe's personal beliefs: while the authorities at Cambridge claimed he was a Catholic dissident, the Privy Council stressed his "faithful dealing" for the Queen, and thus by implication his dedication to Protestantism.

Marlowe's murder in May of 1593 adds more pieces to the puzzle about his religious beliefs. He was stabbed to death by Ingram Frizer after a quarrel over the bill for supper, referred to in the murder report as the "reckoning." Frizer and others present in Deptford that day were also involved in the secret service. In light of Marlowe's reputation for atheism and the series of events in May and June of 1593, it is quite possible that the state, which apparently employed him as a spy, ultimately turned against him for his dissident religious views. On May 18 the Privy Council ordered his arrest for an unknown reason; sometime around May 27 Marlowe's colleague Richard

Baines provided a list of Marlowe's atheistic opinions to the Privy Council; and on May 30 Frizer killed him.

Recent discussions of Marlowe's involvement in espionage do little to clarify the murky picture of his religious affiliations. The world of espionage would have positioned him at some of the most unstable faultlines of his day, where "faithful dealing" was, at the same time, deceitful dealing. Charles Nicholl speculates that Marlowe had Catholic sympathies, as did many of Sir Francis Walsingham's spies. But this is hard to believe in view of the numerous anti-Catholic expressions in his plays. There have been other attempts to link Marlowe to a specific group or faith: Nicholl believes he may have been murdered by the Essex faction as part of a larger attack on Ralegh; Breight makes the case that he was part of an anti-Cecil faction;[9] and Paul Hammer argues against conspiracy theories or political explanations *tout court*, suggesting that the murder of Marlowe was not planned but rather an accident having to do with debt or some other banality that would fit the world of "quick money men and con-artists."[10]

As we will see later in this chapter, Marlowe's plays appear to reflect the anti-Catholicism we might expect from someone who worked for the secret service. In many cases, the authority of the Catholic church comes under attack, such as when Faustus boxes the Pope's ears, or Edward the Second threatens to "enforce the Papal towers to kiss the lowly ground." A brutal expression of anti-Catholicism can be found in a bizarre connection between one of his plays and the world of espionage. In 1582, Richard Baines got carried away with his work spying on English Catholics in Rheims and decided to kill everyone at the seminary by poisoning a well. Roughly ten years later Marlowe alluded to the episode in *The Jew of Malta* when Barabas, angry at his daughter for converting to Catholicism, poisons the pottage of a nunnery, thus murdering all the nuns, including his own daughter.

If we now turn to look at a few of the charges Baines made against Marlowe we find that, if anything, Marlowe appears to have been at least as hostile to the Protestants as he was to the Catholics, if not more so. Baines made a confession from prison in France that included anti-Christian ideas strikingly similar to those he would deliver ten years later in a series of charges against Marlowe in 1593, shortly after the playwright's death at Deptford. Thus, Roy Kendall believes that the later report on Marlowe restated some of Baines's own atheistic views.[11] Still, Kendall, like most Marlowe scholars, believes that the report does provide information about Marlowe's own beliefs, even if he acquired some of them from Baines.[12]

According to Baines, Marlowe attacked the apostle Paul, whose Epistle to the Romans is echoed in the "Homily against Disobedience and Willful Rebellion." Paul's letter states, "Let everie soul be subject unto the higher powers: for there is no power but of God: & the powers that be, are ordeined of God."[13] Marlowe allegedly objected: "Paull only had wit but he was a timerous fellow in bidding men to be subject to magistrates against his Conscience." The statement turns Paul's idea on its head: whereas Paul says that conscience leads us to obey authority, this line tells us that his commandment is itself "against his conscience." The word "timerous" suggests that Paul was merely being obedient to the authorities without truly believing that God had chosen the "governing authorities" as his earthly representatives.

Baines's Marlowe also invokes the English understanding of Machiavelli when he says "That the first beginning of religion was to keep men in awe." As a statement about the origins of religion this may not be accurate, but it does address the fusion of church and state created by the Reformation. After all, the state religion had changed repeatedly over the course of the sixteenth century, and, as David Riggs points out, such Machiavellian thinking "simply took the Tudor mandate of uniformity-in-religion enforced by princely rule to its logical destination. On the grassroots level, even the humblest parishioner could well ask 'is not religion a policy to keep people in obedience?'"[14] Riggs does not claim that many parishioners did in fact say such things. We do know, however, that a few writers made similar points albeit with less seditious intent. Robert Burton, for example, wrote that politicians "maintain religion or superstition, which they determine of, alter and vary upon all occasions, as to them seems best; they make religion a mere policy, a cloak, a human invention."[15] Burton's diagnosis of "religious melancholy" suggests that politicians have been placed under a demonic spell that leads them to treat religion as a mere means to keep the "masses under control." Yet he also concedes that many politicans are truly "zealous and religious

themselves." The damage, however, has been done: Burton sees
Machiavellians lurking around every corner, making religion
appear a "cloak, a human invention." Such radical Machiavellian interpretations of religion do not emerge very often in
texts from the period. Still, we might speculate that many people would have developed a similar perspective after witnessing decades of political wrangling over the state religion.

Another of Baines's charges merges Christian and American
Indian practice. Marlowe allegedly insisted that tobacco smoking improves the Christian form of sacrament: "That if Christ
would have instituted the sacrament with more Ceremoniall
Reverence it would have bin had in more admiration, that it
would have bin much better being administered in a Tobacco
pipe." This subject is one we encountered earlier when discuss-
ing Thomas Harriot. The report taps into one of the most deli-
cate theological puzzles of the Reformation: what could have
been more divisive and controversial during this time than the
proper practice of the sacrament? Luther had attacked the
Catholic system of sacraments, especially the mass, asserting
instead the importance of the Word of God and the faith that
connected the worshiper to God.[16] Luther still believed in the
physical presence of God in the Eucharist, but as the Reformation progressed this idea fell into serious dispute and was
abandoned in the official doctrine of the Anglican church. Yet,
as Baines suggests, diverse views on this issue remained. Indeed, we might read the charge as a parody of Luther's attempt
at reforming Catholic practice. Instead of searching for the
true Christian form of sacrament (uncorrupted by the Catholic
church), Marlowe allegedly turns to a pagan practice as the solution.

Baines's charge also gets at the heart of Elizabethan anxieties about the relation between religious and cultural norms:
once a central doctrine of religion is challenged, all sorts of un-
conventional practices appear on the scene. Tobacco was often
described by Elizabethans as a filthy, noxious weed. John Davies put it succinctly: "Tobacco is a weed of so great power/
That it (like Earth) doth what it feedes devoure."[17] To some,
tobacco connoted false religion: "The saint they worship a tobacco pipe/ and their bedawbd loosenes is their God."[18] For
Baines's Marlowe, on the other hand, tobacco provides a better
way of performing the sacrament and leads to an improvement

in or broadening of one's sexuality. Baines charges that Marlowe blasphemously stated that "St John the Evangelist was bedfellow to Christ" and "those that love not Tobacco & boies were fooles."[19] Thus Baines links Marlowe to practices—homosexuality, pagan religion, and tobacco smoking—that were often perceived as a threat to Elizabethan collective beliefs and cultural norms.[20] The report resonates with a commonplace idea in Tudor and Stuart England: "A man without religion is like a horse without a bridle,"[21] or, to use Dostoevsky's modern aperçu: if God is dead anything is permitted.

Baines also tells us about Marlowe's anti-Protestant beliefs: "That if there be any god or any good Religion, then it is in the papistes because the service of god is performed with more Cerimonies, as Elevation of the mass, organs, singing men, Shaven Crownes & cta. That all protestantes are Hypocritical asses." The word "hypocrite," commonplace in antitheatrical writing, derives from the Greek word for "actor." The idea here is that Protestants are hypocrites because they denounce Catholic ceremonies. If Protestantism itself is also a kind of performance, then the Protestant attack on idolatrous forms of worship can be turned against the Protestants themselves.

The mass, of course, was a particularly contentious issue. Queen Elizabeth decided, for example, to remove the elevation of the mass from her coronation ceremony because it "was the visible sign which proclaimed the doctrine of transubstantiation."[22] The elevation of the host and the chalice in the Eucharist became, in the late twelfth century, the crucial sign of consecration, an exhibit of Christ's body for the laity. Priests would elevate the host after saying "hoc est corpus meum," and thereby excite the devotion and faith of believers.[23] From the very beginning of her reign, Elizabeth turned away from such papist practices, thus discarding the Catholicism recently reinstated by Mary Tudor. Baines's Marlowe, however, poses a challenge to any rejection of Catholic ceremony by insisting that the dismissal of the Catholic Eucharist would not necessarily lead to a more pure, authentic Christianity. Indeed, he tells us that the Protestant state would find its own way to keep people in a state of mystification.

Another charge in the report is that Marlowe claimed that Moses learned "the artes of the Egiptians to abuse the Jewes." Baines's Marlowe challenges the orthodox opposition between the Jews and Egyptians, and thus calls into doubt divinely sanctioned magic. Moses is maintained to have learned his magical art from the Egyptians rather than God. Conversely, the Book of Exodus makes the distinction between Egyptian and Mosaic magic clear:

> Then there shal be a great crye throughout all the land of Egypt, suche as was never none like, nor shalbe. But against none of the children of Israel shal a dog move his tongue, nether against man nor beast, that ye may knowe that the Lord putteth a difference betweene the Egyptians and Israel.[24]

Dismantling this "difference" between the Egyptians and the Jews is an extraordinarily heretical act. Had Moses been a cynic and an unscrupulous trickster, scripture would be built on a false foundation, and the unity of Christian worship through God's word would be impossible.

This distinction between the miracles of God and the magic of the Egyptians was often clarified in Elizabethan texts. The orthodox position stated that God permitted the magicians of Egypt to get assistance from the devil and thus imitate some of the miracles God had given to Moses. In order to make them see that Moses alone had the power of God behind him, God did not allow the Egyptians to imitate the most essential miracles.[25] Exodus, then, gives legitimacy and divine authority to Moses: "Beholde, I have made thee Pharaohs God . . . but I will harden Pharaoh's heart, and multiplie my miracles and my wondres in the land of Egypt" (7:1–3).

For Marlowe, the orthodox biblical reading cannot account for the way in which signs and wonders can be used to manipulate a credulous people. According to the Bible, Moses and Aaron serve as mediators or spokesmen, and they bring the word of God to the people: "Thou shalt take this rod," God says, "in thine hand, wherewith thou shalt do miracles" (4:17). This mediation opens up the narrative to charges that the leaders are themselves self-interested; the people believe Moses because he puts on a good show. Moses the performer stands alone, pulling the wool over the eyes of the "rude and gross" Jewish people for personal advantage.

Baines concludes the report: Marlowe "persuades men to Atheism willing them not to be afeard of bugbeares and hobgoblins, and utterly scorning both god and his ministers." The scorn of God's ministers is crucial to our picture of Marlowe's historical position and reputation: he was responding not merely to religious doctrine but to the Christian political ideology that made loyalty to the church equivalent to loyalty to the state. "Ministers," in this context, are those in political authority, especially the monarch, whom Tudor homilies referred to as "God's minister." Since Protestantism buttressed the authority of the state and instilled civil obedience, the rejection of religion amounted to an act of treason. Baines's charge of atheism, then, was also a charge of treason.

We have seen that Marlowe's ultimate religious beliefs can best be described as heterodox. To what extent did the world of spy and counterspy encourage the seditious thinking reported by Baines? This question could also be reframed: was Marlowe drawn to that world because he already held heterodox views of religion? Elizabeth's spymaster Walsingham was once described as "a most subtle searcher of hidden secrets." Is it possible that Marlowe, who may have entered into his service, took such searching in a more unorthodox direction? If he was a spy for Walsingham's secret service, he may have had an ambiguous religious affiliation; in fact, he may have become an "ambodexter" in the service of the Queen.[26] We have examples of such spies, including Roger Walton, once described as one who "showeth himself a great papist, to others a protestant, but as they take him who haunteth him most, he hath neither God nor religion, a very evil condition, a swearer without measure and tearer of God, a notable whoremaster."[27] Marlowe's plays, as we will see, and the numerous charges against him, suggest that he lacked Walsingham's intense commitment to the Protestant church and state. Marlowe, then, may have been "a subtle searcher," but his bonds of allegiance to the state were also rather slippery and tenuous. We turn next to an examination of the ways in which Marlowe challenges the authority of church and state in *Doctor Faustus*.

II

In this section I will explore two contradictory aspects of magic in *Doctor Faustus*: on the one hand, the play portrays magic as a defiant gesture and a genuine alternative to the state-approved form of worship; on the other, the play leaves us perplexed as to why the Hermetic "metaphysics of magic" that often seems so empowering for Faustus is ultimately not taken seriously. In fact, the play's lack of commitment to magical miracles has skeptical, even irreligious implications, which I will discuss alongside the Baines report. Magic is first seen as a rebellion against the state-sanctioned religion, but as we will see in *King Lear*, the skepticism is soon taken further, to encompass all religion.[28]

Throughout the Middle Ages, the Church tried to maintain control over magical practices, condemning those pursued outside its authority while approving the healing power of saints, holy water, and the mass.[29] The Church, of course, did not consider its own practices to be mere "magic" (as the charge was later made by Protestants) as it tried to crack down on rituals that did not meet ecclesiastical approval. Miracles performed by Christ and the Apostles were prominent in the New Testament, and the Catholic church continued to recognize miraculous events in the world. But the church was inconsistent in its condemnation of magic practiced by the laity: it allowed, for example, people to use certain incantations or charms that included Christian language and gestures.

By the sixteenth century, however, when the Reformation and Counter-Reformation demanded new, carefully drawn boundaries between superstition and religion, magic was widely despised and marginalized. The line between white and black magic, for example, may have been clear to occult practitioners, but for most people the two were hard to distinguish. Some of the most extreme opponents of magic called for the execution of anyone caught practicing white or black magic (the latter also known to Elizabethans as witchcraft). In fact, the ordinary acts of divination, soothsaying, and charming, which had thrived for centuries, were now labeled demonic. For George Gifford, "witch" might describe enchanters, diviners, and virtually all of the "cunning" men and women practicing in English villages.[30]

When Marlowe's source for *Doctor Faustus*—an English translation of the German *Faustbuch*—arrived in England in 1587, the nation had recently witnessed an intensification of witch persecutions. Thus the story of a real magician, Johannes

Faustus, who had been executed amid the German witch-hunts in the early part of the century, would have had a powerful effect on an Elizabethan audience. Was Marlowe adding more fuel to the fire in his dramatic version of this story by portraying Faustus as a witch rather than a white magician or thaumaturge?[31] How did audiences respond to the play's depictions of the evil practices of magic? The play may have inspired greater hostility toward anyone suspected of black magic; but it is also possible that some members of the audience enjoyed a new experience, that of identifying with a transgressive "over-reacher," a magician who obtains power beyond anything possessed by the church and state.[32] Marlowe chose a black magician (what I will also call a "witch") as his overreacher, thus portraying as powerful one of the most oppressed, marginalized subject positions in Elizabethan England. Faustus is not, of course, a reflection of village witches, the most politically powerless, poor, and abject people of his day. Nevertheless, he would have called to mind an assortment of people—men and women, rich and poor—brought to trial and/or execution by the state for making contact with demons. Marlowe's selection of a black magician was in keeping with his rebellious reputation: at a time when witches and magicians faced intense persecution, he created the character of Doctor Faustus, whose magic gave him an alternative to the state-approved form of worship.

One of the aspiring minds Marlowe had as a model for Doctor Faustus was well known throughout sixteenth-century England: John Dee. Although Dee's magic got him into trouble with certain authorities, his professed commitment to the Protestant religion never wavered. By the time *Faustus* was written and performed, Dee's reputation had been tarnished despite his many expressions of devotion to the Christian faith. Throughout the 1580s, he traveled to Renaissance courts and worked with his friend Edward Kelley at angelic magic and raising spirits from the dead. Upon returning to England, his reputation as a black magician had spread.[33] Defending his magic in letters to Elizabeth and James,[34] Dee describes his "briefe Discourse Apologetical" as a "plaine demonstration, and fervant Protestation, for the lawfull, sincere, and very Christian course, of the philosophical studies and exercises, of a certain studious Gentleman."[35]

The Tragicall Histoɪ
of the Life and Death
of Doctor FAVSTVS.

With new Additions.

Written by *Ch. Mar.*

Printed at London for *John Wright,* and are to be sold at his
shop without Newgate, 1624.

Title page of Christopher Marlowe's *Doctor Faustus* (1624)

There is no reason to doubt Dee's sincerity. Like Pico della Mirandola and Marcilio Ficino, he saw magic in Christian, spiritual terms. One means he had of improving his standing was to stay in favor with Queen Elizabeth, supporting her future global expansion of the "British Empire." He believed that a Royal Navy could procure "manifold great Commodities" for the "British Monarchy."[36] In his tract on navigation, Dee envisions Queen Elizabeth at the helm of this new regime: the "most Excellent Royall majesty" will be "sitting at the helm of this imperiall monarchy: or, rather, at the helm of the imperiall ship, of the most parte of Christendome." Dee dedicates this Hermetic tract "unto the Aeternal, Royall, and Heroicall Honor, and Renown of our incomparable Gracious Queene Elizabeth that, all the whole world over, yea, among the Heathen, as well as Christen: what language so ever they speak."[37] The navy would provide the "master key" to open the "locks hindering English Empire." Dee speaks of the public as the British Nation while also considering the "whole world," heathen and Christian, which will "sing and extoll her Princely Benefit therein."[38]

Nevertheless, the Christian devotion behind Dee's work failed to convince those who despised magic of any kind. That devotion, however, was important to his magic. Dee, like others interested in Hermeticism, believed that human beings had a spark of the divine. Hermeticists sought a pre-Christian knowledge based on the work of the Egyptian Hermes Trismegistus, who, they believed, lived during the time of Moses. This rediscovery of ancient wisdom was essential to their mystical Christian interests.[39] Human beings might achieve a certain level of divinity by following the path of mystical contemplation. In the *Monas Hieroglyphica*, for example, Dee says, "the logos of the creative universe works by rules so that man, godly-minded and born of God, may learn by straightforward work and by theological and mystical language."[40] Faustus, then, can be seen as a magician in some ways like Dee, but one who was criticizing the Protestantism that criticized Dee.

Dee and other magi were placed in an awkward position given the changes brought by the Reformation. One of the central doctrines of the reformed religion was that miracles, so important in the earliest years of Christianity, had long since ceased. As we saw in the first chapter, Protestants hoped to discredit the miracles of the Catholic church and distance themselves from the magical practices of the medieval period. For the Anglican church, communion was a reminder that there had been miracles in biblical times but that these were no more: priests could not bring the real physical presence of Christ into wine and bread. While Protestants were trying to do away with the miraculous in such rituals as transubstantiation, the Catholic church countered that the weakness of the Protestant religion could be seen in the fact that it was unable to work miracles. Indeed, it would be hard to overstate the importance of the Protestant break with the miraculous in medieval culture: "The miraculous," Miri Rubin says, "was widely perceived as part of nature which provided a paradigm for the explanation of the world and its apparent aberrations."[41] Rubin describes the eucharistic miracles—for example, the appearance of the Christ child in the host—that inspired worshipers and supposedly renewed the faith of skeptics or even inspired Jews to convert. By the late sixteenth century, however, when Dee's thaumaturgical wisdom was at its zenith, the miracles of magic looked to Protestants like nothing more than acts of fraud.

Faustus's first act of defiance to Protestant doctrine occurs when he strives to become a worker of miracles. His theological study has left him unsatisfied, so he turns to the creation of miracles as an alternative to religion. Disenchanted with philosophy, law, and medicine as well, Faustus vows to practice the miracles of magic. In his opening speech the magus tries to "settle" his studies and "sound the depth of that [he] wilt profess" (1.1–2).[42] After rejecting Aristotle, he turns to Galen and medicine: "Be a physician, Faustus. Heap up gold,/And be eternized for some wondrous cure" (1.1.14–15). But the egoistic goal of becoming a famous physician gives way to a hubristic desire to work miracles: "Couldst thou make men to live eternally,/Or, being dead, raise them to life again, /Then this profession were to be esteemed." Unable to remain "settled" about his profession, Faustus blasphemously imagines himself rising above the human condition by obtaining Christ's power to raise the dead.

Faustus's rejection of Protestantism springs out of a crucial development of the Reformation, the collapse of a single authoritative reading of scripture. Luther opened the door for religious anarchy when he said that believers are entitled to interpret the scriptures for themselves. The Roman Church, he insisted, should no longer have control over the interpretation of scripture. But with no central authority in the Protestant church, who would finally determine the truth about scripture? Reformers who had assumed that there would be collective agreement in their interpretations were, of course, mistaken.[43]

Ignoring the promise of grace offered in Paul's letter to the Romans, Faustus takes advantage of the individualist reading practices supported by Luther and other reformers. Paul writes, "For the wages of sin is death, but the free gift of God is eternal life in Christ Jesus our Lord" (6:23). Faustus interprets this as: "If we say that we have no sin,/We deceive ourselves, and there's no truth in us. Why then belike we must sin,/And so consequently die" (1.42–45). By repeating only the first part of Paul's letter, Faustus calls attention to the Calvinist doctrine of predestination and takes the perspective of the damned. Why adhere to a religious dogma that leaves worshipers feeling helpless? Even if he had cited the passages in their entirety, the contradictions of Calvinist thinking would remain; if the worshiper suspects he or she is one of the damned ("che sera, sera"), why not go on sinning? Indeed, why not sell one's soul to the devil for twenty-four years of pleasure?

Nevertheless, despite such rebelliousness, Faustus shows some signs of religious faith as well. On several occasions he appears to seek the rituals of the old religion, another act of defiance toward Protestantism. Thus his religious desire matches his desire for magic: he seeks an alternative to the unsatisfactory state-approved forms of worship. The most powerful example of this arrives at the play's end, when he yearns for the kind of spiritual satisfaction that Protestantism cannot supply: "O I'll leap up to my God! Who pulls me down?/See, see where Christ's blood streams in the firmament!" As C. L. Barber has shown, Faustus here hungers for the gratification of Christ's physical presence, a gratification that only the Catholic religion offers.[44] The Anglican church may have done away with the material aspect of the Eucharist, but it could not get rid of the individual's desire for that physical presence. Christopher Haigh has even argued that while there was a national church with a Protestant liturgy, the Elizabethan laity remained largely non-Protestant. He observes that "the ecclesiological and liturgical rules of 1559 were implemented reluctantly, and often over ten or twenty years." For instance, one example of resistance to the reformed church was the use of communion wafers rather than ordinary bread. Haigh notes that although royal injunctions forbade such a papist practice, parishes throughout England continued to perform aspects of the Catholic Mass.[45] Thus Marlowe's magus, facing imminent damnation for his sinful ways, alludes in his final moments to a Catholic practice that many Elizabethans continued to hold on to despite the laws forbidding it. While I am not suggesting that the play ultimately affirms the Catholic religion, I think it is significant that Faustus rebels against Protestant doctrines through the use of magic and the desire for the physical presence of Christ offered by the Catholic Church.

The report by Richard Baines, we recall, claimed that Marlowe spoke of Protestants as "hypocrites" for abandoning the ceremonies of the Catholic church. Luther, like so many reformers after him, argued that the mass was an idolatrous performance and that Christians should do without "vestments, ornaments, chants, prayers, organs, candles, and the whole pageantry of things visible."[46] Luther also says, in a discussion of baptism in "The Pagan Servitude of the Church": "let us open our eyes, and learn to pay more attention to the word than to the sign, to faith than to works or ritual."[47] Baines's charge states the precise opposite: Protestants are themselves performers, and by relinquishing the ceremonies of Catholicism, they merely weaken the power of their religion.

Indeed, the idea was not unfounded: the Elizabethan regime, attempting to fill the void left by the Reformation, appropriated many visual forms of Catholic culture. For example, portraits of the Virgin Queen made her into an object of worship not unlike the Virgin Mary. In the famous Ditchley portrait, Elizabeth is depicted as a divine power controlling the cosmic elements while standing like an empress on a map of Europe. Her disembodied form emphasizes her chaste, virginal condition. Also, Elizabeth's royal entry might be compared to public processions in Corpus Christi celebrations.[48] During the summer feast of Corpus Christi, the public procession included priests carrying the Eucharist behind those holding flags, crosses, and relics. The procession symbolized the entry of

Christ into Jerusalem.[49] Elizabeth's royal entry and other processions may have partly filled the cultural void created once
Corpus Christi celebrations had been banned.[50] In both cases—
the portraits and the procession—the Elizabethan state can be
seen as substituting its own rituals for those provided by the
Catholic church.

We can see Baines's charge exemplified in *Doctor Faustus*.
Marlowe might have been presenting Faustus's transgressive
turn toward magic as a critique of the Protestant doctrine on
communion and other ceremonies. The ritual of magic, which
shares much of the symbolism in Catholic ceremonies, can be
read as a substitute for the state-approved form of worship.
Faustus, for example, conjures spirits in Latin, reminding us of
Catholic rituals like transubstantiation or exorcism. He speaks
the abbreviated names of holy saints as he "tries the uttermost
magic can perform" (3.3.14). Such scenes in the play must have
reminded its audience of the ceremonies and rituals that had
been given up during the Reformation.

Nevertheless, skepticism ultimately overtakes magic as well.
Doctor Faustus has long been regarded as an emblem for the
"aspiring mind" of the Renaissance. But it has also been noted
that the play undermines the glorious intellectual aspirations
of its protagonist. Faustus does not remain devoted to the
Hermetic "metaphysics of magic," and the miracles of magic
rapidly begin to look like silly parlor tricks. If the great Renaissance magus Pico della Mirandola turned to the Hermetic
notion of man as *Magnum Miraculum*, Marlowe seems to have
viewed man as human, all-too-human, rather than as a participant in miracles. With the assistance of the information provided by Baines, we can locate a deep skeptical dimension in
the play's disengagement not just with Protestantism, but with
the miraculous in general.[51]

The devout magic of the Renaissance, which bestowed Neoplatonic respectability and Christian divinity on people who
might otherwise have been considered black magicians, was
based on a severe contempt for mere matter. Frances Yates describes the magician capturing *spiritus* and bringing it into
materia as an "operator" who can "canalise" occult proper-
ties.[52] Both kinds of gnosis in Hermetic thinking—optimistic
and pessimistic—suggest that matter without divine spirit is
contemptible (the latter sees matter as evil and the former sees

it as "impregnated with the divine"). This dualistic, Christian spirituality in the Hermetic view of the "aspiring mind" is best articulated by the *Asclepius* (believed at the time to be written by Hermes Trismegistus):

> Because of this, Asclepius, a human being is a great wonder, a living thing to be worshipped and honored: for he changes his nature into a god's, as if he were a god; he knows the demonic kind inasmuch as he recognizes that he originated among them; he despises the part of him that is human nature, having put his trust in the divinity of his other part.[53]

Pico della Mirandola echoes the *Asclepius* in the *Oration on the Dignity of Man*: "O supreme generosity of God the Father, O highest and most marvelous felicity of man! To him is granted to have whatever he chooses, to whatever he wills." The *Asclepius* and the *Oration* promise to teach human beings how to use their intellect to escape their material, human qualities and approach the divinity of God.

The *Asclepius* also presents an astrological system of celestial influences. For John Dee, Cornelius Agrippa, Marcilio Ficino, Pico della Mirandola, and other Neoplatonic magi, magical images capture the essence of heavenly stars and other supracelestial qualities. Magical images, which require transcendence of the physical senses, come through mystical and ineffable contact with the divine Logos, the word of God. Pico, as Frances Yates tells us, was the one who "first boldly formulated a new position for European man, man as Magus using both Magia and Cabala to act upon the world, to control his destiny by science."[54]

Faustus's fellow magician Cornelius says that "The miracles that magic will perform will make thee vow to study nothing else" (1.1.138–39). Yet after his initial yearning for the "metaphysics of magicians," Faustus loses interest in what Pico della Mirandola called the "spirit of the divine" and other contemplative pleasures celebrated by magic. Although Faustus says he "will be as cunning as Agrippa was," the contemplative life so dear to magicians like Cornelius Agrippa or Pico della Mirandola is distant from Marlowe's portrayal of Faustus's desire for profit and delight.[55] Debasing Pico's magic and the Hermetic tradition, Marlowe virtually eliminates the pious, noble, and esoteric quest for logos and divine *mens*. Faustus does not pursue the magical contemplation so admired by historians like Yates, who argues that Hermeticism and Cabala gave the Renaissance magician a new legitimated status.

Once Faustus makes a pact with the devil, material delights, not spiritual ones, capture his imagination; the spiritual powers of Hermeticism recede as he becomes "wanton and lascivious," and the god he serves is "his own appetite." He shifts abruptly from such profound questions about heaven and hell to those of his lascivious desires as he asks Mephistopheles for a wife because he is "wanton." The devil discourages marriage and promises him instead the fairest courtesans for his bed. Here we see that the magic initially presented as a spiritual alternative to Protestantism is losing any claim to divine sanction. Faustus seems to be posing a skeptical question, then, about humans' ability to transcend their material nature.

The comic scenes of the play further expose the earthy and unhermetic nature of Faustian desire.[56] Robin the clown debases the metaphysics of the play's opening scene and makes the vices of Faustian magic clear. His enthusiasm upon stealing the magical books ("O, this is admirable!") resonates with Faustus's reaction to the power of magic ("O, this cheers my soul!"). The clown continues: "I mean to search some circles for my own use. Now will I make all the maidens in our parish dance at my pleasure stark naked before me, and so by that means I shall see more than e'er I felt or saw yet" (2.2.3–5). In another scene the clown mocks Faustus's pact with the devil, saying he would sell his soul for a "well roasted shoulder of mutton with a good sauce."

Thus, Faustus's conjuring practice never comes close to the transcendence of Hermetic magic; in fact, for him, magic becomes yet another empty ceremony, a set of cheap tricks. Faustus engages in what some Protestants would have called "popish" practices, mere juggling tricks to please the senses, such as throwing fireworks among the friars who chant "maledicat dominus." His magical rituals turn out to be just as empty as the repetitious Catholic ones. Profit and delight are merely "promised" to the student of magic; magic never delivers the desired fulfillment. There is no object for his fantasy other than magical rumination, but the scholar fails as well to find satisfaction in magic. Skepticism is once again taken to its ultimate chaotic conclusion: if state-sanctioned religion cannot bring us closer to God, what reason do we have to think we can reach divinity on our own?

It is possible that Marlowe was inspired by accounts of John Dee and Edward Kelley on the continent and chose to parody their quest to speak to the dead. When Faustus travels to the court of the Emperor Charles V, he raises images of Alexander the Great and his paramour, and when he visits the Duke and Duchess of Vanholt, he conjures grapes in the dead of winter. But these are his more noble performances of the "black art"; his other tricks include boxing the pope's ears and making horses disappear. When Faustus actually obtains magical power, it does not enable him to bring the dead back to life; magic serves only to raise up images (spirits) from the past, without the substance of real bodies. The dead are brought back to life for a show of appearances, a means of impressing the emperor. Faustus ruminates on "necromantic skill," which often looks like the ability to impress people through natural rather than supernatural (or divine) means. Thus the word "heavenly" has a twofold irony: first, Faustus uses it as an adjective for "necromantic books"; second, his magical "lines, circles, signs, letters, and characters" do not ultimately approach the divinity described in the Hermetic tradition.

Placed in blasphemous contexts, the signifier "heavenly" describes a world of profit and delight as well as the phantasmagoric Helen. Instead of the spiritual heaven of Christianity, Faustus finds bliss in material pleasures. Guided by Mephistopheles, he strives for immortality through a kiss with Helena. Marlowe saves the most poetically inspiring lines of the play for Faustus's substitute for Christian grace, the heavenly Helen.

> Was this the face that launched a thousand ships,
> And burnt the topless towers of Ilium?
> Sweet Helen, make me immortal with a kiss:
> Her lips sucks forth my soul, see where it flies!
> Come Helen, come, give me my soul again.
> Here will I dwell, for heaven be in these lips,
> And all is dross that is not Helena!
>
> (12.81–87)

The lines put the "soul" squarely in a material position; Helen's kiss "sucks forth" his soul, and, finding this kiss pleasurable,

Faustus, imagining "immortality" from Helen's lips, cries out for more. Instead of ascending to heaven, his soul descends into Helen's mouth as if his soul were an internal organ being extracted from his body. These lines on the page and particularly on the stage, where music accompanies Helen's ethereal presence, have left many readers and audiences feeling as though Faustus has at last found his summum bonum: physical pleasure. Neither the metaphysics of magicians nor the grace of God's heaven ever look this attractive to him.

Even when Faustus confronts eternal damnation, he turns in desperation to the possibility that the soul is mortal. In his final moments, Faustus pleads for the annihilation that a Lucretian-Epicurean, materialist cosmos would provide as the antidote to the torments of hell. Extreme pain, the desire for corporal dissolution, and the cruelty of Marlowe's God combine in the play to lend support to the subversive ideas of Lucretius. "Why wert thou not a creature wanting soul?" Faustus asks.

> All beasts are happy, for, when they die,
> Their souls are soon dissolved in elements;
> But mine must live still to be plagued in hell.
>
> (5.2.102–4)

In *De Rerum Natura*, Lucretius argued that the notion of death as a final form of total annihilation should be comforting, rather than terrifying. Marlowe, unlike orthodox Christians, would not dismiss the possibility of utter annihilation entirely. In addition, he was acquainted with ancient ideas found in Aristotle and Epicurus that the soul is mortal. William Empson makes the tantalizing claim that the original, uncensored play did not end with the damnation of Faustus, but rather with the more radically skeptical conclusion that earthly pleasure and pain are all there is.[57] But even with the damnation scene as it is we have the sense that the physical joys of the libertine, rather than eternal bliss in heaven or the divine experiences of Hermetic magic, are Marlowe's primary interest.[58]

The move away from the divinity of magic repeats the pattern established when Faustus rejects religion in his opening speech. As he rejects Protestantism as a route to divinity, so he eventually rejects magic as a means to transcend his base humanity. The magician is driven by bodily desires that block his goal of reaching heaven. It hardly suffices to describe Faustus's desire as sinful gluttony. When he asks for Helen, for example, Faustus says to Mephistopheles "One thing, good servant, let me crave of thee,/To glut the longing of my heart's desire." When he first plans to conjure demons, he says, "How am I glutted with conceit of this!" One of the irreligious notions that springs out of the play's fixation on physical desires is a variation on the Epicureanism mentioned above. The chorus might complain that Faustus turns away from the "heavenly matters of theology," but the endless needs and desires of the body would seem to offer him no choice other than to pursue heaven on earth.

We recall that the Baines report further suggests Marlowe himself turned his attention away from the miracles of heaven. Protestants insisted that miracles had ceased sometime around the seventh century AD. Marlowe, on the other hand, appears to have believed that the miracles of early Christianity and pre-Christianity, like the miracles of magic in the Renaissance, simply did not exist.

Of course, Marlowe's alleged assertion that Moses was but a juggler might be read as affirming the wisdom of the Hermeticists, who believed that Moses the law-giver lived at the same time as Hermes Trismegistus, an Egyptian Moses, and a law-giver himself. Marlowe, it might be argued, may have been interested in the heretical version of Hermeticism developed by Giordano Bruno, who valued Egyptian magic over and above the Hebrew religion.[59] But Bruno's magic challenged orthodox Christianity while remaining focused on the human capacity to connect with the divine. Baines's Marlowe, on the other hand, moves in a more anti-Christian direction, as will be apparent if we briefly compare the charge about Moses to what Reginald Scot has to say on the same matter.

Scot's *Discoverie of Witchcraft* (1584), we recall, exposes the fraud of magicians and argues that witches are merely melancholic old women. In order to demystify the "papist" practices that remained in a reformed England, he reexamines Pharaoh's magicians in the Book of Exodus, distancing the work of the Egyptians as far as possible from the miracles of God: "These magicians did rather seeme to doo these woonders, than worke them indeed. And if they made but prestigious shewes of things, I saie it was more than our witches can doo." Scot declares that all miracles have ceased and that no one can perform real magic or witchcraft anymore. As we might expect, Scot's hostility toward contemporary magic does not extend to the true miracles of Moses and Christ. Responding to charges in works by Pliny, Tacitus, Strabo, and Apollonius that Moses was a juggler, he says, "For Moses differed as much from a magician, as truth from falshood, and pieties from vanitie." His miracles came from "the finger of God," while contemporary magicians used mere illusions.[60]

Scot's rationalism put him on the margins of witchcraft discourse; but Marlowe's alleged remarks put him in a much more dangerous position vis-à-vis the state religion, and indeed all Christianity. For Marlowe, a similar logic undermines the charismatic authority not only of contemporary charlatans, but of Moses and Jesus as well. Scot is precisely what the Baines note describes as a Protestant "hypocrite" since he attacks transubstantiation and other displays in the Catholic church without recognizing that Protestantism is itself a fraudulent performance. Marlowe pushes the envelope further by questioning scriptural accounts of miracles and the sacred, turning the unmasking of popish practices against Protestantism itself.

In sum, *Doctor Faustus* and the Baines note lead us to believe that while the Protestant nation was growing in power, there was much ideological and spiritual instability remaining in England long after the Catholic religion appeared defeated. With *Faustus*, Marlowe took the skeptical uncertainty regarding the true form of Christianity further, to question Christianity itself and humanity's ability to reach Christian goals.

III

More than any other of Marlowe's plays, *Doctor Faustus* devotes its energies to religious matters. In fact, when we consider the censorship confronting plays with religious content, it is hard to believe that it ever saw the light of day. The Privy Council minutes of November 17, 1589, describe matters "unfytt" for plays and asks the players to "deliver unto them [the Master of the Revelles, the Archbishop Canterbury, and the

Lord Mayor of London] their bookes, that they maye consider of the matters of their comedyes and tragedyes, and thereuppon to stryke out or reforme suche partes and matters as they shall fynde unfytt and undecent to be handled in playes, bothe for Divinitie and State. . . ."[61] We cannot be certain that *Doctor Faustus* and *The Jew of Malta* were affected by this censorship. Despite its warnings about the representation of "Divinitie" on stage, the state was either uninterested in or unconcerned with much of Marlowe's work. One wonders, for example, why the censors did not extract Faustus's blasphemous words upon signing the contract to sell his soul: "consummatum est" (it is completed), he says, repeating the final words of Christ before his death.

Doctor Faustus may focus intensely on religious matters, but *The Jew of Malta* (1590) is Marlowe's most vicious satire on Christianity. In this section I will demonstrate that one of the sources for the play's religious skepticism is radical economic change. Critics have long recognized that *The Jew of Malta* confronts economic matters that were pressing in Elizabethan England, including mercantile interests in the New World, usury, acquisitiveness, and the severing of social bonds. These developments, the play indicates, posed a challenge to religious piety and conventional morality. Marlowe's Barabas, a composite of anti-Semitic stereotypes inherited from the medieval period, reveals the anxieties of a nation undergoing rapid religious and economic change.

Marlowe's protagonists often mention New World trade, one of the major contributing factors of sixteenth-century capitalist development. In his opening soliloquy, Barabas boasts about his expansive commercial investments, including "Spanish oils," the "wines of Greece," "spices and silks from Alexandria," and the metal of "Indian mines." The New World is seen obsessively as land to be pillaged, as we saw in chapter two: in the *Massacre at Paris*, Guise observes that "the Catholic Philip, king of Spain,/Ere I shall want, will cause his Indians,/To rip the golden bowels of America" (18.63–65); as he is dying Tamburlaine laments that he will not be able to conquer the New World and bring back "all the golden mines, Inestimable drugs and precious stones" (5.3.145–46). Faustus brags that his slavish servants will "ransack the ocean for orient pearl,/and search all corners of the new found world/For pleasant

fruits and princely delicates" (1.83–85). In all of these instances, New World discovery is associated strictly with the
greed of commercial expansion, what Marx once referred to as
the "icy water of egoistic calculation."[62]

Barabas's second soliloquy praises heaven for bringing him
this wealth from around the world. Although it is couched in
anti-Semitic language, the speech presents a materialist perspective held by just about everyone in Malta—Jew, Christian,
and Muslim alike.

> Thus trowls our fortune in by land and sea,
> And thus are we on every side enriched:
> These are the blessings promised to the Jews,
> And herein was old Abram's happiness:
> What more may heaven do for earthly man
> Than thus to pour out plenty in their laps,
> Ripping the bowels of the earth for them,
> Making the sea their servant, and the winds
> To drive their substance with successful blasts?[63]

Note that there is nothing spiritual about this "heaven": it
merely aids "earthly man" in his aggressive quest for material
gain. Barabas's biblical interpretation, as James R. Siemon reminds us, derives from the anti-Semitic arguments of Christian theologians who thought that Jews treated God's blessing
as "carnal."[64] Nevertheless, Barabas is not the only one who
thinks in these terms. The Bashaw confesses that the wind that
drives him to Malta is "the wind that bloweth all the world be-
sides/Desire of gold" (3.5.3–4). Moreover, the "we" in Barabas's
passage refers not to the Jewish community, but rather to the
merchants whose ships have just arrived. Barabas, whose
motto is "ego mihimet sum semper proximus" (I am always
closest to myself), does not feel any solidarity with the other
Jews of Malta. He does, however, enjoy his position as Malta's
wealthiest merchant. In fact, his materialist outlook is more
indebted to the mercantile culture around him than it is to Ju-
daism.[65] Economic identity is here presented as overtaking religious identity, to the point of nullifying religious bonds. The
skepticism engendered by extreme economic turmoil threatens
to erode religion itself.

As we saw in *Doctor Faustus*, Marlowe depicts religion as

subordinate to material desires by detaching the word "heaven" from its traditional spiritual meanings. In the above passage, the word "more" is crucial: for Barabas, there is nothing more "heaven" can do than enable man to violently extract riches from nature. Indeed, "heaven" does not look any different from nature. Barabas praises the wind for sending ships abroad and the land for spilling forth "plenty." The divine intelligence behind it all seems unimportant, and the more traditional connotations of "heaven," especially the afterlife, are beside the point.

It is hard to ignore the anti-Semitism behind this portrait of Barabas.[66] But it is important to note that Marlowe's work was inspired by the new voyages of discovery and the mercantile culture of Protestants in England. The first two sections of Thomas Harriot's *Briefe and True Report*, we recall, catalog the "marchantable commodities" of Virginia. As we have seen, Harriot prioritizes his study of the land's natural resources— silk, hemp, sassafras, cedar, furs, iron, copper. Like James Rosier, who described the vegetation on the coast of New England as "the profits and fruits which are naturally on these Ilands," Harriot perceived the New World through the lens of the profit motive. Moreover, if we think that Marlowe's language for the extraction of wealth from the New World is merely a caricature of what we find in travel narratives of his day, we need only look at Sir Walter Ralegh's *Discovery of Guiana* (1595), which states that "Guiana is a country that hath yet her maidenhead, never sacked, turned, nor wrought, the face of the earth hath not been torn, nor the virtue and salt of the soil spent by manurance, the graves have not been opened for gold, the mines not broken with sledges, nor their images pulled down out of their temples."[67] Evangelism, as well as profit, motivated many voyages to the New World. Yet we wouldn't know that from reading Marlowe's plays, which remind us only of the desire to plunder the land of riches. Thus it is the advent of capitalism that is a source of Marlowe's skepticism: religion, the play suggests, is compromised by the excesses of international trade. The acquisitive impulses, evident in narratives by Ralegh, Harriot, and countless others, might well lead a skeptic like Marlowe to satirize the hypocrisy of Christians who claim to place religious goals above material desires.

In *The Jew of Malta*, we learn from Ferneze, the Governor

of Malta, that Barabas is a usurer as well as a merchant. In Elizabethan England, usury—defined as lending money with interest—generated much more apprehension than did mercantilism, and its critics harped on the economic, social, and religious dangers it presented. Gerard Malynes warned that usury might "overthroweth the harmony of the strings of the good government of a commonwealth, by too much enriching some, and by oppressing and impoverishing some others, bringing the instrument out of tune: when as every member for the same should live contented in his vocation and execute his charge according to his profession."[68] Usury was seen as dangerous, then, not only because it creates vast inequalities, but also because it disrupts the social order in which everyone is bound to a particular vocation and position in the hierarchy. Sixteenth-century laws against usury did indeed take this problem into consideration. Many Elizabethans were concerned that lending money with interest could enrich people of lowly rank, thus enabling them to rise above their God-given social positions.

Nevertheless, Elizabethans depended on usury even as they feared it would create disharmony in society. Those who sought to liberalize laws against usury recognized that lending and borrowing at interest were an essential part of trade that could benefit large numbers of people. Even after Edward VI placed a total ban on usury, the practice did not go away. In fact, as Normon Jones tells us, a new bill had to be introduced in 1571 because "people were lending and borrowing at interest all over England, for good purposes and for bad. All lenders ran the risk of molestation by the informers, and the borrowers were being gouged by very high interest rates—rates that were partly the result of the prohibition of usury."[69] Usury was a reality in England, and no amount of moralizing or preaching could put a stop to it.

Ferneze, in a passage rich with irony, uses the word "covetousness" twice, echoing the language of anti-usury tracts as he reveals that Barabas was himself a usurer.

> Out wretched Barabas,
> Sham'st thou not thus to justify thyself,
> As if we knew not thy profession?
> If thou rely upon thy righteousness,

> Be patient and thy riches will increase.
> Excess of wealth is cause of covetousness:
> And covetousness, oh 'tis a monstrous sin.
>
> (1.2.119–125)

The words "excess," "covetousness," and "sin" are ubiquitous in the anti-usury tracts. The preacher in Thomas Wilson's dialogue, *A Discourse Upon Usury*, published two years before the usury law of 1571, states, "And therefore, as Lucifer for pride fel down from heaen, so usurers for covetousnes wil fall down from earth to the dark dungeion of hel."[70] And in his preface to the dialogue Wilson describes the "ouglie, detestable and hurtefull synne of usurie, whiche, being but one in grossenes of name, caries many a mischief linked into it in nature, the same synne beinge nowe so rancke throughout all England. . . ."[71] When such moralistic language is uttered by the deceitful Ferneze, however, the result is satire. The Governor feels no shame when he takes away half the property of the impoverished Jews in Malta, nor does he feel remorse when he converts Barabas's home into a nunnery. Ferneze, the character who most stands for religious piety and moral rectitude, is himself driven by covetousness.

Barabas exposes the religious danger that confronted Elizabethans as their economic system changed: usury, many believed, violated the law of God; it was "unnatural" for money to beget more money. The widespread conservative position on usury followed the biblical prohibition in the Old and New Testaments. Yet debate was extensive and there was no consensus on the matter. In fact, the laws changed repeatedly. During the seventeenth century, the anti-usury rhetoric of Thomas Wilson became obsolete as the activities of the market and "God's Law" increasingly occupied separate ideological spheres.[72]

The Jew of Malta poses the question of what happens when economic practices clash with religious values. In Barabas's case, the result is skepticism: throughout the play religion comes under deep suspicion for the way in which it hides baser economic motives. "Religion," Barabas tells his daughter Abigail, "hides many things from suspicion." The play does not suggest that there is an alternative way to be authentically religious either, since, with the exception of Abigail, everyone is caught either deceiving others or deceiving themselves into believing that religious values are not tainted by economic motives.

Thus many Elizabethans, expecting to see a play that followed traditional moralizing against usury and covetousness, may have been surprised at the complexity of this work. To be sure, *The Jew of Malta* seems to follow the structure of other Tudor homiletic plays by showing the covetous and cruel Barabas meet a violent death in the end. Barabas carries his vindictive behavior so far that he is ultimately hoisted with his own petard when he falls into the boiling cauldron he meant for Calymath. But true to his sardonic reputation, Marlowe does not allow the audience to leave the theater thinking of the Jewish merchant simply as the "other." In Malta, covetousness is part of the zeitgeist: slaves stand in a market where "every one's price is written on his back," friars seek money and sex, and the governor, Ferneze, is as venal as they come. In addition, the audience may well have recognized that economic changes in England made it impossible to avoid the acquisitiveness attributed to usurers by Ferneze. To be sure, the stage Jew may have functioned as a scapegoat, but it is also possible that he, like other avaricious characters such as Ben Jonson's Volpone, provided a mirror in which the audience might, as Hamlet puts it, see in "the very age and body of the time his form and pressure."

Furthermore, as if it wasn't enough to make Barabas a deceitful usurer, Marlowe also casts him as a Machiavellian. As we saw in chapter two, Machiavellian theory (as opposed to the theatrical Machiavel) had become known to the politically astute by the end of the sixteenth century.[73] Robert Burton, for example, recalls Marlowe's Machiavellian interrogations in the Baines report: the ubiquitous English Machiavellians find that there is "No way to curb than superstition, to terrify men's consciences, and to keep them in awe: they make new laws, statutes, invent new religions, ceremonies, as so many stalking-horses, to their ends."[74] But some familiarity with Machiavellianism may also have enabled theater audiences to come to understand the economic changes in their midst. Unlike the Italian Machiavelli, who was hardly interested in using deceit for economic gain, the English stage version often exhibited acquisitive values.[75]

On the Elizabethan stage, the Machiavell was a comic villain who treated religion with disdain or regarded it as a form of "policy," a means to a political end. Loosely based on Machiavelli, who was placed on the index in 1559, the stage Machiavell was a shape-shifter, a chameleon whose existence defied the possibility of divine providence. *The Jew of Malta* opens with a direct address to the audience by the atheistic Machevill, who challenges the authority of religion in order to foreground the unlimited scope of Barabas's possessive individualism: he will "present the tragedy of a Jew, /Who smiles to see how full his bags are crammed,/Which money was not got without my means" (prologue, 30–32). Authority, he demonstrates, relies heavily on the process of ascribing objective meaning to nature or seeing a moral order outside the human will-to-power: "Birds of the aire will tell of murders past?/I am ashamed to hear of such fooleries" (prologue, 16–17). This naturalistic critique could apply to pagan and Christian ways of thinking about the supernatural or divine providence. Hamlet's line, "There is a special providence in the fall of a sparrow," for example, echoes Calvin's *Institutes* as well as the New Testament.[76]

The prologue focuses on religious authority, especially that of the Catholic church: the followers of Machiavelli are able to obtain "Peter's chair" (the papacy) by denouncing him in public while secretly following his ideas. Political authority is based on deception, since laws are really just the product of earthly power. In other words, might makes right: "What right had Caesar to the empire?/Might first made kings, and laws were then most sure/When like the Draco's they were writ in blood" (prologue, 19–21).

Whereas both Machevill and Barabas argue early on that "policy" can be a means of "profit," Barabas points out at the end of the play that "he that liveth in authority,/And neither gets him friends, nor fills his bags,/Lives like the ass that Aesop speaketh of,/That labours with a load of bread and wine,/And leaves it off to snap on thistle tops" (5.1.38–42). This characterization, which alludes to the limitations placed on Jews in early modern Europe, shows that Barabas has little interest in the public sphere that is so important to Machiavelli's political philosophy.[77] Barabas does not want to occupy a position of authority, nor does he expect to be controlled by any authority.

His real aim is to enjoy the endless accumulation of wealth without the interference of religious or political authority.

Barabas's egoistic obsession with private gain must have been somewhat shocking to many Elizabethans who were coping with economic change. Although large networks of market relations had expanded and the social structure of medieval life no longer held sway, the English had not immediately transformed into rational, Smithian economists. Egoism had been anathema in the medieval period, when private gain was considered less important than the public good, and up until the eighteenth century the amoral and self-interested thinking represented by Barabas could hardly be said to have characterized any kind of cultural norm.[78] Even as market relations rapidly expanded, people continued to rely on communal bonds in financial transactions.[79] Thus many Elizabethans, still attached to a pre-capitalist morality, would have despised Barabas's individualistic affirmation of private accumulation.

Nevertheless, market forces had unquestionably entered into sixteenth-century life, and thus the characters of Machevill and Barabas would have tapped into English anxieties that economic motives would affect religious faith. Thomas Wilson, for example, saw usury as a threat to God's law and charitable dealing that would cause people to worship Mammon instead of God, give them a "hardenes of harte," and ultimately destroy the world: "I do verely beleve, the ende of thys worlde is nyghe at hande."[80]

Although the prologue tells the audience that Barabas has become rich through Machiavellian means, Ferneze is in many respects a greater Machiavell since he uses religion as a means to further the state's interests.[81] Masking his deeper economic motives by invoking "heaven" in justification for his actions, Ferneze exemplifies Christian hypocrisy. When he is forced to pay tribute money to the Turks, he in turn expropriates Barabas's fortune. "Will you then steal my goods?" Barabas asks, "Is theft the ground of your religion?" (1.1.95–96). Ferneze claims that because the Jews "stand accursed in the sight of heaven," he is justified in robbing them of their wealth. Thus his final lines are ironic and hypocritical: "So march away and let due praise be given /neither to fate nor fortune, but to heaven." From the prologue on, Marlowe makes it clear that pious references to "heaven" or the transcendent in general merely serve to cover up baser self-interests.

Religion is also debased in this play by the hedonism of the friars Bernardine and Jacomo. Bernardine adds to the last words of Abigail ("And witness that I die a Christian") by saying, "Ay, and a virgin too, that grieves me most." The friars also give Marlowe an opportunity to satirize confession and repentance. When Barabas dissembles a desire to repent, confess, and convert to Christianity, the two friars fight over who will gain his possessions. This struggle reenacts Ferneze's attempt to take all of Barabas's wealth while threatening to convert him. Hence, the friars exemplify Barabas's point that it is better to dissemble knowingly (as he does) than to be a hypocrite without knowing it. While Barabas is fully aware of the implications of his behavior, the friars, like the other Christians, cannot even recognize the hypocrisy of their lust for material gain.

Marlowe also shows how social bonds, like religious values, are affected by economic change. As Marx observes on the rise of capitalism: "the bourgeoisie has torn away from the family its sentimental veil, and has reduced the family relation to a mere money relation."[82] In *The Jew of Malta*, familial and romantic love take on a new character in a commodified world. Barabas, armed with his motto—*ego mihimet sum semper proximus*—tells his slave, Ithamore, "First be thou void of these affections,/Compassion, love, vain hope, and heartless fear" (2.3.171–72). When Barabas does announce his love, his language is rich with irony; while hugging the moneybags rescued by Abigail, he comically and mockingly expresses affection for her: "Oh girl, oh gold, oh beauty, oh my bliss!" When Abigail converts to Christianity, her father turns to his slave as a source of filial affection. But the love of his Turkish slave Ithamore is really a bond of accompliceship in murder, rather than a substitute for filial bonds. Fearing that Abigail might reveal his murder of the two friars, Barabas decides to poison her and the entire nunnery that occupies his former home: "Very well, Ithamore, then now be secret;/And for thy sake, whom I so dearly love, /Now shalt thou see the death of Abigail,/That thou mayst freely live to be my heir" (3.4.60–64). Barabas shifts his affection to his slave with ease, even offering to make him his heir. In the commodified world of Malta, Ithamore, a Turk, can easily replace a Jewish daughter, so long as he can protect the wealth and safety of Barabas.

The behavior of Ferneze and other Christians in Malta leads Barabas to make the most skeptical point in the play, that religion is a means of "hiding" wicked deeds from suspicion. It was common for Machiavellian villains to put this idea into practice on stage. Shakespeare's irreligious Richard of Gloucester, for example, stands between two clergymen carrying a prayer book in order to impress the citizens and get their support for his reign. But Marlowe adds a subversive twist: Barabas has learned this way of operating from the economic practices of the Christians themselves. As we have seen, Ferneze demonstrates the truth of Barabas's point that religion is an excellent means of concealing mischievous economic behavior. As he accuses Barabas of covetousness, he prepares to expropriate his home and money. Thus, when Barabas has Abigail feign a conversion to Catholicism in order to regain some of his money, he is following the same behavior as the Christians.

Barabas, like the Marlowe we have seen in scandalous reports, relentlessly demystifies the religious practices of his society. His cynical wisdom on hypocrisy is a fine example: "As good dissemble that thou never mean'st/As first mean truth and then dissemble it; /A counterfeit profesion is better/ Than unseen hypocrisy" (1.2.290–93). Everyone dissembles, he suggests, but those who do it intentionally are at least not hypocritical. Having unmasked the deception of others, Barabas paradoxically insists that in the absence of truth, it is better to be cynically aware of one's deception. Peter Sloterdijk has described this mentality as cynical distance. The cynic, he argues, shows "evidence of a radical, ironic treatment of ethics and of social conventions, as if universal laws existed only for the stupid, while that fatally clever smile plays on the lips of those in the know."[83] At times, Barabas suggests that Ferneze and his knights themselves exhibit a Machiavellian form of cynical distance: "Ah, Policy? That's their profession,/ And not simplicity, as they suggest" (1.2.161–62). In his speech about dissembling, however, Barabas notes that while the Christians are guilty of "unseen hypocrisy," he, being more enlightened, is aware of his dissembling nature from the start. This ironic disposition casts doubt on religious truths, especially since there is no rebuttal to such cynical wisdom in the play. Instead, the other characters merely confirm the validity of Barabas's point by using religion (consciously or unconsciously) as a flimsy justification for seizing Jewish property.

Despite his self-consciousness and his ability to demystify other people's hypocrisy, Barabas lacks a grounding in any ethical norm; indeed, he is guided by the fantasy of revenge and the love of money. We might consider, for example, his comic boasting of extreme villainous acts: "As for myself, I walk abroad a-nights/And kill sick people groaning under walls:/Sometimes I go about and poison wells" (2.3.176–77). He then tells us he once practiced medicine and "enriched the priests with burials." He was an engineer who "slew friend and enemy" and a usurer who made young orphans hang themselves. This list suggests that the character of Barabas is not one person but a composite of cynical villains. Despite the cynical distance that enables him to critique the behavior of the Christians, Barabas remains blind to the power of his own fantasy.[84] He is unable to break free from economic motivations that guide his every action.

This bizarre account of Barabas's social dislocation explains much of his skepticism. We are made aware that he has traveled in many places and taken on different subject positions: usurer, engineer, doctor. Such a scattered, fragmented existence would account in part for his religious doubt and unethical behavior. For example, having informed us of his cynical view of "conscience"—"Happily some hapless man hath conscience,/And for his conscience lives in beggary"—Barabas makes it clear that he does not feel any guilt over his sexual transgressions since they occurred "in another country." When the two friars come to charge him with murder, he interrupts them by admitting to a different sin:

> *Bernardine:* Thou hast committed—
> *Barabas:* Fornication?
> But that was in another country:
> And besides, the wench is dead.

The passage combines religious and philosophical doubt. Having laughed off the idea of repentance elsewhere, he shows no commitment whatsoever to Christian ethics here either; he is a skeptic about all religious norms. Futhermore, Barabas shares the amoral, irreligious perspective of his teacher Machevill, who says "I count religion but a childish toy,/And hold there is no sin but ignorance" (prologue, 15–16). Like his teacher, he fears no divine punishment for his sins.

This religious doubt reflects a view of custom similar to that espoused by Greek Pyrrhonism. Like the Pyrrhonist skeptical relativism on "custom," the line "that was in another country" seems to undermine universal ethical norms. The tenth mode of skepticism by Sextus Empiricus states:

> We oppose dogmatic suppositions to one another when we say that some people assert that there is one element, others infinitely many; some that the soul is mortal, others immortal; some that human affairs are directed by divine providence, others non-providentially.[85]

The skeptic suspends judgment by using the method "in utramque partem"—"opposed to every account there is an equal account." Because there is no fixed, universal truth guiding ethical behavior, the skeptic decides simply to follow the customs determined in whatever location he or she happens to be in. Barabas implies that his fornication cannot be judged because he is no longer in the country where the fornication took place; the customs of that country might call for a different judgment upon him. But the question of what the ultimate judgment should be simply has no answer, to the skeptic.

Thus, in Marlowe's Elizabethan context, Barabas would signal that "the time is out of joint." He is a caricature of the "new man," the subject position that took on increasing importance in a burgeoning market society. The term describes merchants, entrepreneurs, investors, and others whose status was based solely on their ability to make money. Barabas has no connection or commitment to any particular geographical location, family, or political regime, and his Jewish background largely supplies material only for anti-Semitic farce. Hence, since his only attachment is to money and he lacks a genuine religious affiliation, his identity seems to depend wholly on the fetishism of commodities. Indeed, this *homo economicus* is a fine embodiment of what Jean-Christophe Agnew calls the "placeless market" and the "protean social world" in which "the conventional signposts of social and individual identity had become mobile and manipulable reference points."[86] Social identity in an emerging capitalist economy, Agnew argues, took on theatrical qualities. Thus Jacques's line in *As You Like It*—"All the world's a stage,/ And all the men and women merely players"— represented a new cultural situation in which people might recognize their identities as contingent and changeable rather than fixed in nature. Barabas, then, like other protean characters on the Renaissance stage, is a figure of the "placeless market," in that his fungible identity appears to mirror the new system of commodity exchange.[87] This merchant or "new man" reflects an experience of self that did not fit into the traditional structures inherited from the medieval period.

Barabas would have reminded audiences of the rampant confusion and anxiety created by social mobility. The traditional picture of a social order based on degree in nature could not account for the dislocations of the market, in which, as William Harrison put it, merchants "often change estate with gentlemen, as gentlemen do with them, by a mutual conversion of the one into the other."[88] Often regarded as ignoble by those who did not sully their hands in the work of trade, merchants nevertheless often did establish the status of gentlemen by amassing large quantities of wealth. Merchants may not have fit into the traditional status hierarchy, but given the importance of trade in Shakespeare's England, they increasingly carried more influence, power, and prestige.[89]

The Jew of Malta suggests that economic change would have had a profound impact on many facets of English culture, including religion. The powerful satire does not leave Barabas as the scapegoat on whom the Christians in Marlowe's theater might place all the blame for their economic woes, however. Indeed, the Jew becomes a strong critic who exposes the hypocrisy and cunning of those pious individuals who use religion as a means of covering up their sinful actions. Moreover, the sacred and the spiritual take on a whole new appearance in such an economic system, as signifiers like "heaven" call for a suspicious response when baser interests often lurk beneath the surface of religious piety. Elizabethan audiences may have congratulated themselves on not being as covetous as Barabas, but it is likely he also caused them some spiritual anxiety: Medieval morality had long preached that worshipers ought to turn their attention on the world to come and not focus on material pleasures in the present. But with expanding markets throughout Europe, new items of consumption appeared daily, and it became harder to follow the medieval *contemptus mundi*.

Marlowe's plays may well have led many to ask if religious faith would soon be subordinated to material desires. As we have seen, he takes religious skepticism to a radical conclusion in *Doctor Faustus*, suggesting that humanity's ability to reach spiritual truth, through either sanctioned religious or magical means, is severely curtailed. We ultimately remain slaves to physical delights. In *The Jew of Malta*, we have seen the corrosive skeptical impact of the emerging capitalist economy: under such tenuous and greed-driven conditions, money alone, not religion or social status, makes the man.

4

"And that's true too": Skepticism in *King Lear* and *Timon of Athens*

SHAKESPEARE WROTE *KING LEAR* AND *TIMON OF ATHENS*, PLAYS that present similar economic themes, sometime between 1605 and 1606. The two plays display a striking sense of exigency, an apocalyptic anxiety over socioeconomic disorder best expressed by Gloucester in *Lear*: "Love cools, friendship falls off, brothers divide: in countries, discord; in palaces, treason; and the bond cracked 'twixt son and father" (1.2.108–10).[1] Historians have long asserted that the English economy virtually collapsed in the 1590s. As poor harvests and unemployment increasingly strained the social order, the government took measures to solve the crisis: laws were passed to "relieve" the poor, often by putting them in workhouses or in prison. By the time James I inherited the throne in 1603, conditions were no better. That year a terrible plague descended upon London, adding exponentially to the misery of the city's poor. In the London suburbs, where many of Shakespeare's plays were performed, crime, poverty, and plague seemed implacable. Thomas Dekker described the plague of 1603 as a "Spanish leaguer or rather like a stalking Tamberlain," fighting a war in "the sinfully polluted suburbs."[2] In the early years of James's reign, the English were painfully aware that changes in their economy—increasing social mobility, new markets, a widening gap between rich and poor—were slowly corroding their religion and culture. Religious and philosophical skepticism flourished in such an environment, as economic anxiety led people to raise fundamental questions about their precarious position in a time out of joint. It is not all that surprising, then, that Shakespeare's tragedies in the early years of the seventeenth century so often confront the turmoil and distress of economic and intellectual change.

Often regarded as one of Shakespeare's most skeptical plays, *King Lear* forges a strong connection between economic struggle and crises of knowledge. The play reworks some of the tropes of Sextus Empiricus—the absence of final truths, the unreliability of sense perception, the weakness of human reason, and the relativity of social customs. One possible response to skepticism is stoicism, a calm acceptance in the face of the uncertainty. But as we shall see, the skepticism of *King Lear* never achieves *ataraxia*, or peace of mind (the goal of ancient skepticism), because it is too firmly rooted in the pain and struggle that result from economic dislocation. For example, Gloucester suffers severely from the economic crisis unleashed by Lear's division of the kingdom. After Edmund conspires to obtain his brother's land, Gloucester's eyes are ripped out, a symbolic rendering of the father's failure to believe in the filial devotion of his son Edgar. In the final act, Edgar offers a bit of stoic wisdom to Gloucester, whose reply alludes to the skeptical trope of equipollence, the notion that there is no fixed truth or absolute knowledge since "opposed to every account there is an equal account":[3]

> *Edgar* What! in ill thoughts again? Men must endure
>   Their going hence even as their coming hither.
>   Ripeness is all. Come on.
> *Glouc.* And that's true too.
>
>   (5.2.9–12)

Note the significance of Gloucester's last word. Rather than accepting Edgar's advice and embracing a stoic forbearance, Gloucester lets us know with the word "too" that no morsel of truth or wisdom can attain a dominant status. Even the consolation of stoicism is presented as just one possibility among others. Thus the play ultimately falls short of offering solace: in the absence of any metaphysical or dramatic closure, what seem to be certainties are negated, and new truths are disclosed only to go on to be negated as well.

In *King Lear,* skepticism both arises from and exacerbates the pressures of social and economic flux: Edmund challenges the beliefs of his father and his society because he resents his inferior status as a bastard and a younger brother; Edmund's brother Edgar, negating his identity and taking on the position of the Bedlam Beggar ("Edgar I nothing am"), further aggravates the crisis of knowledge that threatens to undermine social order; Lear provides a powerful critique of economic injustice only after he has lost his reason and lives in uncertainty and confusion. These crises, as Stanley Cavell argues, have to do with traumatic interpersonal relationships, the skeptical refusal to accept knowledge about the self and the other.[4] Yet these crises are also socioeconomic in nature, leading us to look to the historical conditions that inspired Shakespeare to write *King Lear*.

This chapter will explore the socioeconomic context for the widespread epistemological and religious doubt in the play, from Edmund's naturalism to Lear's "reason in madness."[5] The first section will set up the historical context of shifting economic conditions by looking at *Timon of Athens*. The second section looks at how Edmund's skeptical, naturalistic philosophy supports his rise in power and further threatens the social order. The third covers three types of skepticism represented by Edgar/Poor Tom that relate to conditions of poverty in *Lear* and Jacobean England. The fourth section examines the skeptical alternatives to reason presented by King Lear and his Fool.

I

Examining the skeptical engagement of *Timon of Athens* with an economic crisis, the emergence of capitalism, offers us a better understanding of the context of skepticism in *Lear*. Economic change, Timon tells us, generates moral confusion and calls all knowledge about the social and natural world into doubt. The new economic conditions, symbolized in the play by gold, will "knit and break religions," destroy our sense-perception (black becomes white, foul becomes fair), and undermine all authority. There is no possibility of returning to a world of intrinsic authority and order. So when the parsimonious values of Timon's society take over, he attempts to find solace in the other extreme, the natural world in which "nothing" offers "all things."

In the first act we find that Timon's aristocratic largesse has gone awry: his "free love," his generosity, knows no bounds.

After freeing his friend Ventidius from prison by paying his debts for him, Timon proceeds to supply his servant Lucilius with the financial means to marry above his station. The unreciprocal, excessive nature of Timon's bounty becomes apparent in the feast he provides his fellow lords. As one of his flattering guests puts it: "He pours it out. Plutus the god of gold/Is but his steward. No meed but he repays/Seven-fold above itself: no gift to him/But breeds the giver a return exceeding /All use of quittance" (1.2.275–79).[6] This "use of quittance," the interest on the repayment of loans, will in fact come back to ruin him. While Timon believes that the festive occasion represents the true reciprocity of friendship, Apemantus, the play's satirical commentator, recognizes that the lords, given the opportunity, will feast *on* Timon, not with him: "What a number of men eats Timon, and he sees 'em not! It grieves me to see so many dip their meat in one man's blood; and all the madness is, he cheers them up too" (1.2.39–42). Timon, who only realizes later that "unwisely, not ignobly have I given," imagines himself living in an idealized feudal economy, hosting an estate like Ben Jonson's Penshurst, "Whose liberal board doth flow/With all that hospitality doth know."[7] But at Penshurst—a nostalgic vision of an organic society, an old-time *gemeinschaft* if there ever was one—no one arrives empty-handed. Timon, however, finds that he is the only aristocrat so eager to assist others. Indeed, his friends do not help him recover from the debt he incurs through his indiscriminate largesse.

Having foolishly given huge sums of money to his friends, Timon goes mad when they abandon him. His confrontation with usurers leads him to flee Athens for a cave by the sea, where he rants about the evils of gold:

> Gold? Yellow, glittering, precious gold?
> No, gods, I am no idle votarist.
> Roots, you clear heavens! Thus much of this will make
> Black, white; foul, fair; wrong, right;
> Base, noble; old, young; coward, valiant.
> Ha, you gods! Why this? What this, you gods? Why, this
> Will lug your priests and servants from your sides,
> Pluck stout men's pillows from below their heads.
> This yellow slave

Will knit and break religions, bless th'accurs'd,
Make the hoar leprosy ador'd, place thieves,
And give them title, knee and approbation
With senators on the bench. This is it
That makes the wappen'd widow wed again:
She whom the spital-house and ulcerous sores
Would cast the gorge at, this embalms and spices
To th'April day again. Come, damn'd earth,
Thou common whore of mankind, that puts odds
Among the rout of nations, I will make thee
Do thy right nature.

(4.3. 26–44)

Here gold is a metaphor not simply for wealth but for the new wealth made possible by capitalism. For Timon, April is the cruelest month because spring is no longer part of the natural cycle of birth and decay. The new economy will enable the "wappen'd widow" to wed again after she covers up the signs of age by purchasing the means to "embalm" or "spice" her body. Timon, like King Lear, lashes out at female sexuality, treating women as somehow the culprits of an economic crisis. The "wappen'd widow" becomes a symbol of everything "unnatural" in the new economy. What bonds will tie people together once natural bonds are severed? Timon sees only confusion and chaos, believing that, in a capitalist economy, gold, the "common whore" of humanity, has a strong negative influence on natural bodies and natural social relations: with enough gold, anyone can appear noble, beautiful, or powerful. True nobility, we infer, is based on the blood of aristocratic lineage; true beauty doesn't require "embalming"; and true power comes from inherited wealth rather than the ruthless competition of the market.[8] But as parsimonious, commercial values subsume the feudal values of bountiful gift-giving, new money threatens to destroy true nobility, beauty, and power.

Timon represents a common reaction of his time. As we saw in the previous chapter, renaissance moralists often complained that usury was an unnatural means of acquiring profit. Gerald de Malynes is as vociferous as Timon in his rant against usury: "Since the hellhound has been raging, concord has been broken, charity has grown cold, and inequality has crept in through the falsification of measure."[9] Timon insists that the new commercial values create a moral crisis: wrong becomes right, authority collapses, the distinction between priests and servants disappears, thieves are given "place" and "title" so that people will kneel before them. In an acquisitive society, authority becomes an extrinsic rather than intrinsic quality; it can no longer be based on the hierarchical order fixed in nature.

But the new economy, according to Timon, not only destroys social bonds, it also unsettles human sense-perception and belief. In other words, once we enter a capitalist economy, we lose our grasp of natural qualities, the way things really are, and become trapped in a skeptical worldview. The skeptical thinking on natural qualities is best described by Sextus Empiricus: "It is unclear, then, whether in reality it [the apple] has these qualities alone, or has only one quality but appears different depending on the different constitution of the sense-organs."[10] In other words, given that our perception of the object is relative to our senses, it is impossible to know the nature of the object in itself—not how it is perceived, but how it *is*, regardless of our perceptions of it. Shakespeare adds a more historical dimension to such an epistemological problem: once the market has subverted older, communal bonds, humans lack a common world and sense-perception is undermined.[11] For example, appearances can no longer be trusted to reveal whether one is of noble birth. For Timon, once innate bonds of loyalty are lost, all of humanity is set adrift. Capitalism is a "sweet king-killer" that divorces "natural son and sire," corrupting sense-perception by destroying natural qualities and replacing them with economic quantities.

The collapse of Timon's normative idea of nature has other epistemological implications. Nature, no longer a benevolent presence, is henceforth described as a festering, plague-ridden breeding ground for monstrous births and beasts of prey. Indeed, the world will eventually self-destruct. Michel de Montaigne makes the connection between skepticism and imminent doom we see in *Timon of Athens*: "case we our eyes about us, and in a generall survay, consider all the world; all is tottering, all is out of frame."[12] In addition, Montaigne argues, the capacity for reason in such a deteriorating state of nature is diminished and philosophical skepticism is the result: "Thus, seeing all things are subject to passe from one change to another, reason, which therein seeketh a reall subsistence, findes herself deceived as unable to apprehend any thing subsistent and permanent."[13] Timon's apocalyptic rage puts the human capacity for knowledge in jeopardy as well, since, in the decaying, commodified world of Athens, "all is obliquy" (obliquity) and gold is the "visible god" that "sold'rest close impossibilities,/And mak'st them kiss" (4.3.390–91). There can only be epistemological uncertainty in a world of "impossibilities" and "contraries": black becomes white; foul becomes fair. Having metamorphosed from philanthrope to misanthrope overnight, Timon himself becomes ensnared in uncertainty: reason and sense-perception cannot be trusted after such a complete collapse of the socioeconomic order.

The pessimistic notion of decay, which was widespread in Jacobean England,[14] first appears in the play's opening dialogue when a poet asks a painter "how goes the world?" and the latter responds, "It wears, sir, as it grows." Acts four and five, overloaded with images of decay and disease, develop this philosophy. Timon curses Athens with plagues, leprosy, itches, and chilblains; he calls for the sun to "infect the air" and hopes that gold will become a "planetary plague" and "consumptions" will "sow in hollow bones of man" (4.3.153–54). In her classic study of Shakespeare's imagery, Caroline Spurgeon argues that Shakespeare's central image in this play is the dog—"dogs fawning and eating and lapping and licking"—and yet she somehow overlooks the centrality of decay and disease.[15] The two image-clusters are related, however, in that they both develop a pessimistic understanding of the world. Human beings, Timon insists, should be ranked somewhere beneath dogs; indeed, "arrogant man" comes from the same womb of nature as the "black toad and adder blue, the gilded newt and eyeless venom'd worm." [16] Nature herself is diseased, and her womb can "breed" only monsters, infection, and viscious beasts of prey.

Such imagery, created soon after a terrifying outbreak of plague in London, contributes to the play's metaphorical understanding of the practice of usury. Usury, many believed, was a form of improper or unnatural breeding. The complaint goes back to Aristotle, who insisted that "usury is most reasonably hated, because its gain comes from money itself and not from that for the sake of which money was invented."[17] According to Aristotle, usury is "unnatural" because nothing is exchanged in the act other than money. Money, he says, was invented for the purpose of exchanging goods, and usury defies that natural use since money is bought only for money. Aristotle also saw what he called "chrematistic exchange" as inferior because it took money outside the limited sphere of the household and placed it in the sphere of unlimited and purposeless exchange on the market.

In his nihilistic despair, Timon comes to recognize that an unnatural breeding has undermined his mode of exchange: the creditors who demand repayment ruin Timon by charging interest. The first person to demand payment is a senator whose credit will be destroyed by Timon's tardiness: "My uses cry to me. I must serve my turn/Out of mine own; his days and times are past,/And my reliances on his fracted dates/Have smit my credit" (2.1.20–23). Later on, a number of servants, referred to as "usurers," flock to Timon's estate demanding payment. But in Timon's idealized—indeed, magical—economy, bounty is endless; it can grow beyond measure so long as it is based on friendship. With no grasp of the calculating, economic motives of his fellow lords, he is doomed to move from one extreme of profligate generosity to the other of misanthropy once he sees the error in his ways. Whereas Timon sees the exchange of goods in Aristotelian terms as serving the needs of the household—liberality and hospitality—in reality he is ensnared in the world of usurious, unlimited exchange, an economy of rational and egoistic calculation. The extent to which Timon has foolishly believed in the economy of hospitality is evident in the similarity his name bears to Timandra, a woman he labels a whore: "Be a whore still. They love thee not that use thee." Timon, of course, is also used by those who do not love him. Worst of all, he has discovered that "love" and friendship have been false all along, since his fair-weather friends saw accumulation as an end in itself rather than a means to greater bonds of love.

Timon depicts the English aristocrat in decline, since he defies the real workings of the market and mistakenly believes that his largesse can go on indefinitely. Lawrence Stone tells us that most of the English nobility had learned to be more economical by the seventeenth century; but Timon's predicament was very real up to and beyond the date of *Lear*. Many men "stuck to the old country ways under the new conditions," men who "continued to keep open house to all comers, to dispense lavish charity, to keep hordes of domestic servants and retainers; to live, in short, as a great medieval prince."[18] When it turns out that Timon's friends won't return his magnanimity, the time for him becomes "out of joint," chaotic, nonsensical:

> Piety, and fear,
> Religion to the Gods, peace, justice, truth,
> Domestic awe, night-rest, and neighbourhood,
> Instruction, manners, mysteries, and trades,
> Degrees, observances, customs, and laws,
> Decline to your confounding contraries;
> And yet confusion live!
>
> (4.1.15–21)

Timon envisions a world of endless change and confusion. Jacobean economic conditions hardly supported his hostility to change, since the medieval economy, which allowed for very little alteration in status, had long been challenged by mercantile activity. In fact, the usury that ultimately destroys Timon's fortunes could not be stopped. Francis Bacon summed up the pro-usury position that would gain many adherents: "since there must be borrowing and lending, and men are so hard of heart as they will not lend freely, usury must be permitted."[19] In light of widespread international finance, especially the availability of loans for commercial ventures, complaints like Timon's were futile.[20]

Timon's "confounding contraries," the "confusions" of economic change, reappear in the skeptical world of Lear, where reason and truth are elusive, perception fails, knowledge disintegrates, and the gods are nowhere to be found. Lear's Edmund, as we will see, hints at one of the changes mentioned by Timon: "Let me, if not by birth, have lands by wit: / All with me's meet that I can fashion fit" (1.2.180–81). This acquisitive impulse is precisely what Timon fears about the new economic life: Edmund seeks to break free of the status he has been given by birth, challenging "degrees, observance, customs, and laws" in the process.

II

A Jacobean audience would have immediately recognized a dangerous religious skepticism in Gloucester's son Edmund.

Even in a pagan context, his naturalism marks him as a threat to fundamental Christian beliefs.[21] In his first soliloquy, Edmund tells us that he serves the goddess Nature and that he is not bound by morality of any kind, since there is no Christian "natural law" or God-given, universal moral structure guiding human behavior:

> Thou, Nature, art my goddess; to thy law
> My services are bound. Wherefore should I
> Stand in the plague of custom, and permit
> The curiosity of nations to deprive me?
> For that I am some twelve or fourteen moonshines
> Lag of a brother? Why bastard? Wherefore base?
> When my dimensions are as well compact,
> My mind as generous and my shape as true
> As honest madam's issue? Why brand they us
> With base? With baseness, bastardy? Base, base?
> Who in the lusty stealth of nature take
> More composition and fierce quality
> Than doth within a dull stale tired bed
> Go to the creating of a whole tribe of fops
> Got 'tween a sleep and wake. Well, then,
> Legitimate Edgar, I must have your land.
> Our father's love is to the bastard Edmund
> As to the legitimate. Fine word, "legitimate"!
> Well, my legitimate, if this letter speed
> And my invention thrive, Edmund the base
> Shall top the legitimate. I grow, I prosper:
> Now gods, stand up for bastards!

                                                    (1.2.1–22)

Here we see that Edmund cherishes the vital forces of nature such as sexual instinct—the "lusty stealth of nature." More important, he lives for the feeling of power that appears to be an extension of natural force—"I grow, I prosper." According to this vitalistic philosophy, power is the essential force in nature, and all other forms of power that do not enhance one's feeling of domination are worthless. Given his naturalism and his repudiation of traditional religious authority, Edmund avoids any fear of divine retribution for his actions. He even suggests that, since all service of others is ultimately egotistical, the gods are simply our own anthropomorphic projections: "Now, gods," he commands, "stand up for bastards." By the end of his soliloquy, Edmund has gone from saying he is in the service of the goddess Nature to ordering the gods to serve him.

A Jacobean audience would have quickly acknowledged the link between Edmund's religious skepticism and the complex socioeconomic problems he confronts. While they would see him in a negative light, they could also sympathize with his situation and perhaps even identify with his longing to defy the hierarchical social structure. Adopting a naturalistic philosophy in which there are no supernatural forces constraining human action, Edmund focuses on his goal of rising in power regardless of any ethical consequences. Accordingly, he questions the stigma attached to bastards: "Why brand they us with base? with baseness? bastardy? base, base?" (1.2. 9–10). As the epitome of the ambitious and disobedient subject that Tudor homilies warned against, Edmund wants to rise above his supposedly God-given station. Nevertheless, this intense questioning of norms ascribed to nature in Jacobean England would hardly mark Edmund strictly as a villain with no legitimate resentment, since parliament had the power to nullify the official illegitimacy of bastards. Sir Thomas Smith, a great advocate of parliamentary power under Elizabeth, insisted that

> The parliament abrogateth old laws, maketh new, giveth orders for things past, and for things hereafter to be followed, changeth rights, and possessions of private men, legitimateth bastards, establisheth forms of religion.[22]

Edmund, then, has a point: bastards need not be "branded" as base, since that social position is not so fixed in nature that it cannot be ameliorated by an act of parliament.

Edmund would also suffer from his economic status as determined by primogeniture, a hotly contested law: why, he asks, should he be treated as inferior merely because he is "some twelve or fourteen moonshines /Lag of a brother?" Thus Edmund articulates a common dilemma for younger brothers, even though not all were denied an inheritance. Smith, for example, tells us that there were many exceptions to "the rule of common law," and he adds, "but these being but particular customes of certaine places and out of the rule of the common law, doe litle appertain to the dispute of the policie of the whole Realme, and may be infinite" (135). So there was in fact much flexibility on this matter, according to Smith, though the debate over the policy was a real one. Smith's views may well have been more pragmatic than those of his colleagues; nevertheless, such examples suggest that Edmund's views on the plasticity and variety of "customs" would not have been completely beyond the pale.

Edmund's goal of shaping a new identity is one of the characteristics that mark him as a "new man," a controversial and dubious status. He tells us later in act one that since he has been assigned an inferior position by birth, he intends to use his wit as a means of forging a new identity. Social mobility was often reviled, but it was also recognized as inevitable and even valuable. It was possible, as one anonymous sixteenth-century writer shows us, for people to have a somewhat favorable view of upstarts:

> he which is born of a low degre . . . which men taking his beginning of a poor kyndered by his virtue, wyt, pollicie, industry, knowledge in lawes, valliancy in armes, or such like honest meanes becometh a welbeloved and high esteemed manne, preferred then to a great office . . . eversomuch as he becommeth a post or stay of the commune wealth and so growing rich, doth thereby avance . . . the rest of his poore line of kindred: then are the children of suche one commonly called gentleman, of whiche sorts of gentlemen we have nowe in Inglande very many, wherby it should appeare that vertue florisheth among us.[23]

So there was at that time a concept of upward social mobility as one's reward for being virtuous. Edmund, of course, is not an entirely virtuous upstart; the concept had a negative side as well. Even Smith, who is fairly supportive of the emerging capitalist market, condemns a variety of upstarts. And note that the anonymous writer also says here that only the children of these upstarts could attain the status of gentleman.

Edmund's challenge to the fixedness of his place in the natural order would have marked him as a morally reprehensible figure who nevertheless pointed to important gaps in the Tudor and Stuart ideology of degree. During the Stuart period there was increasingly a split in the ruling class about this ideology. As Christopher Hill puts it, "there was a rivalry between those who wanted to preserve a static hierarchical society and those who were busy shaping a more fluid society in which men of ability and means would be able to make their way to the top."[24] Elizabethan homilies on order declared that all subjects must remain in positions that were fixed in the social hierarchy. But this dogma could not control the Babylonian confusion of Elizabethan life. In fact, historians have long recognized that the ideology of a static, hierarchical order ordained by God was itself a response to the disturbing changes in the sixteenth century, rather than, say, a long-standing tradition that was finally giving way.[25] Ideas of hierarchy and authority had always been latent in the culture, but it was only when explicitly threatened that they surged to the fore. Edmund, then, was not alone in believing that the social hierarchy was not irrevocably inscribed in the natural order. Yet he negates the ideology of "degree" without replacing it with any sense of community or collective praxis for the oppressed; "bastard" was not a subject position for advocates of genuine political change. Given his society's ambivalent definition of him, he would have been largely powerless.

Edmund does exhibit some of the stereotypical characteristics of bastards as destructive and immoral. Still, he is not an entirely unsympathetic villain. He often reveals a particularly writerly mentality, as he turns the word "legitimate" around in his mind, or when he enters the interrogatory mode: "Why brand they us with base?" Like some of the other great soliloquies of the age, this one reveals a reflective subject at work. Edmund, whose thought is never static, exhibits a lively intelligence as he is engaged in reconsidering the nature of power and order. In this sense he shares certain dramatic attributes with Hamlet, Doctor Faustus, and other characters who are not marked so clearly as villains. Like Hamlet, Edmund often occupies what Robert Weimann calls a platea position from which to question authority:[26] he is at some distance from the privileged and hence more sympathetic. Derived from that of the villain of the morality play, Edmund's dramatic role was one of the most exciting in the popular dramatic tradition. His skepticism of the validity of the social order may well have aroused deep sympathy from an audience aware of the arbitrary nature of a hierarchical structure that left younger brothers destitute.

As such, it must have been enthralling to watch his rise in status. Edmund's power undergoes a massive increase prior to his demise: his potency is thus most conspicuous when he says that bastards are great in part because the "lusty stealth of nature" creates a more "fierce quality/ Than doth, within a dull, stale, tired bed" (1.2.11–13). Moreover, as Edmund's economic fortunes rise, Lear's diminish: when Lear gives up his land, his daughters eliminate his retainers and, ultimately, he loses his reason along with his potency.[27] Edmund's worship of nature energizes his rise in power while others find themselves in decline.

Thus, in Edmund, the social position of bastard is treated seriously, offering the audience opportunity to identify with his plight while acknowledging the dubious nature of his tactics. The Fool, on the other hand, offers a bawdy metaphor that brings out the comic nature of the bastard's rise in sexual and economic power. Addressing the audience in a concluding remark appropriate to the action preceding it (Goneril and Regan's downsizing of Lear's retainers), he says, "She that's a maid now, and laughs at my departure,/Shall not be a maid long, unless things be cut shorter (1.5.49–50). The fool jokingly hints at deflowering the maidens in the audience unless his "thing" is "cut shorter." More important, the line alludes to the diminution of Lear's phallic power at a time when Edmund gains both economic power as his father's new favorite, and sexual power over Goneril and Regan, who compete for a position in his bed. In Edmund's case, then, "things" expand or grow. As Goneril points out seductively to him: "this kiss, if it durst speak,/Would stretch thy spirits up into the air" (4. 2.22). The bastard, of course, responds to their desires by plotting to take political as well as sexual advantage of them: "Which of them shall I take? Both? One? Or neither?" (5.1.58–59).

Edmund as bastard is portrayed as one who takes natural power into his own hands and rebels against the social hierarchy. But, although Edmund may be an outsider with subversive views, he also wants to obtain legitimate aristocratic and state power at any cost by resuscitating aristocratic norms of manly, warrior power. Edmund's traditional masculine traits—unemotional, courageous—are evident in his exchange with the officer who hangs Cordelia.

> *Edm.* Come hither, captain, hark:
> Take thou this note. Go, follow them to prison.

> One step I have advanced thee. If thou dost
> As this instructs thee, thou dost make thy way
> To noble fortunes. Know thou this, that men
> Are as the time is; to be tender-minded
> Does not become a sword. Thy great employment
> Will not bear question: either way thou'lt do't,
> Or thrive by other means.
> *Offi.* I'll do't, my Lord.
> *Edm.* About it and write "happy" when thou'st done't.
> Mark, I say, instantly; and carry it so
> As I have set it down.
> *Offi.* I cannot draw a cart nor eat dried oats;
> If it be man's work I'll do't.
>
> (5.3. 27–40)

Envisioning a future of "noble fortunes" for himself, Edmund offers the captain the same vision as bait for the murderous task of hanging Cordelia. In this way, Edmund does not fit the model of the effete, effeminate courtier used by Kent to describe the upstarts (Edmund, Oswald, Cornwall). But the bastard's pride in his masculinity does fit his naturalistic worldview: he sees his sexual power as part of the uncontrollable energies of nature. Further, it fits with his religious skepticism: there are no gods around to stop his rise in economic power or his heinous crimes. In addition, Edmund links his masculinity to a skeptical Machiavellian idea that "men are as the time is." Human nature is not fixed and, as Machiavelli says, men should fashion their political activities according to the needs of their historical moment. Divine providence plays no role in Edmund's skeptical, naturalistic worldview or in his Machiavellian political philosophy.

Here and elsewhere, Edmund articulates a common Tudor and Stuart concern with rank and the cash nexus. In the passage above, the officer is concerned about falling to the rank of a day laborer, the lowest or meanest sort of person whose standard of living worsened under the rule of the Stuarts.[28] Anxiety over social status is here seen as a driving force in the officer's behavior. Like the officer, a large segment of the population feared dropping to the lowest social position. In the officer's case, however, resentment leads to the horrible act of hanging Cordelia: thus the socioeconomic disorder is shown to lead to tragedy. After Edmund promises that aristocratic *virtù* can help the lowest wage-laborer conquer fortune and become noble rather than base, the officer's monstrous resentment bursts into the open and the breach of nature allows for the base to top the legitimate. By depicting an ideology of "degree" that clashes with the forces of mobility and social struggle, the tragedy confronts the consequences of hierarchy and the bitter resentment it creates.

As we have seen, Edmund's religious skepticism goes hand in hand with his quest for economic mobility. Infused with a sense of power from nature, indifferent to any supernatural force that might punish his behavior, the bastard advances his cause through cruelty and cunning. Edmund's brother Edgar, prior to his ultimate rise in power, suffers a horrible decline in economic fortunes as a result of his brother's deception. Indeed, the brothers are two sides of one coin: one attempts to rise in social status, the other pretends to be a beggar. Edgar's skeptical thinking, like his brother's, matches the economic conditions that surround him.

III

Edgar's profound negation of his identity, "Edgar I nothing am," inaugurates scenes filled with allusions to wretched conditions in Jacobean England.[29] A code word for the materialist philosophy of Lucretius, "nothing" appears frequently in Lear: The King tells Cordelia, "nothing will come of nothing," and when the Fool asks, "Can you make no use of nothing?" Lear replies, "Why, no, boy; nothing can be made out of nothing." When Lear encounters Poor Tom (Edgar's new identity), he wonders "is man no more than this? . . . thou art the thing in itself; unaccomodated man is no more but such a poor, bare, forked animal as thou art." The word "nothing" in these lines, especially Lear's response to Cordelia, resonates with the traditional skeptical idea we encountered in the philosophy of Thomas Harriot—the materialist ex nihilo nihil fit—but it also introduces something we have not yet encountered: the deflation of human reason, the debasing of man's position in the Great Chain of Being. This section will address three skeptical problems posed by Edgar: the identity of self and other, the absence of the gods, and the fragility of human reason.

At every turn, Poor Tom reminds us of the conditions facing the poor in London, a city teeming with rogues and vagabonds. The title page of the first quarto mentions Poor Tom (most likely because he would draw an audience): "With the unfortunate life of Edgar, sonne and heire to the Earle of Gloster, and his sullen and assumed humor of Tom of Bedlam." For a Jacobean audience in particular, Poor Tom addressed a pressing social concern: what to do with the hundreds of unemployed and poverty-stricken people flooding into London. Charity, an essential part of a moral economy, had long been a means of helping the poor in England. The title page of the first quarto also informs us that *Lear* was "played before the Kings Maiestie at Whitehall upon S. Stephans night in Christmas Hollidayes." The festival of St. Stephen's day, a day of noblesse oblige, would decline in significance as England turned toward new means of dealing with the poor. The new morality would champion hard work and discipline rather than aristocratic largesse, and older Christian forms of charity were supplanted by the state's imperative of work and the disciplining, and in some cases torturing, of the unemployed. Alluding to the punishments of vagabonds who failed to find gainful employment, Poor Tom tells us that in addition to eating frogs and cowdung, he is "shipp'd from tithing to tithing, and stock-punished, and imprison'd" (3.4.125–32). A. L. Beier points out that the punishment of vagabonds dramatically increased in frequency and intensity toward the end of the sixteenth century, building on trends that had started long before: "Although good works, including acts of charity, continued to be popular, many of the learned now questioned their spiritual value. They mocked friars and pilgrims as impious frauds."[30] Acts of charity did not disappear entirely, but the state discouraged begging and the relief of poverty through charity by rounding up large numbers of the poor for punishment.

In addition, many people, appalled by beggars' allegedly feigned madness, began to refuse charity to the poor. A Jacobean audience would have recognized in Poor Tom the popular stereotype of the Bedlam madman, who, as William Carroll observes, were often considered a "species of actor."[31] Here we are confronted with a deep skepticism about the identity of the self and other: how can we know that others are what they seem—especially when they are driven to extremes by severe economic hardship? On the one hand, *Lear* cries out for charity, if not social justice and economic reform; on the other hand, the play alludes to charlatans who might well elicit a less sympathetic response that precludes charity. Should we, as Lear puts it, come to "feel what wretches feel"? Or should we beware that the feelings of the wretched are merely being performed, just as Edmund pretends his brother Edgar gave him a wound that was, in fact, self-inflicted? The dramatic nature of Edgar's role is complex: he is play-acting a charlatan as an allusion to beggars in England who were often thought to be—and likely sometimes were in fact—charlatans.

Throughout the play we find a flurry of questions about Poor Tom's identity: "What's he?" Lear wonders at Poor Tom in the hovel. Kent's "who's there? What is't you seek?" is followed by Gloucester's "What are you there? Your names?" (3.4.121–23). Edgar takes on a baffling array of roles—a mad beggar, a rural peasant, a knight, and a messenger. The collapse of stable social hierarchy and fixed social roles can be seen in his decentered sense of self. Like the beggars of London, Poor Tom owns virtually nothing, and the skeptical negation of his identity is a result of the severe challenges of poverty.

One of the play's long-standing mysteries is why Edgar chooses to wait so long before revealing his identity to his father. Upon encountering his blind, suicidal father being led by a loyal old tenant, Edgar does not reveal that he is Gloucester's son. Despite his father's emotional plea—"Might I but live to see thee [Edgar] in my touch,/I'd say I had eyes again"—Edgar stubbornly maintains the role of Poor Tom. Edgar, of course, insists that his goal is a benevolent one: "Why do I trifle thus with his despair/Is done to cure it" (4.6.32–33). But if Edgar/Poor Tom's deceit of Gloucester is supposed to reaffirm their familial bond, it also seems clearly to create distance and lack of feeling. Harry Berger, one of the leading proponents of a darker view of Edgar, argues that the cliff scene is "an act of symbolic parricide." Even though they might be "reborn together," Berger notes, "Edgar can never fully rid himself of the fiend, and in his second attempt to cure Gloucester the parricide is less symbolic."[32] Cruelty would seem the only convincing explanation for his delay.[33] Moreover, Edgar's deceit of Gloucester creates a playful negation of identity that would not seem, as Edgar suggests, to cure his father's despair. Again we find a deep skepticism about self-identity, resulting from economic strife that ends in tragedy.

Edgar creates more confusion of identity by toying with his father's blindness. When Gloucester recognizes a change in his son's voice, Edgar replies, "You're much deceived; in nothing am I changed/But in my garments" (4.6.8–9). The blind Gloucester, seeking to end his life, asks to be taken to Dover where he will have Poor Tom push him off a cliff, thus putting an end to his misery. They never arrive at the cliff, however, and Tom presents a visual tableau instead.

> Come on, sir, here's the place. Stand still: how fearful
> And dizzy 'tis to cast one's eyes so low.
> The crows and choughs that wing the midway air
> Show scarce so gross as beetles. Half-way down
> Hangs one that gathers samphire, dreadful trade;
> Methinks he seems no bigger than his head.
> The fishermen that walk upon the beach
> Appear like mice, and yond tall anchoring barque
> Diminish'd to her cock, her cock a buoy
> Almost too small for sight. The murmuring surge
> That on th'unnumber'd idle pebble chafes,
> Cannot be heard so high. I'll look no more,
> Lest my brain turn, and the deficient sight
> Topple down headlong.
>
> (4.6.11–24)

Edgar's tableau adds to the skeptical confusion of identity by further distorting his father's perception of the world around him. Edgar then proceeds to baffle his father even more by playing with his limited sense perception, describing the beggar who stood on the cliff with Gloucester as a demon with eyes like "two full moons," a "thousand noses," and horns.

The tableau also offers a glimpse of nonaristocratic members of the kingdom in an oddly diminished form (a samphire gatherer and fishermen). The samphire gatherer seems "no bigger than his head," and the fishermen "appear like mice." By representing base members of society to be "low," the illusion fills a blind spot in Lear's vision of the kingdom: the people ignored by those in power are represented for a moment, even if only in an imaginary scene. The socioeconomic import of the tableau fits into the play's skeptical crisis of knowledge: once Lear divides the kingdom and traditional social bonds are destroyed, the problematic relation of self and other comes to the fore. New identities—the fishermen and samphire gatherer—emerge, reminding us of Lear's lack of knowledge of the people in his own kingdom. The perspectival image of Dover creates a feeling of madness—"I'll look no more,/Lest my brain turn, and the deficient sight/Topple down headlong" (4.6.22–24). Edgar reminds us of the repeated failures to see the truth, including Lear's failure to recognize the humanity and very existence of the less privileged people in his kingdom. Harsh economic reality effects a pervasive skeptical crisis of identity of the self and other.

A second form of skepticism emerges from Edgar's interaction with Gloucester: the absence of the gods. Throughout the play we find that anguished cries for divine intervention leave only the impression that there is nothing in the heavens. Prescient of the disasters to come in the final act, Albany says, "If that the heavens do not their visible spirits/Send quickly down to tame these vile offences,/It will come: Humanity must perforce prey on itself,/Like monsters of the deep" (4.2.47–51). That is precisely what happens. Despite many pleadings, the "visible spirits" never arrive, and the repetition of the word "nothing" throughout the play leads us to the conclusion that there are no gods in heaven to respond to human needs.

Such skepticism, we find, is clearly tied to economic distress. As Edgar leads the way to the imaginary cliff, Gloucester cries out to the gods for social justice:

> Heavens, deal so still!
> Let the superfluous and lust-dieted man
> That slaves your ordinance, that will not see
> Because he does not feel, feel your power quickly:
> So distribution should undo excess,
> And each man have enough. Dost thou know Dover?
>
> (4.1.69–74)

These bootless utopian cries for divine intervention are ultimately mocked by Edgar, whose actions further establish human finitude and isolation from the gods. The redistribution of wealth Gloucester calls for never comes, for the gods are either nonexistent or too distant from the suffering of the poor to intervene. The act of making Gloucester believe he has been pushed off the cliff, actually just a small step over the stage, may well have appeared bathetic rather than pathetic, eliciting nervous laughter from the audience.[34] Taken more seriously, the scene on the imaginary cliff drains the hope from transcendental, utopian longings. The gods appear much more distant once Gloucester's appeal to them is negated by Edgar's fiction. The call for redistribution, which notably goes well beyond the noblesse oblige of St. Stephen's Day, is hardly taken seriously, since the gods, like the Christian *deus absconditus*, never show themselves.

Jacobean audiences might well have applied this skeptical crisis to the dislocation in their own society. Despite government intervention in the form of Poor Laws, poverty increased throughout the sixteenth and early seventeenth centuries. Noblesse oblige, the tradition of a moral economy quickly becoming out of date, no longer seemed to provide a solution, but neither did the new form of governmental control. Paul Slack demonstrates that the problem of poverty was particularly severe at the turn of the century, and that the legislation of 1598 and 1601 attempted to alleviate the situation. Population increases since the 1520s may have been the root of the problem, and by the end of the century wages dropped, illegitimacy rose, and crime increased. Starvation became more common after bad harvests in the late 1590s.[35] Poor Laws were not successful in maintaining social order, however, and we can well imagine certain members of a Jacobean audience identifying with Gloucester's appeal to the gods that "distribution should undo excess/and each man have enough." But, how, precisely, could that happen in such an inegalitarian society? It is only appropriate, then, that Gloucester's appeal would go unheeded, for undoing "excess" would radically challenge the ideological foundation of English society.

A third form of skepticism represented by Edgar is the fragility of human reason. Scholars looking for Shakespeare's sources often turn to the "Apology for Raymond Sebond," Montaigne's great Pyrrhonist statement about the status of reason in human affairs.[36] The human capacity for reason, he argues, is not unique; reason is not as potent and autonomous as philosophers make it out to be. Reason, he says in the *Apology*, is "an instrument very supple, pliable, and yeelding to all shapes." And he wonders how it has come to pass that such puny creatures who cannot even master themselves pretend to be masters of the universe. Man, the most arrogant creature in the universe, mistakenly believes he is separate from the "horde of other creatures" roaming about the earth. *King Lear* and *Timon of Athens*, filled with bestial images, likewise portray reason as fallible; indeed, once the social order collapses, reason can hardly be said to place humanity in an exalted position. As Gloucester says of Poor Tom: "I'the last night's storm I such a fellow say,/Which made me think a man a worm" (4.1.34–35).

During their encounter, Lear calls Poor Tom a "philosopher," very likely alluding to Diogenes, the naked ascetic who, like Montaigne, questions the power of human reason:

> *Lear*　First let me talk with this philosopher:
> 　　　　[to Edgar] What is the cause of thunder?
> *Kent*　Take his offer, go into the house.
> *Lear*　I'll talk a word with this same learned Theban:
> 　　　　What is your study?
>
> 　　　　　　　　　　　　　　(3.4.150–55)

Diogenes, Lear's "learned Theban," was famous for abandoning all superfluous possessions and sitting naked in his tub in Athens.[37] Mocking Plato's definition of "man" with his lewd behavior in public, Diogenes reminded his fellow Athenians that the human capacity for reason is hardly superior to that of other animals. He was also famous as a cynical moralist who advocated a simple life in which only the bare necessities were needed for pleasure. There was a highly performative quality to this cynicism, since it was a public display rather than a private diatribe against human mores.

Poor Tom, who continually plays on the meaning of "nothing" and "the worst" or what it means to be reduced to the most "dejected thing of Fortune," is much like the laughing Diogenes in Montaigne's essay, "Of Democritus and Heraclitus." Blending skepticism with classical cynicism, Montaigne says that although both of these philosophers recognized the folly of human beings, he prefers the mocking and laughing Diogenes for his recognition that humans are like "bladders puft with wind."

Bewailing and commiseration, are commixed with some estimation of the thing moaned and wailed. Things scorned and con-
temned, are thought to be of no worth. I cannot be perswaded,
there can be so much ill lucke in us, as there is apparant vanitie,
nor so much malice, as sottishnesse. We are not so full of evill, as
of voydnesse and insanitie. We are not so miserable, as base and
abject. Even so Diogenes, who did nothing but trifle, toy, and dally
with himselfe, in rumbling and rowling of his tub, and flurting at
Alexander, accompting us but flies, and bladders puft with winde,
was a more sharp, a more bitter, and a more stinging judge, and by
consequence, more just and fitting my humor, than Timon, sur-
named the hater of all mankinde. For looke what a man hateth, the
same thing he takes to hart.[38]

Montaigne argues that laughter at the "sottishnesse," "voydnesse," and "insanitie" of humanity is preferable to misanthropy. Lear doesn't identify Edgar as Diogenes because he is
a "stinging judge," but rather because he seems to embody humanity in its most primitive state. Poor Tom is the "thing itself," the "unaccomodated man."

Thus Poor Tom is modeled on Diogenes, a philosopher of
urban simplicity, and the Bedlam Beggar. Like Diogenes,
Edgar/Poor Tom inspires people to question their attachment
to possessions (Diogenes was critical of the rich or power-hun-
gry members of the polis). Lear even begins to disrobe after his
encounter with the naked madman. For a brief moment at
least, Poor Tom makes us think of poverty as freedom, hope,
and laughter: "The lamentable change is from the best,/The
worst returns to laughter" (4.1.5–6). Poor Tom also offers an
alternative to Timon of Athens, "the hater of all mankinde,"
whose rage led him to solitude and suicide. While Timon bears
the burden of human wickedness, Poor Tom, like Diogenes in
his tub, deflates human reason and arrogance with a mocking
amusement.

How, then, do we respond to this complex representation of
poverty? We might follow Grigori Kozintsev, who, inspired by
Tom to "feel what wretches feel," produced unforgettable images of poor peasants roaming the countryside. Conversely, we
might take to heart the popular Jacobean stereotype of the
Bedlam Beggar, the fake madman seeking alms on city streets,
and, distancing ourselves from empathy, treat this representative of the poor as a fraud, an actor who would seem to confirm

the crisis of knowledge running throughout *Lear*. The three
kinds of skepticism discussed in this section—the identity of
self and other, the absence of the gods, and the fragility of reason—all point to the hopeless and miserable condition of the
fictive Poor Tom and his real-life model, the Bedlam Beggar.
"The country gives me proof and precedent," Edgar says as he
dresses up as Poor Tom, "Of Bedlam beggars, who, with roaring voices/Strike in their numbed and mortified bare arms/
Pins, wooden pricks, nails, sprigs or rosemary" (2.2.184–87).

IV

Lear's uncertainty grows out of conditions not unlike what
we saw in *Timon of Athens*: the social order, comprising natural, human bonds, seems to have disintegrated. But for Lear,
"matter and impertinency" mix, and the disorder of the world
becomes an opportunity for him to criticize specific social
practices. After he goes mad, Lear learns to "feel what
wretches feel" and launches a powerful critique of the institutions that oppress the poor. The speech calls for an alternative
way of seeing, asking us to reconsider how we make sense of
the world: "A man may see how this world goes with no eyes.
Look with thine ears."

Lear reinforces the ocularcentric metaphors of Western philosophy by describing the loss of reason in terms of the loss of
vision.[39] One of the strongest pieces of evidence given by Sextus Empiricus for the deficiency of human reason is the weakness of human sense-perception, especially vision. If vision
cannot accurately grasp the nature of objects in the external
world, given the prevalence of illusions and simple mistakes, it
follows that our capacity for reason is extremely limited. Classical skepticism, in other words, argues that we cannot obtain
genuine knowledge about the real world since we are unable to
get beyond mere appearances: "But if the senses do not apprehend external objects, the intellect is not able to apprehend
them either (since its guides fail it), so by means of this argument too we shall be thought to conclude to suspension of
judgement about external existing objects."[40] In Lear's mad
condition, he lacks the sense-perception to grasp Truth; but,
paradoxically, he finds an alternative to reason—"matter and

impertinency mixed"—that enables him to offer forceful social criticism.

Lear's vision, a metaphor for his ability to grasp the truth, had been weak for quite some time; it further degenerates when he banishes Cordelia and gives his land to his wicked daughters. Kent insists: "See better, Lear; and let me still remain/The true blank of thine eye." Lear, like Gloucester, has come to realize that he did not know the truth, so he abandons ocularcentric reason, opening up the possibility that he might gain new knowledge about his past and the plight of the oppressed in his kingdom. As Kent's paradoxical word "blank" suggests, vision may have been a weak means of grasping the truth long before Lear gave up his land: "blank" can mean an emptiness or "nothingness" as well as the center of the eye.

While Lear's satirical speech seems to convey the truth about social injustice, that truth is folded back into its own folly and mad contempt for the evils of the world. For all its perspicacity, Lear's social criticism only generates greater uncertainty, in keeping with the play's extreme skepticism:

> Lear What! art mad? A man may see how this world goes
> with no eyes.
> Look with thine ears. See how yon justice rails upon
> yon simple thief.
> Hark, in thine ear: change places and handy-dandy,
> which is the justice, which is the thief? Thou hast
> seen a farmer's dog bark at a beggar?
> Glouc. Ay, Sir.
> Lear And the creature run from the cur—there thou
> might'st behold the great image of authority: a
> dog's obeyed in office.
> Thou rascal beadle, hold thy bloody hand;
> Why dost thou lash that whore? Strip thine own
> back,
> Thou hotly lusts to use her in that kind
> For which thou whipp'st her. The usurer hangs the
> cozener.
> Through tattered clothes small vices do appear;
> Robes and furred gowns hide all. Plate sin with
> gold,
> And the strong lance of justice hurtless breaks;
> Arm it in rags, a pigmy's straw does pierce it.

> None does offend, none, I say, none. I'll able 'em:
> Take that of me, my friend, who have the power
> To seal th'accuser's lips. Get thee glass eyes,
> And, like a scurvy politician, seem
> To see the things thou dost not.
>
> (4.6.146–69)

This speech, which covers particular abuses of power—religious hypocrisy, legal and political corruption—also attacks the "great image of Authority." Again, economic injustice is placed at the heart of oppression, and gold creates class divisions that enable the rich to get away with anything: "Through tattered clothes small vices do appear; Robes and furred gowns hide all." The world has been blind, we are told, as no one has been able to see the truth behind false appearances. But skepticism ultimately undermines the belief that the truth can ever be uncovered: without the means of "seeing" the truth, we are trapped in our subjective sense-perception. Like Gloucester and the "scurvy politician," we can only "seem" to see things in the external world. Following the dramatic structure of inversion that we also find in the Fool's speech, Lear turns the world upside down, or rather shows that the world is itself in a state of carnivalesque confusion: a "dog's obeyed in office," the beadle is lustful, the usurer hangs the cozener. With the world in such disarray, an alternative to ocularcentric reason seems in order.

Lear incorporates the mock-king tradition with a major adjustment: the "dogs" in office, Lear's daughters, suggest not only that Lear needs to reconsider his nature as king, but also that the very "image of Authority," including the office of king, can be called into question. A utopian critique almost emerges from this satirical "handy-dandy," but Lear's madness crushes even that much knowledge about the world, once more taking skepticism to its radical conclusion: if nothing is certain, there is no firm place to stand from which to offer a critique—there is only madness.

The negation of vision—"Look with thine ears"—indicates that these powerful lines fall short of what we are tempted to call "demystification" or "critique." The passage insists that the prosthetic device of "glass eyes" (for Gloucester) would make him only another hypocrite in power who pretends to see the truth. The punishments meted out would be unjust because the eyes are an inherently evil seat of cynical deception. Class interests dictate justice (as Marx would say of the bourgeoisie), and one's position of power and wealth, rather than truth, determines one's perspective on the world. While the speech shows how appearances hide the truth, it does not allow for the possibility of any truth to penetrate such deception, and thus the social criticism collapses into its own skepticism. Even with a new pair of eyes, Gloucester (or anyone else) would remain like a scurvy politician, who *seems* to "see things thou dost not." Glass eyes, haunting emblems of powerlessness, are a reflective surface, like "sin plated with gold." Shimmering surfaces present a cover for those corrupt power-mongers to hide their true wickedness. The loss of real eyes represents the devastating fear that authenticity and feeling (especially as revealed by tears) could be completely destroyed by the cynicism of those in power.

Playing with the language of the gospels, Lear's speech suggests that power corrupts and that absolute power corrupts absolutely. Lear offers a fairly standard Christian glorification of the meek, who must follow Christ and learn to develop a sense of moral superiority in their private realm of suffering. In the absence of a just king (who is sane) no clarity is brought to bear on a system of power, but only a remystification through a reliance on Lear in his madness. "When I do stare, see how the subject quakes," Lear says in his self-deception earlier in the scene. Part of the mad, skeptical discourse of the play, this speech is not really a demystification of power. As Jacques Derrida argues, terms like "critique" and "demystification" contain the brand of Western metaphysics with its metaphor of vision as Truth.[41] In *Lear*, all such visions are shown to be faulty; any critique of or insight into ideology must remain partial, murky, or unreliable.

Furthermore, by insisting that feeling is more reliable than vision or ocularcentric truth, Lear and the Fool ask us to "stop making sense" and, in the process, rethink the sociopolitical order. Although Lear, with his loss of reason, does not move beyond surface appearances to an exposure of "true" power relations, his unmasking challenges the idea that all subjects ought to bow down in fear at the loss of an absolute authority. The moment of danger (a dog is obeyed in office) provides an opportunity, a gap in history for a mad social criticism to emerge. Denouncing the lust of the eyes and those who manipulate appearances to maintain power, Lear's diatribe adds to the moralistic discourse of the play (Edgar's cruel moralism about "the dark and vicious place," the site of his father's adultery, also comes to mind).

At the same time, the skeptical nature of Lear's speech implies that (as any Pyrrhonist would tells us) we cannot transcend appearances. In these scenes, Lear is the one with the power of the gaze, but he, too, has been a corrupt politician. Initially, Lear fails to recognize that he has only a partial perspective—he has the illusion of total control while he does not even know that his own daughters will turn against him. Lacking reason and an accurate visual perception, Lear adopts a perspectival, relativistic view of the world. The perspectival nature of Lear's grasp of reality is made clear when he is captured:

> No, no, no no! Come, let's away to prison;
> We two alone will sing like birds i'th'cage.
> When thou dost ask me blessing I'll kneel down
> And ask of thee forgiveness. So we'll live,
> And pray, and sing, and tell old tales, and laugh
> At gilded butterflies, and hear poor rogues
> Talk of court news; and we'll talk with them too—
> Who loses and who wins; who's in, who's out—
> And take upon's the mystery of things
> As if we were Gods' spies. And we'll wear out,
> In a walled prison, packs and sects of great ones
> That ebb and flow by the moon.

(5.3.8–18)

These new perspectives for Lear reveal that once he begins to encounter the margins of political and social life, the public is replaced by the private. Now that Edmund is no longer on the margins but is in power, Lear and Cordelia join the world of rogues and find a perspective as outsiders. The private sphere is a retreat for those who are unable to confront the violent, corrupt, and decaying (sublunary) world of the court. Thus we encounter the impotence and despair of a private/public dualism that allows only for (inter)personal redemption as an alternative to courtly power. Once Lear is "out" he can think only about those who are "in," a mad subject trapped by the deprivation of private sense perception.

Lear, as we saw in the previous section on Edgar, teaches us that human reason is fragile and fallible, and that we are not as superior to other animals as we might think. As Florio's Montaigne puts it, man "who perceiveth and seeth himselfe placed here, amidst their filth and mire of the world, the vilest corner of the house, and farthest from heavens coape." It is only vanity, he says, that allows us to separate ourselves from other animals.[42] Humans cannot escape the flux of the material world; they are not, as Lear puts it, "ague proof." Confronted with a world that makes no sense, where reason and truth have become debilitated, Lear, out of hatred for his daughters, singles out women for particular contempt as representative of the bestial state of humankind.

Thus the socioeconomic collapse has further ramifications for Lear's relation to the natural world. No longer in possession of authority, Lear finds that all of nature becomes a chaotic and horrifying threat to his masculinity. Lear's misogynistic perspective, which arrives with the rise of an atomized, Hobbesian world of each against all, forces women to carry the burden of a society in transition.[43] Women, like centaurs, become dangerous exemplars of hybridity: "Down from the waist they are centaurs, though women all above" (4.6.121–22). The play does not, however, simply warn us that in the absence of authority, the proper boundary between the human and the animal, civilization and nature, will collapse. Instead, the human/animal dualism itself is called into question. And when the boundary between the human and the animal breaks down, female sexuality appears untamed: "The fitchew nor the soiled horse goes to't/With a more riotous appetite" (4.6.121–22). Lear, like Timon of Athens, sees a complete collapse of the "human," as those who exhibit "monstrous ingratitude" aggressively seek economic gain. Given socioeconomic collapse, the natural world seems more threatening in its uncivilized state.

Lear's social criticism follows the festive language of inversion developed by his Fool. Folly continues to fill his thought as rational judgment departs: "O Lear, Lear, Lear! Beat at this gate, that let thy folly in, And thy dear judgement out!" (1.4.262–64). Folly is not simply the error he made in judging his daughters; it becomes a way of thinking about the world he has learned from the inverted language of his all-licensed Fool. The Fool's prophecy in act three shares the skeptical thinking of Lear. Both characters find a skeptical alternative to ocular-centric reason and, lacking fixed truths about the external world, nevertheless remain insightful about the state of the world. In the Fool's case, an alternative "vision," a muddled, nonsensical prophecy, engages socioeconomic instability.

The Fool's prophecy, like Lear's mad speech, follows a utopian structure. We are given, in some of the lines, a clear vision of an alternative future: "When every case in law is right/No squire in debt, nor no poor knight." Lear and the Fool provide forms of "reason in madness" or "matter and impertinency mixed" that grapple with usury, law, and poverty in the hope that there might be a new way of organizing socioeconomic life. The tradition of *homo festivus*, alive and well in the Middle Ages, allowed people to act up, make fun of those in power, and imagine a radically different world.[44] Carnival was only one calendrical event, one small part of a larger culture of *homo festivus*. For a short time, the world would cease to make sense as society was allowed to fall into disorder, or, as Falstaff puts it, to be "out of all compass." This period of licensed confusion was a means of clarifying, interrogating, and possibly challenging the social roles of everyday life.[45] By the time of *King Lear*, however, when the feudal structure had collapsed, carnival had lost much of its special meaning. Everyday life had already become, to some extent, carnivalesque, as social roles once rigidly assigned by birth now lacked clarity and definition.

The Fool's prophecy reflects these new conditions of carnivalesque confusion. The passage doesn't exactly fit the traditional structure of inversion, as it refuses to put forth any knowledge or clarification about socioeconomic life:

> When priests are more in word than matter,
> When brewers mar their malt with water,
> When nobles are their tailors' tutors,
> No heretics burn'd, but wenches' suitors;
> When every case in law is right
> No squire in debt, nor no poor knight;
> When slanders do not live in tongues;

Nor cut-purses come not to throngs,
When usurers tell their gold i'th'field,
And bawds and whores do churches build,
Then shall the realm of Albion
Come to great confusion:
Then comes the time, who lives to see't,
That going shall be us'd with feet.
This prophecy Merlin shall make, for I live before his time.

                                        (3.2.81–96)[46]

The Fool juxtaposes disorder with utopian order, but he makes no clear boundary between the two. After a presentation of what seems like a utopian order, the Fool says, "Then shall the realm of Albion/Come to great confusion." The confusion appears to be the prophecy itself, which negates the dream of order in the lines preceding and following it. Even what seems like progress has a peculiar moral ambiguity: "And bawds and whores do churches build." The reformation of the former is dubious in nature; in fact, this may be the Church of Bawds and Whores. The passage produces a historical disjunction in its last line, where the fool negates his own lines by saying "This prophecy Merlin shall make: for I live before his time." Commenting on the present only through a radical historical disjunction, the passage exhibits a heightened awareness of its own form and content and does not allow for a positive vision of the future to develop. Thus, although these lines are structurally utopian, they are also a parodic form concerned with their own conditions of possibility. Cutting short the prophetic mode of temporality and metaphysics, the Fool says, "I'll speak a prophecy ere I go" and finishes the passage by negating and deferring the lines he has already spoken. The Fool's utopianism is a form of festive madness that cannot be contained by the dramatic structure of inversion. Utopia is thus given a complex, satirical debunking that negates its own vision of an alternative social hierarchy. A discombobulated negativity vitiates any genuine sustained critique of social conditions.[47]

The first line of the prophecy deconstructs the binary opposition of word and matter. We see this problematic opposition early in the play: Goneril's inauthentic expression of love to Lear, "Sir, I love you more than word can wield the matter," may be an indication that she is a wicked flatterer, but it is also an indication that love is hard to express, since words never equal matter. The Fool reminds us that matter is known only through words, yet words are always somehow detached from matter. Since Merlin has not even made the prophecy yet, there is no matter in the Fool's prophecy, and thus it exists as a collection of words with no real temporal substance. The Fool cannot offer a prediction of the future because words are mired in the materiality of the present. Despite or perhaps because of its confusion, the passage seems to question utopian prophecy by commenting obliquely on the metaphysical idea that the immaterial future can be foretold by words in the material present. The Fool does not offer a visionary escape from disorder and the reality principle, but he does grapple with the moral confusion of reality itself through negation. Unlike the witches in *Macbeth*, the fool cannot "look into the seeds of time/And say which grain will grow, and which will not" (1.3.58–59).[48]

Traditionally, the prophet's foresight comes from his blindness and his subsequent ability to see in alternative, metaphysical ways. Crying, an alternative to ocularcentric displays of power, is an activity that separates the compassionate characters, including the Fool, from the mean-spirited ones. As Jacques Derrida points out,

> If the eyes of all animals are destined for sight, and perhaps from there to the scopic knowledge of the *animale rationale*, only man knows how to go beyond seeing and knowing because only he knows how to cry. . . . Only he knows that tears are the essence of the eye—and not sight. . . . Revelatory blindness, apocalyptic blindness, that which reveals the very truth of the eyes, this would be the gaze veiled by tears.[49]

The Fool's prophecy, Lear's handy-dandy, and Cordelia's tears are modes of feeling opposed to the calculating visual deceit of Edmund, Cornwall, Goneril, and Regan. Blindness, often an alternative path to truth in Renaissance discourse on folly, is less powerful than crying. "When we are born, we cry that we are come/To this great stage of fools," Lear says shortly after his speech on the maltreatment of the poor. Upon meeting Cordelia, he remains uncertain who she is: "Methinks I should know you and know this man;/Yet I am doubtful"(4.7.64–65).

Cordelia's tears, in Derrida's words, become "the essence of the eye," as Lear's visual perception is not up to the task of fully recognizing his daughter. Lear's "yet I am doubtful" haunts the conclusion of the play, but a skeptical alternative to seeing—crying—offers a possible means of going beyond the vision and knowledge that have led to the tragic denouement.

The Fool's riddling prophecy, which cannot be untangled to reveal any kind of clear truth about the world, suggests that the world of *Lear* is opaque. Timon's rant on economic change creates a similar picture. He complains that an entire social order has been lost: "Degrees, observances, customs, and laws, Decline to your confounding contraries; And yet confusion live!" (4.1.19–21). In both speeches we encounter responses to the fluidity of society. In Timon's case, however, we find something similar to the common conservative position in Shakespeare's England that significant change in economic life signaled the end of all social order. Timon has a particular ideal of society in mind: it is an organic or "natural" collectivity in which people know their place and noblesse oblige keeps the nobility in power and the poor fed. Thus Timon echoes religious and political doctrines that condemned the acquisitiveness and social climbing of "base" people like Edmund, or, for that matter, William Shakespeare himself, who came from fairly humble origins but wound up owning the largest house in Stratford, obtaining a coat of arms, and receiving the name "William Shakespeare of Stratford-upon-Avon, gentleman."

Yet, as *King Lear* reveals, fixed boundaries had been breaking down for quite some time as new opportunities emerged in the market economy. Merchants, investors, and usurers took advantage of opportunities to make money from trade in luxury goods. Robert Burton commented on the situation: "In a word, every man for his own ends. Our Summum bonum is commodity, and the goddess we adore Dea Moneta, Queen Money, to whom we daily offer sacrifice, which steers our hearts, hands, affections, all."[50] And John Lyly made this change explicit to his theater audience in the induction of *Midas*: "Traffique and travell hath woven the nature of all Nations into ours, and made this Land like Arras, full of devise, which was Broad-cloth, full of workmanship. Time hath confounded our mindes. . . . the world is become an Hodgepodge."[51] Lyly depicts a world of constant change in which cultural and economic boundaries are redrawn every day. The opacity in *Lear* is a symptom of such economic change: social mobility, the expansion of capital investments, unemployment, and poverty forced people to question the supposedly immutable order that assigned them a fixed identity and social position. Lear and his fool, like Timon, recognize the challenge of obtaining true knowledge about the world when traditional social bonds have disintegrated and no alternative ideology is available for guidance. When the time is out of joint, there is no way to set it right because the time is always already being transformed into something new and unknown.

As we have seen, skepticism became widespread in England when the traditional ideology of order could no longer account for the realities of social and economic change. How can people feel secure in having a genuine knowledge of the world when, as Timon laments, intrinsic value has been replaced by market value? As Troilus asks in Shakespeare's *Troilus and Cressida*, "What's aught, but as 'tis valew'd?"[52] Religious beliefs would seem unstable as a result of such change as well. Timon's concern that "this yellow slave will knit and break religions" had been voiced many times in the works of religious authorities who feared that worshipers might follow the skeptical path of Edmund, ignoring the power of God and turning their attention to their own economic gain. Calvin, for instance, described the rampant idolatrous worship of gold instead of God: "Man . . . would have the metal which he has deified to be regarded as God."[53] The new economy, many believed, provided the opportunity to ignore or reject religious faith and turn to a life of sensuous pleasure and possessive individualism, which it was feared would only lead to ruin.

In this chapter we have seen how Shakespeare uses skeptical motifs to illustrate how pervasive and powerful were the effects of shifting socioeconomic conditions during his time. In the characters of Timon, Edmund, Edgar/Poor Tom, Lear and his Fool, we see various forms of skepticism toward religious authority, self-knowledge, and knowledge of others, as well as various attempts to respond to such uncertainty. Ultimately, the moral is bleak: given such chaotic shifts in the socioeconomic structure, the only possible solace is madness, laughter, or tears.

Conclusion

"THE CAUSES OF ATHEISM," FRANCIS BACON WROTE, "ARE: DIVI-sions in religion, if they be many; for any one main division ad-deth zeal to both sides; but many divisions introduce Atheism." By "atheism" Bacon meant the belief that "this universal frame is without mind."[1] Definitions of the word were rarely so clear in the sixteenth and seventeenth centuries, however, since it was often applied to people who supposedly strayed in any way from the path of the "true religion." Thus in practice the word covered a broad range of possibilities, including any radical departure from the religious norms of the day. People executed for atheism included, in 1579, a number of Unitarians in En-gland who denied the Holy Trinity and the divinity of Christ.[2] Five years earlier, in France, a man was executed for being an atheist when in fact he maintained a belief in God while dis-mantling the central tenets of the major religious faiths.[3]

If Bacon was correct about religious division—that it leads to skepticism about the existence of God—atheism must have flourished in the sixteenth and seventeenth centuries. To be sure, there was a "main division," that between Protestantism and Catholicism, which engendered "zeal to both sides," and there were often divisions within these religions as well. Radi-cal sects of Christianity, like the Family of Love, who did not believe in Christ's divinity, or the Anabaptists, who did not practice infant baptism, were denounced as "atheistic." Thus Bacon's claim about the source of atheism might well be read as a warning against such sectarianism: uniformity in religion must be maintained, for the ultimate end of sectarianism is un-belief and eternal damnation. The number of people who did in fact abandon the belief in God as a result of the fact of reli-gious division remains unknown, but it does seem likely that at the very least many would have been tempted toward skepti-cism.

Why did the word "atheism," seldom seen prior to the six-

167

teenth century, appear so frequently in Shakespeare's England? The religious dislocation covered in this book clearly
had much to do with it. The shift from Catholicism to Protestantism resulted in furious accusations of atheism as the nation struggled to consolidate the new religion. Protestants,
anxious to criticize the Catholic religion, spoke of the many
"atheists" in Rome. Similarly, Catholics charged Protestants
with the very creation of atheism, since, as Bacon observed, religious division itself could inspire skepticism.

But note that the charges of atheism did not necessarily
spread because there were in fact more atheists. The word was
bandied about more frequently because people feared that the
many streams of doubt running through Europe were leading
to a sea of unbelief. One way to try to contain the rise in religious and philosophical doubt was to condemn it as "atheistic." Thomas Nashe, for example, maintained that atheists
were drawn to Pyrrhonist philosophy, a link that would have
discouraged many people from pursuing skepticism or at least
admitting it in public. Charges of atheism, then, arose to meet
the challenge presented by the proliferation of religious and
philosophical doubt, as a means of curtailing the ensuing social disorder. Thus, as skepticism expanded, so did charges of
atheism.

As such, a charge of atheism was often much more than a
vicious means of slandering an enemy for personal or political
reasons. Sir Walter Ralegh, who was indeed the victim of such
slander, provides a fine example. Throughout his lifetime, Ralegh was embroiled in contentious and treacherous political issues. The power brokers of the Jacobean regime, who were
clearly unhappy with his political activities, took revenge by
denouncing him as an atheist.[4] During Ralegh's trial for treason in 1603, James's Attorney-General, Sir Edmund Coke, declared that Ralegh had a "Spanish heart" and that he was a
"damnable atheist." The ideological import of this charge extended beyond Coke's immediate political goals. By labeling
Ralegh an atheist, the Jacobean regime could gain greater control over one of the prominent skeptical minds of the period.

Ralegh's penchant for skeptical inquiry—interrogating dogmatic philosophical and religious ideas and critiquing religious institutions—was well known by the end of the sixteenth
century. His poem "The Lie," which champions the immortal

soul while exposing the deceptions of religious and political institutions, reflects the spirit of Ralegh's skepticism: "Say to the court, it glows/And shines like rotten wood;/Say to the church, it shows/What's good, and doth no good/If church and court reply,/Then give them both the lie."[5] Unlike Greek Pyrrhonism, the poem holds out hope for truth; indeed, truth is the "warrant" that enables the soul to interrogate the falsehoods of the world. Nevertheless, the poem shares the classical skeptic's awareness of truth's elusiveness: "Tell schools, they want profoundness,/And stand too much on seeming." Whether the soul will find anything but "seeming" is left an open question. Moreover, the poem promotes a form of religious skepticism as well. True faith and virtue remain elusive, it suggests, and, without substantial institutional change, they may be impossible to achieve: "Tell faith, it's fled the city;/Tell how the country erreth." Although the poem maintains hope for truth and genuine faith, it also insists that, given the disjunction between appearance and reality, these goals will be difficult, and perhaps impossible, to attain. Truth might be the basis of the soul's critique, but we are left to wonder whether the soul itself, while operating in the material world, must remain part of "the lie" as well.[6] In other words, we cannot be entirely certain that the soul, although immortal, is not implicated in the world of decay and deception that surrounds it.

Thus the charges of atheism launched against skeptics like Ralegh served an ideological function: in a time of religious, social, and cultural change, the notion of atheism fostered an image of wholeness, a perception of a stable "reality" that was being threatened by outsiders and nonbelievers. In this way, declarations of atheism enabled ideological boundaries to be drawn between self and other; the charges created a useful fiction of cultural cohesion. Whether or not Ralegh, or for that matter Marlowe or Harriot, were atheists (in the modern sense, of people who really did deny the existence of God) becomes beside the point. Ideology, Althusser points out, does not describe reality; it is an expression of desire, hope, or nostalgia.[7] In a time out of joint, the notion of atheism preserved a sense of order by reinscribing ideological boundaries that pushed some skeptics beyond the pale of true belief.

As we have seen, numerous charges of blasphemy and unbelief also plagued Marlowe during his final years. Wrestling with his own personal demons, Robert Greene found in Marlowe a clear representation of the "damnable practices" of actors and playwrights. When Greene warned his fellow playwrights to repent and abandon their disreputable careers, he singled out Marlowe as an atheist. In *Greene's Groatsworth of Wit* (1592), he says, "Wonder not, (for with thee wil I first begin) thou famous gracer of Tragedians, that Greene, who hath said with thee (like the foole in his heart) There is no God, shoulde now give glorie unto his greatnes: for penetrating is his power, his hand lies heavie upon me."[8] Writing from his deathbed, Greene rues the "folly of his youth" and repents his former lack of belief in God. He also implies that "making plaies" might be the source of irreligion; he condemns his entire life and warns everyone else to leave the theater for purer pursuits.

In fact, antitheatrical critics had been charging players with irreligion and debauchery long before Marlowe and Greene appeared in the world of the theater. In a time of religious upheaval, it seemed especially scandalous that many people spent more time in the theater than they did in church. Phillip Stubbes was another who denounced the un-Christian practices in the theater, seeing them as one of the most serious threats to the reformed religion and social order in England. Theatergoers, he wrote, "go to these houses where players frequent, they go to Venus pallace and Satans synagogue to worship devils, and betray Christ Jesus. . . . Is he a Christian that spendeth all his life in wanton pleasures and pleasant delights."[9] Connecting the word "synagogue" with Satan is significant here, as it would have tapped into the anti-Semitism of his readers. Charges of ungodliness or atheism often linked various sorts of heresies together, as we find in the title of Philip Mornay's work, translated from the French by Arthur Golding in 1587 as *The Trewnesse of the Christian Religion: Against Atheists, Epicures, Paynims, Jewes, Mahumetists, and other Infidels.* According to Stubbes, all theatergoers had decided to follow in the footsteps of Marlowe's doomed Faustus.[10] The theater represented the disorder of a society insufficiently committed to God. The players were, essentially, treated as vagabonds, with no proper place in the social order; they blasphemed God, engaged in homosexuality, and followed Machiavelli.[11]

Greene enjoined his fellow playwrights to "abhorre those Epicures, whose loose life hath made religion lothsome to your eares." "Epicureanism" connoted a life devoted to pleasure with no attention to God or the consequences of one's lack of devotion to God. In the Renaissance, this signified atheism: though it did not mean that the practitioners doubted the existence of God, it did mean that they were dangerously close to doing so and were risking eternal damnation. Thus Greene's charge links religious unbelief to a dissolute, immoral life. Thomas Nashe, in his extensive review of different kinds of atheism, says something similar: "Too much joy of this world," he says of the atheist, "hath made him drunke. . . . He forgets he had a Maker, or that there is a Hevaen above him which controules him."[12] The operative word here is "controls": what critics feared most was that skeptics would turn out to be like Edmund in *King Lear*, unafraid of God's wrath (or not even believing in it) and thereby destroying a social order that was dependent on religious ideology.

The theater was, in fact, an ideal site for skeptics or at least people who did not write plays expressing a commitment to a specific faith. After the government banned the older religious plays for their Catholic leanings, most drama was no longer overtly religious. Although censorship was heavy, the abandonment of older religious drama did not entail the creation of a new, Protestant drama. So, for all their bluster and hyperbole, the antitheatrical writers had a point: the theaters could indeed provide a distraction from the "true word of God." The theater was not under the control of the church, and, by keeping drama relatively secular, writers managed to smuggle in skeptical ideas of all kinds that would have otherwise raised alarms. Thus, as we have seen, Marlowe could address the religious dislocations of his society without necessarily having to fear reprisal by the church and state.

In the same text on his repentance, Greene attacks William Shakespeare as an "upstart crowe."[13] He does not, of course, charge Shakespeare with atheism, and he does not mention his religion. Although the question of Shakespeare's religion is beyond the scope of this book, it deserves brief mention since we have discussed the religious views of Scot, Harriot, and Marlowe. Shakespeare has been thought to have been an Anglican, a Puritan, a Catholic, and even an agnostic. His hometown of Stratford was well known as a hotbed of resistance to the Protestant Reformation. John Shakespeare, his father, apparently held onto his Catholic faith, and even signed a "Last Will of the Soul" to which he added that he was "an unworthy member of the Holy Catholik religion." We of course have no evidence that William, like his father, was a recusant, nor have we any direct evidence of William's private religious views.[14] *King Lear*, *Hamlet*, *Othello*, *Timon of Athens*, and many other plays certainly reveal that he found skepticism—both religious and philosophical—to be of great interest. Whether he was ultimately a skeptic remains unclear. But, although there is no evidence that he pursued anything like Marlowe's deep interrogations of Christianity, Shakespeare's plays undeniably reflect a skeptical rather than dogmatic orientation, a point Keats made long ago with his notion of "negative capability," which praised the mind that "is capable of being in uncertainties, mysteries, and doubts." The medium of drama, of course, does not encourage a writer to expose a personal attachment to a particular philosophical or religious school. Marlowe, we have seen, was an exception, and there were others, including Ben Jonson, whose personal views made some kind of appearance in their plays.

The skepticism of Reginald Scot, on the other hand, makes for a sharp contrast. His empirical outlook does not entail anything like "negative capability," since his strong commitment to the Protestant faith never wavers in *The Discoverie of Witchcraft*. Nevertheless, the hostility to Scot's position on witchcraft was at times fierce and reminds us of the uncertainty that surrounded religious doctrines in the sixteenth century. As far as I know, it was not until the twentieth century that Scot was called an atheist in print.[15] But he was condemned as a heretic by no less than King James, who states on the first page of his preface to the reader of the *Daemonologie* that he was writing "against the damnable opinions of two principally in an age, whereof the one called SCOT an Englishman, is not ashamed in publike print to deny that ther can be such a thing as Witch-craft: and so mainteines the old error of the Sadducees, in denying spirits."[16] The Sadducees, members of an ancient Jewish sect, did not believe in angels or the resurrection of the dead. James's charge is itself strictly an error, since Scot denied only the corporeality of spirits, and he certainly did not challenge the Christian notion of the resurrection. Thomas Nashe argued that atheists in his own day were

Sadducees: "what are these Atheists but Saducaean sectaries that deny the resurrection?"[17] If James's view was shared by others, it is quite possible that Scot was regarded as an atheist for his doubt about the material existence of demonic spirits.

James sets out, he says, to "resolve the doubting hearts of many," and he denounces Scot's position as "damnable" before the argument of the *Daemonologie* even gets off the ground. This treatment of Scot resonates with the discourse on atheism, which branded anyone who departed from established religious norms as a threat to the belief in God. With religious doctrines within the Protestant church in a state of flux, it is not too surprising that witchcraft debates could be so controversial. Even a staunch anti-Catholic and supporter of the Anglican church like Scot could come under fire for "damnable opinions."

Scot himself, as we have seen, was no religious pluralist. He made it all too clear that he thought of atheism as "unnatural" and that all those who do not believe in God ought to be executed or severely punished. Early in the *Discoverie,* he lists fifteen crimes determined by the famous French jurist Jean Bodin, and gives the reader his own answers. The first is:

> They denie God, and all religion
> Answere: Then let them die therefore, or at the least be used like infidels, or apostates. (18)

The inquisition, he says, is justified in burning heretics, because their depravity is within the bounds of nature, and these heretics are thus a genuine threat to the Christian church. But when the inquisitors condemn the practice of witchcraft, which is not within the bounds of nature, they are themselves entering into the darkness they should dispel.

Thomas Harriot, like William Shakespeare, had no similar inclination to take such a vigorous stance against heretics. Indeed, he himself fell victim to England's internal religious and political strife. In the 1590s and the first decade of the seventeenth century, he was branded a witch, a heretic, and an atheist. One of the many charges against him was made by a Jesuit, Robert Parsons, who had been engaged in an ongoing battle to maintain a Catholic presence in England by converting Protestants. Parsons fueled the suspicions against Harriot by implicating him in a school of atheism with his friend and patron, Sir Walter Ralegh. The next decade turned out to be just as difficult for Harriot. During Ralegh's trial for treason, Harriot, like his patron, was declared an atheist. The Chief Justice in the case, Sir John Popham told Ralegh: "And let not Heriott nor any such Doctor perswade you there is no Eternity."[18]

Charges of atheism were first launched against Harriot shortly after the publication of *A Briefe and True Report of the New Found Land of Virginia*. Thus the report would seem to be one of the reasons people questioned Harriot's religious orthodoxy. And in general, we find that travel around the globe sparked fears of relativism in religion and epistemology. Thomas Nashe's *Christ's Tears over Jerusalem*, which, as I argued in the second chapter, implicates Harriot in atheism, expresses this fear: atheists, he says, "followe the Pironicks, whose position and opinion it is that there is no Hel or misery but opinion. Impudently they persist in it, that the late discovered Indians are able to shew antiquities thousands before Adam." The first part of this quotation shows that Nashe must have been familiar with the 1590 translation of Sextus Empiricus, which has long been attributed to Sir Walter Ralegh. "Different people believe in different gods," Ralegh as translator says, "some in providence; others not. . . . As to what is true, then, let suspension of judgment be our practice."[19] The second sentence in the quotation from Nashe implies some felt connection between the discovery of new information provided by the Indians and the views of Pyrrhonists. Indeed, as the line above from "The Skeptic" tells us, there is no one true religion. It seems at least plausible that the voyages to America did inspire relativistic ideas about religion and culture—but it is undeniable that there was much anxiety that they were doing so.[20] In Harriot's case, we saw evidence of what I called ethnographic receptivity, if not exactly relativism. Nashe's protest may not reflect the actual existence of such atheists so much as a deep anxiety about relativism. Nashe, and many others like him, plagued by the fear of what Bacon called "divisions" in religion, may easily have come to the conclusion that dangerous relativists were lurking everywhere, waiting to convince others that with so many religions fighting for control, no one could be certain that any one sect in particular could be sure in its claims to truth.[21]

With a great deal of religious dissonance and social confusion at home, it also seems probable that the English were not entirely confident about their evangelistic practices abroad. Evangelical colonialism relied heavily on feelings of cultural superiority: the natives were "uncivilized," meaning they lacked European social customs, and they worshiped what the English considered to be false gods. But as we have seen, English social norms were themselves in disarray at this time. As Karen Kupperman observes, the early contact between the English and the Indians came at a time when the English were concerned about their own social demarcations:

> Social boundaries and their demarcators mattered to early modern English men and women. As foreign influences were increasingly felt through "apish and servile Imitation," commentators worried that categories were becoming blurred, and the foundations of good order undermined.[22]

Thus, much of the concern over atheism derived from this fear that boundaries were being destroyed by increased contact with foreign lands, in continental Europe as well as the New World. Once again, we hear from Thomas Nashe: "Italy, the Paradice of the earth and the Epicures heaven, how doth it form our yong master? . . . From thence he brings the art of atheisme, the art of epicurizing."[23] From America the English discovered that biblical chronology was wrong, and from Italy they received the "art of epicurizing." New ideas about religion were invading England and, people feared, they might destroy the social order. Epicureanism and Pyrrhonism, for example, took away the fear of hell and damnation, leaving practitioners with the option of leading a life of sin with no fear of divine retribution. The fear of hell, of course, was crucial to the ideology of order, which stated that rebellion was an act against God and the state.

As we have seen, skepticism emerged largely as a response to social and religious dislocations. But Gabriel Harvey's response to a natural disaster, the earthquake of 1580, offers us a fine metaphor for skepticism in Shakespeare's England: after a frightening earthquake shook England in 1580, Harvey opened up a skeptical, or, more specifically, naturalistic inquiry into the causes of the event. He put forth that there were natural causes for the quake—"windie exhaltations" and vapors in the bowels of the earth—and questioned the role of divine providence. Did God even have a hand in the disaster? How can humans be so presumptuous as to think they can discern precisely what God's plan is? "To make shorte," he wrote to Edmund Spenser, "I cannot see, and would gladly learne, howe a man on Earth, should be of so great authoritie, and so familiar acquaintance with God in Heaven . . . as to be able in such specialities . . . to reveale his incomprehensible mysteries, and definitively to give sentence of his Majesties secret and inscrutable purposes."[24] Likewise, given the rapidly shifting socioeconomic conditions of Shakespeare's England, the role of God must have seemed increasingly indiscernible in the social realm as well.

Our four skeptics confronted the faultlines of change in a variety of ways. Hoping to end the persecution of witches and advance the cultural and religious reformation of England, Reginald Scot denied the material existence of spirits and demons. Thomas Harriot crossed the boundaries of religious orthodoxy in his ethnography and science, instigating concern among his contemporaries about England's cultural and religious identity. Marlowe may have been an example of Bacon's "atheist," an astute observer of "divisions" in religion who found absolute religious truths unlikely given the internal instability of Christianity with its division and sects. And Shakespeare, no stranger to economic change himself (he became a wealthy landowner in Stratford), presented Jacobeans with an apocalyptic vision based on the turmoil of rapid economic change. In a time so "out of joint," these voices responded with a myriad of challenges to the wisdom of the day.

Notes

INTRODUCTION

1. Quoted in Keith Thomas, *Religion and the Decline of Magic* (New York: Charles Scribner's Sons, 1971), 163.

2. As Sextus Empiricus tells us, Pyrrhonism, which I will refer to as "classical skepticism" or "philosophical skepticism" is an "ability to set out oppositions among things which appear and are thought of in any way at all, an ability by which, because of the equipollence in the opposed objects and accounts, we come first to suspension of judgement and afterwards to tranquility." Thus, the skeptic does not argue that anything is true or false but prefers to suspend judgment, balancing all arguments. Even this idea is negated, however, once the skeptic reaches ataraxia: the practitioner uses negation as a purgative and then negates the negation by purging the method itself. One can reach the state of *eudaimonia* only when one is left totally empty-handed, freed of ideas or beliefs that have any content. Pyrrho of Elis (c. 360–270 BC) disdained to put his ideas in writing, and thus our knowledge of his brand of skepticism largely depends on the work of Sextus Empiricus (c. 200 AD). See Sextus Empiricus, *Outlines of Scepticism*, ed. Julia Annas and Jonathan Barnes (Cambridge: Cambridge University Press, 1994), 4.

3. Unless otherwise indicated, all quotations of *Hamlet* will be from the Arden edition: William Shakespeare, *Hamlet*, ed. Harold Jenkins (London: Routledge, 1982). On the textual indeterminacy of the play, see the analysis of the three available texts in Leah Marcus, *Unediting the Renaissance* (London: Routledge, 1996). See also "'The Cause of This Defect': Hamlet's Editors" in *Hamlet: New Critical Essays* (New York: Routledge, 2002), 115–34.

4. Stephen Greenblatt has recently explored how Shakespeare appropriated the idea of purgatory after it had been dismissed and banned by Protestants. Shakespeare's ideas about mortality, memory, and the afterlife, Greenblatt demonstrates, were vitally connected to sixteenth-century debates about purgatory. See Stephen Greenblatt, *Hamlet in Purgatory* (Princeton: Princeton University Press, 2001).

5. Reginald Scot, *The Discoverie of Witchcraft* (1584), ed. Rev. Montague Summers (1930; rpt., New York: Dover Books, 1972), 262.

6. "An Exhortation against the Fear of Death," in *Certain Sermons or Homilies* (London, 1676), 54.

7. This comic dialogue retains a crucial aspect of the Epicurean/Lucretian philosophy that the soul is mortal. After death, Alexander and Caesar become mere things with use-value. The human being, a temporal configu-

ration or conglomeration of atoms, moves back into the void after death. In Shakespeare's dialogue, the material body dissolves and is then transformed into other objects in the natural world.

8. Scot, *Witchcraft*, 86–87.

9. Thomas, *Religion*, 509.

10. Greenblatt, *Hamlet in Purgatory*, 155–205.

11. Francis Bacon, "Of Envy" in *Francis Bacon*, ed. Brian Vickers (Oxford: Oxford University Press, 1996), 355.

12. Lawrence Stone, *The Causes of the English Revolution 1529–1642* (New York: Harper and Row, 1972), 110.

13. See Keith Wrightson, *English Society 1580–1680* (London: Hutchinson, 1982) and Anthony Fletcher and John Stevenson, *Order and Disorder in Early Modern England* (Cambridge: Cambridge University Press, 1985).

14. Annabel Patterson suggests that "peasant" in this context does not mean an agricultural laborer since the word was symbolic of anyone below the rank of gentleman and yeoman. See *Shakespeare and the Popular Voice* (Oxford: Basil Blackwell, 1989), 32.

15. On Shakespeare and carnival, see Michael Bristol, *Carnival and Theatre* (New York: Methuen, 1985) and Francois Laroque, *Shakespeare's Festive World*, trans. Janet Lloyd (Cambridge: Cambridge University Press, 1991). On changes in the calendar and nationalistic festivities, see David Cressy, *Bonfires and Bells* (Berkeley: University of California Press, 1989).

16. John Donne, "An Anatomy of the World. The First Anniversary" in John Carey, ed., *John Donne* (Oxford: Oxford University Press, 1990). For an impressive analysis of the social, anatomical, and linguistic meanings of the phrase "out of joint," see Marjorie Garber, "Out of Joint," in *The Body in Parts: Fantasies of Corporeality in Early Modern Europe*, ed. David Hillman and Carla Mazzio (New York: Routledge, 1997), 23–52.

17. On the history of the philosophical tradition of skepticism, see Richard Popkin, *The History of Skepticism* (Berkeley: University of California Press, 1979).

18. The problem of criteria has long been part of the philosophical tradition. Stanley Cavell discusses Wittgenstein's use of the problem in *The Claim of Reason: Wittgenstein, Skepticism, Morality, and Tragedy* (Oxford: Oxford University Press, 1979).

19. For more on Pyrrhonism in England, see William M. Hamlin "Skepticism in Shakespeare's England," in *The Shakespearean International Yearbook* 2 (1999): 290–304.

20. The vast majority of recent books on skepticism focus on the epistemological dilemmas that philosophical skepticism poses for modern philosophy. These works generally do not examine the historical context of skeptical thinking and instead tend to consider what is right or wrong with skeptical arguments. See, for example, Charles Landesman, *Skepticism: the Central Issues* (Oxford: Blackwell, 2002). In their introduction to philosophical thinking, Richard Popkin and Avrum Stroll show that skepticism is a crucial step to take in grappling with everyday ethical, political, and religious dilemmas. Popkin and Stroll do take into consideration the "social climate" for older forms of philosophical skepticism. See Richard H. Popkin and Avrum

Stroll, *Skeptical Philosophy for Everyone* (Amherst, Mass.: Prometheus Books, 2002). Ellen Sposky makes a more dramatic break from standard philosophical approaches by combining cognitive science, literary theory, and cultural analysis. See *Satisfying Skepticism* (Aldershot: Ashgate, 2001).

21. Dominick Lacapra has convincingly demonstrated that intellectual history must now be concerned with textuality and a dialogistic understanding of history. See Dominick Lacapra, *Rethinking Intellectual History* (Ithaca: Cornell University Press, 1983).

22. On the relation of social history and the new cultural history, see Victoria Bonnell and Lynn Hunt, eds., *Beyond the Cultural Turn* (Berkeley: University of California Press, 1999) and Lynn Hunt, ed., *The New Cultural History* (Berkeley: University of California Press, 1989).

23. In his discussion of the idea of a "structure," Derrida describes the epochal "event," when deconstruction decentered all notions of "structure": "This was the moment when, in the absence of a center or origin, everything became discourse . . . the absence of the transcendental signified extends the domain and the play of signification infinitely." See Jacques Derrida, *Writing and Difference*, trans. Alan Bass (Chicago: University of Chicago Press, 1978), 280.

24. Wittgenstein says the term " 'language-game' is meant to bring into prominence the fact that the speaking of language is part of an activity, or a form of life." See his *Philosophical Investigations*, paragraph 23. Language can thus be an important part of a concrete historical and institutional setting, not merely Derridean "play." For a compelling use of Wittgenstein in conjunction with Marx and Derrida, see Ernesto Laclau and Chantal Mouffe, *Hegemony and Socialist Strategy* (London: Verso, 1985), 105–14. See also my critique of postmodern politics in "New Reflections on the 'Revolutionary' Politics of Ernesto Laclau and Chantal Mouffe," *boundary 2* 22:3 (1995): 81–111.

25. Ernesto Laclau, *New Reflections on the Revolution of Our Time* (London: Verso, 1990), 92.

26. Louis Althusser, "Ideology and Ideological State Apparatuses," in *Literary Theory: An Anthology*, ed. Julie Rivkin and Michael Ryan (London: Blackwell, 1998), 294–304.

27. Jacques Lacan, "The Mirror Stage as Formative of the Function of the I as Revealed in Psychoanlaytic Experience" in *Literary Theory*, Rivkin and Ryan, 178–84.

28. For more on the irony of this divine retribution, see Stephen Greenblatt, *Renaissance Self-Fashioning* (Berkeley: University of California Press, 1980), 193–221.

29. For such charges against ideology, see Claire McEachern and Deborah Shugar, *Religion and Culture in Renaissance England* (Cambridge: Cambridge University Press, 1997) and Deborah Shugar, *Habits of Thought in the English Renaissance* (Berkeley: University of California Press, 1990).

30. Mary Douglas, "The social preconditions of radical scepticism" in *Power, Action and Belief*, ed. John Law (London: Routledge, 1986), 74.

31. Diogenes Laertius, *Lives of Eminent Philosophers*, volume 2, trans. R. D. Hicks, Loeb Classical Library (Cambridge: Harvard University Press, 1925), 479.

32. Ibid., 481.

33. For the text of the depositions at Cerne Abbas, see Willam Harrison, ed., *Willobie His Avisa* (New York: Barnes and Noble, 1966), Appendix III.

34. Sir Walter Raleigh, "Sir Walter Raleigh's Sceptick" (London: W. Bent ley, 1651), 24, 1. See also William M. Hamlin's recent edition of the text accompanied by new information he has uncovered about the manuscripts: "A Lost Translation Found? An Edition of The Sceptick (c.1590)" in *ELR* 31:1 (2001).

CHAPTER 1. "THE SPIRIT OF BLINDNESS AND ERROR DOOTH SEDUCE THEM"

1. Robert H. West, *Reginald Scot and Renaissance Writings on Witchcraft* (Boston: Twayne, 1984), 42.

2. Brian Easlea, *Witch-Hunting, Magic, and the New Philosophy: An Introduction to the Debates of the Scientific Revolution, 1450–1750* (Sussex: Harvester Press, 1980), 24.

3. Sydney Anglo, "Reginald Scot's *Discoverie of Witchcraft*: Skepticism and Sadduceeism" in *The Damned art: Essays in the Literature of Witchcraft*, ed. Sydney Anglo (London: Routledge and Kagan Paul, 1977), 106–40; quotation from 134. Anglo was the first modern scholar to provide a careful study of Scot. As he puts it, Scot is "often cited but rarely read."

4. Anglo, "Reginald Scot's *Discoverie of Witchcraft*," 135.

5. Although scholars have become more cautious, they continue to offer careless readings of Scot's work. Robin Briggs, for example, responds to Scot's view that the "proofs brought against [witches] are impossibilities contrary to reason, scripture, and nature" by saying "indeed they were." The implication here is that Scot's claim needs no scrutiny, for it is perfectly in line with our own worldview. Once we understand Scot's concepts and his ideological context, however, it becomes much harder to project our modern views on to his texts. See Robin Briggs, *Witches and Neighbors* (New York: Penguin, 1996), 20. Even scholarship on witchcraft that questions the heroic status of early modern skeptics often tends to exacerbate misunderstandings by making Scot and twentieth-century historians themselves out to be part of a long-standing tradition of rationalist misogyny. If Scot is not the hero, they suggest, then he must be the villain. Diane Purkiss, for example, declares that Scot's contempt for women accused of witchcraft "actually exceeded that of his contemporaries" and adds that modern historians "overlap" with Scot and are thus implicated in his misogyny. See Diane Purkiss, *The Witch in History* (New York: Routledge, 1996).

6. Scot's reading of the scripture is, nevertheless, unorthodox, and places him in a marginal position. Although I am not convinced by the argument that Scot was part of the Family of Love or any other radical sect, it is important to acknowledge that his metaphorical, rather than literal, reading of the Bible was highly unusual. He does not appear, however, to have had any affiliation with Puritans, anti-Puritans, or any particular sect. On Scot's possi-

ble connections to the Family of Love, see David Wooton, "Reginald Scot, Abraham Fleming/ the Family of Love," in *Languages of Witchcraft*, ed. Stuart Clark (New York: St. Martin's Press, 2001). On Scot's political motive of anti-Puritanism, see Peter Elmer, "Toward a Politics of Witchcraft in Early Modern England," in the same volume.

7. Reginald Scot, *The Discoverie of Witchcraft*, 165. Unless otherwise noted, all quotations of *The Discoverie* will be from the Dover edition, cited above.

8. For Counter-Reformation thinkers, the appeal to conscience and dependence on the rational interpretation of scripture over the guidance of the church was incoherent. This inner sanctum was illusory since it could not be verified by any traditional doctrine. The sixteenth-century French Jesuit St. Francois de Sales, for example, in referring to the "inner persuasion of the Holy Spirit," said, "Oh God, what a hiding place, what a fog, what a night!" Scot's skepticism, then, differed greatly from the Pyrrhonism of his Catholic, French contemporary, Michel de Montaigne, who believed that all religion had to be based on faith rather than reason. De Sales is cited in Richard Popkin, *The History of Skepticism*, 71.

9. Stuart Clark has analyzed this spiritualization in his brilliant account of Protestant demonology. See Stuart Clark, *Thinking with Demons* (Oxford: Oxford University Press, 1999).

10. Quoted in Philip Corrigan and Derek Sayer, *The Great Arch: English State Formation as Cultural Revolution* (Oxford: Basil Blackwell, 1985), 59.

11. Christina Larner, *Witchcraft and Religion: The Politics of Popular Belief* (New York: Basil Blackwell, 1984), 35–36.

12. Jean Delumeau, *Catholicism Between Luther and Voltaire*, trans. Jeremy Moiser (London: Westminster Press, 1977), 160.

13. Ibid., 161.

14. For a detailed analysis of such rites, see Stephen Wilson, *The Magical Universe: Everyday Ritual and Magic in Pre-Modern Europe* (London: Hambledon and London, 2000).

15. *The Book of Common Prayer*, ed. John Booty (Charlottsville: Folger Shakespeare Library, 1976), 264.

16. This section of Scot's *Discoverie* is essential to his general philosophy yet it has been left out of most editions, including the Dover edition cited throughout this chapter. My references to this section are from Nicholson's edition. See the "Discourse on Devils and Spirits" in Reginald Scot, *The Discoverie of Witchcraft*, ed. Brinsely Nicholson (Totowa, New Jersey: Roman and Littlefield, 1973), 459.

17. Phillip Stubbes, *The Anatomie of Abuses* (1583), facsimile edition (New York: Da Capo Press, 1972), preface.

18. Peter Burke, *Popular Culture in Early Modern Europe* (New York: Harper Torchbooks, 1978), 208. Burke refers to this as "the withdrawal thesis." Some studies have criticized Burke for overlooking the "middling sort" and the blurred nature of categories like "elite" and "popular." See, for example, the essays in Tim Harris, ed., *Popular Culture in England* (New York: St. Martin's Press, 1995).

19. Eamon Duffy, *The Stripping of the Altars: Traditional Religion in England 1400–1580* (New Haven: Yale University Press, 1992), 571.

20. We can contrast Scot's hostility to Puck and other popular superstitions with the magical worldview of the Paracelsians, who understood the natural order as operating, to a large extent, in the hands of diverse spirits or intelligences. An important aspect of the Paracelsian cosmology was that it was steeped in popular culture and included stories of special beings who moved in a separate plane of existence. One might also look to Agricola, who drew on commonly circulated beliefs in dwarves who populated mines and participated in community labor. See Georg Agricola, *De Re Metallica*, trans. Herbert Hoover (New York: Dover, 1950), 217.

21. George Gifford, *A Dialogue Concerning Witches and Witchcraftes* (London, 1583), A4v.

22. Cited in Alan MacFarland, *Witchcraft in Tudor and Stuart England* (London: Routledge and Kegan Paul, 1970), 129.

23. Bernard Capp, *English Almanacs, 1500–1800* (Ithaca: Cornell University Press, 1979), 131.

24. See Robert Muchembled, "Satanic Myths and Cultural Reality," in *Early Modern European Witchcraft*, ed. Bengt Ankarloo and Gustav Henningsen (Oxford: Clarendon Press, 1990), 139–160.

25. Frances E. Dolan, *Dangerous Familiars* (Ithaca: Cornell University Press, 1994), 198. See also Dolan's introduction to *The Taming of the Shrew*, by William Shakespeare (Boston: Bedford Books, 1992).

26. Reprinted in Joan Larsen Klein, ed., *Daughters, Wives, and Widows: Writings by Men about Women and Marriage in England, 1500–1640* (Urbana: University of Illinois Press, 1992), 17.

27. William Perkins, "Christian Economy," in Klein, *Daughters*, 172.

28. Lawrence Stone, *The Family, Sex, and Marriage* (New York: Harper Torchbooks, 1977). See also Allison P. Coudert, "The Myth of the Improved Status of Protestant Women: The Case of the Witchcraze" in *The Politics of Gender in Early Modern Europe*, ed. Jean R. Brink et. al. (Kirksville: Sixteenth Century Journal Publishers, 1989), 61–92.

29. "The Epistle of Paul to the Ephesians," in *The Geneva Bible* (1560), facsimile rpt. (Wisconsin: University of Wisconsin Press, 1969), 5:22–23.

30. "The devilishly clever enemy, sly and cunning, enlists the feminine sex, which is fickle by nature, of little faith, malicious, impatient, melancholy in its inability to control its emotions, and above all the old weaknesses, stupidities and unsteady disposition." French version quoted in Sydney Anglo, "Melancholia and Witchcraft: the debate between Wier, Bodin, and Scot," in *Folie et Déraison à la Renaissance* (Edition de L'université de Bruxelles, 1976), 211–12. Scot holds onto Weyer's misogyny but does not see such an active role for the devil.

31. Cited in Barbara Rosen, ed., *Witchcraft in England: 1558–1618* (Amherst: University of Massachusetts Press, 1969), 105.

32. Heinrich Kramer and James Sprenger, *The Malleus Maleficarum* (1485), trans. Montague Summers (1928, rpt. New York: Dover, 1971), 58.

33. This symbolic battle contributed to the widespread slaughter of women on the continent and also forced people to reassess the role of women in society. Barbara Ehrenreich and others argue that the persecution of so-called witches provided a means for the masculinization of the medical prac-

tice as well as Christianity. The *Malleus Maleficarum*, they argue, set off a wave of terror over midwives by claiming that they were often witches who devoured babies or gave them over to the devil. See Barbara Ehrenreich and Deirdre English, *For Her Own Good: 150 Years of the Expert's Advice to Women* (New York: Vintage Books, 1978). Ehrenreich and English's argument may be overstated, but the case for a historical connection between the persecution of midwives and witches has been presented by a number of historians. For an argument against Ehrenreich and English, see David Harley, "Historians as Demonologists: The Myth of the Midwife-Witch," *Social History of Medicine* 3 (1990), 1–26.

34. Scot, *Discovery of Witchcraft* (1651), A1r

35. See Alan MacFarland, *Witchcraft in Tudor and Stuart England* and Keith Thomas, *Religion and the Decline of Magic*. The more recent book by Robin Briggs makes some significant adjustments to previous social and cultural histories. See Briggs, *Witches and Neighbors*.

36. Thomas, *Religion and the Decline of Magic*, 557.

37. J. Thomas Kelly, *Thorns on the Tudor Rose* (Jackson: University of Mississippi Press, 1977), 62. See also Paul Slack, *The English Poor Law, 1531–1782* (Cambridge: Cambridge University Press, 1990).

38. Richard Halpern writes, "The poor were increasingly viewed with indifference, suspicion, or fear, and instead of being given charity they were frequently persecuted or punished. They became, in a sense, the quintessential 'other' of English society." See *The Poetics of Primitive Accumulation* (Ithaca: Cornell University Press, 1991), 73.

39. A. L. Beier argues that this change began in the fourteenth century but reached its climax in the sixteenth century. It is no accident, then, that witch persecutions increased dramatically in this period. See A. L. Beier, *Masterless Men* (London: Methuen, 1985).

40. All quotations of the play are from Dekker, Ford, and Rowley, *The Witch of Edmonton*, ed. Peter Corbin and Douglas Sedge (Manchester: Manchester University Press, 1999).

41. Henry Goodcole, "The Wonderful Discoverie of Elizabeth Sawyer a Witch . . ." (London, 1621). Goodcole wrote numerous pamphlets identifying sins, crimes, and presenting confessions. His goal with Elizabeth Sawyer, as with other "sinners," was to help them repent and to sensationalize the whole process for popular consumption. For more on Goodcole, see Diane Purkiss, *The Witch in History*, 231–47 and Marion Gibson's commentary and notes in *Early Modern Witches* (London: Routledge, 2000), 299–316. For an excellent analysis of the trope of discovery and the "ocular proof" of witchcraft trials, see Katherine Maus, "Proof and Consequences: Inwardness and its Exposure in the English Renaissance," in *Materialist Shakespeare*, ed. Ivo Kamps (London: Verso, 1995).

42. Goodcole and Scot, for all their differences, do have much in common: the minister criticizes popular practices as absurd and advocates a spiritualized form of worship that attends to "the glorie of God." Goodcole refers to the "ridiculous" customs reported in popular ballads such as "the bewitching of corn," or "a ferret and an owl daily sporting before her [Sawyer]." These stories, he says with the reforming attitude common to the clergy of his day,

are "fitter for an Ale-bench than for a relation of proceeding in Court of Justice." Scot, too, puts considerable effort into debunking such customs.

43. On the play's critique of the law, see Lisa Jardine, "Ladies' Trials: Women and the Law in Three Plays of John Ford," *Cahiers Elisabéthains* 56 (October, 1999): 49–64. Katherine McClusky points out that Dekker often included a "defiant heroine" in his plays, including *The Honest Whore* and *The Roaring Girl*. See Katherine McClusky, *Dekker and Heywood* (New York: St. Martin's Press, 1994), 128–54.

44. Richard Grinnel, "Naming and Social Disintegration in *The Witch of Edmonton*" in *Essays in Theatre/Études théatrales* 16:2 (1998): 212.

45. Some scholars have claimed that the plot on witchcraft is not very important to the play. Leonora Leet Brodwin, for example, says that the treatment of the witch is "a largely unrelated sub-plot to the more fully developed, fictional tragedy of Frank Thorney." See "The Domestic Tragedy of Frank Thorney in *The Witch of Edmonton*," *SEL* 7 (1967): 311–28. Perhaps the best refutation of this argument has been made by Anthony B. Dawson, "Witchcraft/Bigamy: Cultural Conflict in *The Witch of Edmonton*" in *Renaissance Drama* 20 (1989): 77–98.

46. Kathleen McLusky, *Renaissance Dramatists* (New York: Harvester Wheatsheaf, 1989), 68.

47. George Gifford, *A Dialogue Concerning Witches and Witchcrafts*, sig. 1.4v.

48. Larry Champion, "'Factions of Distempered Passions' : The Development of John Ford's Tragic Vision in *The Witch of Edmonton* and *The Lover's Melancholy*," in "*Concord in Discord*": *The Plays of John Ford, 1586–1986*, ed. Donald K. Anderson, Jr. (New York: AMS Press, 1986), 109–110.

49. Gymnosophists were Hindu ascetics who wore little or no clothing and thus, according to Scot, imitated Esau in the book of Genesis.

CHAPTER 2. "THE MAYSTER OF ALL ESSENTIALL
AND TRUE KNOWLEDGE"

1. "De Guiana, Carmen Epicum" in *The Poems of George Chapman*, Phyllis Brooks Bartlett, ed. (New York: Russel and Russel, 1941).

2. Ian Archer, *The Pursuit of Stability: Social Relations in Elizabethan England* (Cambridge: Cambridge University Press, 1991).

3. Thomas Nashe, *The Unfortunate Traveller* (1594) in *The Works of Thomas Nashe*, Ronald McKerrow, ed. (New York: Barnes and Noble, 1966), II, 297.

4. Jeffrey Knapp, *An Empire Nowhere* (Berkeley: University of California Press, 1992), 4. See also Karen Ordahl Kupperman, *Indians & English: Facing Off in Early America* (Ithaca: Cornell University Press, 2000).

5. Greenblatt himself qualified the theory after the essay stirred so much debate: "Even those literary texts that sought most ardently to speak for a monolithic power could be shown to be the sites of institutional and ideological contestation." See Stephen Greenblatt, *Shakespearean Negotiations* (Berkeley: University of California Press, 1988), 2–3. For analysis and criti-

cism of the subversion/containment model, see: Louis Montrose, *The Purpose of Playing* (Chicago: University of Chicago Press, 1996), 7–11; Jean Howard, *The Stage and Social Struggle in Early Modern England* (London: Routledge, 1994), 11–14; Tom McAlindon, "Testing the New Historicism: 'Invisible Bullets' Reconsidered," *SP* 92:4 (fall 1995): 411–38. The theory has also been criticized by those who do not want to see Harriot's work politicized. B. J. Sokol, for example, takes the position that Harriot is a "seeker of truth" and rails against Greenblatt's more negative appraisal. Sokol argues that Greenblatt's portrayal of Harriot uses "stereotypes . . . as unfoundedly as did the labels 'devil or doctor' which were applied to him by his witch-fearing contemporaries." See "The Problem of Assessing Thomas Harriot's *A briefe and true report* of his Discoveries in North America" in *Annals of Science* 51 (1994): 1–16. While Greenblatt's reading is not as crude as Sokol suggests, it does make Harriot an enforcer of "containment."

6. Greenblatt, *Shakespearean Negotiations*, 37. The essay first appeared in *Glyph* 8 (1981): 40–61.

7. See David B. Quinn and John W. Shirley, "A Contemporary List of Harriot References," *Renaissance Quarterly* 22:1 (1969): 9–27.

8. The word "atheism" had a broader meaning than it does today. It was often used to attack people who held unorthodox Christian ideas. The accusation of unbelief often reflected the fear of attackers that the person charged would eventually move from heterodoxy to unbelief. Of course, it was also used simply to ruin reputations. I cover this topic in more detail in the conclusion.

9. See Stephen Clucas, "Thomas Harriot and the Field of Knowledge in the English Renaissance" (Oxford Harriot Lecture, 1994), 45.

10. For an extensive and rigorous analysis of the relation between science and religion in the early modern period, see John Hedley Brooke, *Science and Religion: Some Historical Perspectives* (Cambridge: Cambridge University Press, 1991).

11. The scientific theory of atomism was accepted by Harriot and other members of the Northumberland circle well before it was taken up in the seventeenth century by mechanical materialists.

12. Quoted by Hillary Gatti, "The Natural Philosophy of Thomas Harriot" (Oxford: Lecture at Oriel College, 1993), 7–8.

13. One practitioner of the Northumberland circle, Nicholas Hill, was fully aware of the dangerous social implications of his Epicurean cosmology. Like Giordano Bruno, he understood that his cosmology (especially his view of matter) threatened many basic Christian tenets. For a discussion of Hill, see Jean Jacquot, "Harriot, Hill, Warner and the New Philosophy" in *Thomas Harriot: Renaissance Scientist*, ed. John W. Shirley (Oxford: Clarendon Press, 1974), 107–29.

14. See Francis Bacon, "Of Atheism" in Vickers, *Francis Bacon*, 371. Robert Kargon gives a survey of Bacon's different views on atomism throughout his career. Bacon was heavily influenced by the atomism of the Northumberland circle after 1603. See his essay in Shirley, ed., *Thomas Harriot: Renaissance Scientist*.

15. John Aubrey, *Brief Lives*, ed. Andrew Clark, 2 vols. (Oxford: Clarendon Press, 1898), I. 284–87.

16. Quoted in Shirley, ed., *Thomas Harriot, Renaissance Scientist*, 29. See Shirley's discussion of the circumstances of Harriot's imprisonment. Harriot was arrested along with the "Wizard" Earl of Northumberland after the Gunpowder Plot when James I became concerned that Harriot may have cast his horoscope.

17. The word "written," contradicts Harriot's claim that they have no written history. This could easily be an error by Baines rather than proof that Harriot was not one of the men who shared this view with Marlowe.

18. Another example of potentially subversive humanism can be found in Leonardo da Vinci's manuscripts. While not charged with this heresy, Leonardo questioned biblical knowledge, specifically the event of a universal deluge, in his geological analysis of sea shells in the mountains of Parma See *The Notebooks of Leonardo Da Vinci*, compiled and edited by Jean Paul Richter, 2 vols. (New York: Dover Publications, 1970), 986–91.

19. This quote is from *Christs Tears Over Jerusalem* in R.B. Mckerrow, ed., *The Works of Thomas Nashe*, II: 121–22.

20. Hillary Gatti has found the following curious reference in Harriot's manuscripts to academic skepticism: "Socrates which by oracle was judged the wisest man in this time sayd he knew nothing. And Arcesilas which sayd he knew not much as that, and such with his followers called sceptikes which will not affirme or deny any knowledge to be true or false but do still doubt, yet they make their knowledge playne to doubt assuredly." Hillary Gatti, "The Natural Philosophy of Thomas Harriot," 19.

21. Gatti reviews a list of Harriot's books from the stationer John Bill in 1618 that suggests an encyclopedic knowledge (assuming he read all the books). Gatti, "The Natural Philosophy of Thomas Harriot," 21–28. She notes, "I have myself found no clear and sustained commitment to any one orthodox Christian faith in Harriot, either Anglican or Catholic. Rather he seems to have approached such questions on almost scientific terms, with an open and enquiring mind" (26).

22. John Brereton, *A Briefe and True Relation of the Discoverie of the North Part of Virginia* (London, 1602).

23. The *Briefe and True Report* can be characterized as "ethnographic" since it factors in cultural diversity and acknowledges the epistemological problems inherent in the colonial encounter. On the term "ethnography," see William M. Hamlin, *The Image of America in Montaigne, Spenser, and Shakespeare: Renaissance Ethnography and Literary Reflection* (New York: St. Martin's Press, 1995), 2.

24. Ralph Hamor, *A True Discourse of the Present Estate of Virginia (London, 1615), A 4*.

25. James Rosier's account of a voyage with Captain George Waymouth explained that the "All creating God, with his most liberall hand," had made the beautiful "garden of nature" in Northern Virginia and he had "obscured it to any, except to a purblind generation, whose understanding it hath pleased God so to darken," that they do not acknowledge the Deity of the Almighty giver." Rosier was committed to the "promulgating of Gods holy church by planting Christianity." James Rosier, *A True Relation of the most prosperous voyage made this present yeere 1605* (London, 1605), E1.

26. Ralph Hamor, *A True Discourse*, G2.

27. D. B Quinn, *The Roanoke Voyages*, v.1 (London: Hakluyt Society, 1955), 372. Unless otherwise noted, all quotations of Harriot's *Brief and True Report* will be from this edition.

28. Quoted in D. B. Quinn, *The Roanoke Voyages*, 126–27.

29. I discuss this connection in chapter three.

30. We should characterize Harriot as a Renaissance as well as an early modern scientist. The former gives emphasis to the analogical framework that informed the work of his circle and the latter gives emphasis to the empiricist and mechanistic thinking he helped develop. Brian Vickers suggests that although there is no clear division between analogical or occult thinking and the "scientific tradition," we can see how "in many instances, especially in the late sixteenth and seventeenth centuries, a spectrum of beliefs and attitudes can be distinguished, a continuum from, say absolutely magical to absolutely mechanistic poles." Brian Vickers, "Analogy versus Identity," in Brian Vickers, ed., *Occult & Scientific Mentalities in the Renaissance* (Cambridge: Cambridge University Press, 1984), 95.

31. See Hillary Gatti, *The Renaissance Drama of Knowledge* (London: Routledge, 1989) and Shirley, ed.,*Thomas Harriot*: Renaissance Scientist. See also Julie Solomon's account of Harriot's interests in the occult in "'To Know, To Fly, To Conjure': Situating Baconian Science at the Juncture of Early Modern Modes of Reading," *Renaissance Quarterly* 44:3 (1991).

32. This description of the conjuror accompanies a drawing by John White. Thomas Harriot, *A Briefe and True Report of the Newfound Land of Virginia*, facsimile of De Bry's 1590 edition (New York: Dover, 1972), 54. These drawings along with Harriot's descriptions were published by De Bry.

33. Quoted in John W. Shirley, *Thomas Harriot: A Biography* (Oxford: Clarendon Press, 1983), 180.

34. This form of recognition can also be found in a petition by John Dee to King James in 1604. Dee felt compelled to defend himself against charges of conjuring long before Harriot. This document has been published in *John Dee: Essential Readings*, ed. Gerald Suster (Wellington: Crucible, 1986). See also Ernest Strathmann, "John Dee as Ralegh's 'Conjuror'" in *Huntington Library Quarterly* 10 (1947): 365–72.

35. Alexander Whitaker, *Good News from Virginia* (London, 1612), G3.

36. John Aubrey, *Brief Lives*, I. 285.

37. William Shakespeare, *Henry IV Part 1*, ed. David Bevington (Oxford: Oxford University Press, 1987).

38. The complete line of the poem reads: "And who, in time, knowes whither we may vent/The treasure of our tongue, to what strange shores/This gaine of our best glory shall be sent" (957–59). Samuel Daniel, *Musophilus; containing a general defense of all learning* (West Lafayette: Purdue University Studies, 1965).

39. Andrew Hadfield refers to Harriot's display with the useful phrase, the "metaphysics of technology." See "Writing the 'New World': More 'Invisible Bullets'" in *Literature and History* 2, second series (1991): 3–19. On Harriot's emphasis on visual perception, see Bruce R. Smith, "Mouthpieces: Native American Voices in Thomas Harriot's True and Brief Report (sic) of . . . Vir-

ginia, Gaspar Pérez de Villagra's Historia de la Nuevo México, and John Smith's General History of Virginia," *New Literary History* 32:3 (2001): 501–17.

40. Harriot's role here is not unlike the one he and John Dee played as mathematicians or conjurors in England. The "simple sort" in England were, like the indigenous in Virginia, often mystified by the work of natural philosophers and mathematicians. See J. Peter Zetterberg, "The Mistaking of 'the Mathematicks' for Magic in Tudor and Stuart England," *Sixteenth Century Journal* XI, No.1 (1980): 83–97. Peter French discusses John Dee's relation to popular conceptions of mathematics at length. See also Frances Yates, *Theatre of the World* (Chicago: University of Chicago Press, 1969).

41. For example, Mario Biagioli has shown that Galileo's discoveries of the moons around Jupiter came in handy for the Medici court. See *Galileo Courtier* (Chicago: University of Chicago Press, 1993).

42. Robert Laneham, *A Letter Describing the Entertainment of the Queen at Kenilworth* (1575), reprinted in William Shakespeare, *A Midsummer Night's Dream*, eds. Gail Kern Paster and Skiles Howard (Boston: Bedford, 1999), 129. Fireworks were a rarity in the early modern period. They typically appeared only at festivals of state such as the entry of Maximilian II into Nuremberg in 1570. For an illustrated history, see Susan Boorsch, *Fireworks! Four Centuries of Pyrotechnics in Prints and Drawings* (New York: Metropolitan Museum, 2000).

43. Shirley, *Thomas Harriot: A Biography*, 255.

44. Sir Humphrey Gilbert, "Queen Elizabeth's Academy," 4–5.

45. For more on Harriot's connection to Gresham college, geography, universities, and the state, see Leslie Cormack, *Charting an Empire* (Chicago: University of Chicago Press, 1997).

46. The bond is reprinted in Leah Marcus et. al., eds., *Elizabeth I: Collected Works* (Chicago: University of Chicago Press, 2000), 183–85.

47. Blaise Pascal, *Pensées*, trans. Honor Levi (Oxford: Oxford University Press, 1995), 148.

48. I am indebted to Julie Solomon, who points out that "Harriot here reads European religious desire into the gesture of the Indian, but in so doing, he reduces Christian faith to pantomime, finding religious truth in ignorance and a gesture of faith in friendly mimcry." Harriot, she says, is in danger of reducing religion to a "farce." See Solomon, "'To Know, To Fly, To Conjure,'" 539.

49. See "Richard Mulcaster's account of Queen Elizabeth's Speech and Prayer" in Marcus et al., *Elizabeth I: Collected Works*, 55.

50. William Peetz links the idea of the fetish to early modern colonial encounters. See "The Problem of the Fetish I" *RES* 9 (1983): 5–17.

51. Machiavelli has often mistakenly been characterized as an atheist for his idea that religion can and should be used as a means of civic or military discipline. Elizabethans tended to make this fallacy. Harriot does follow Machiavelli in treating religion as a form of civic discipline and political manipulation (see discussion below).

52. See Felix Raab, *The English Face of Machiavelli* (London: Routledge, 1964), 51–76.

53. Ralegh's interest in Machiavelli can be found in his "Cabinet Council" and "Maxims of State." Ralegh had a popular reputation as a Machiavellian. See Christopher Hill, *Intellectual Origins of the English Revolution* (Oxford: Clarendon Press, 1980).

54. Niccolo Machiavelli, *The Prince and the Discourses* (New York: Modern Library, 1950), 150.

55. See Edward Rosen, "Harriot's Science: The Intellectual Background," in *Thomas Harriot, Renaissance Scientist*, Shirley, ed., 4.

56. See Niccolo Machiavelli, *The Prince*, trans. George Bull (New York: Penguin Books, 1961), 101.

57. See Bernard Sheehan, *Savagism and Civility* (Cambridge: Cambridge University Press, 1980).

58. *The Complete Essays of Montaigne*, trans. Donald Frame (Stanford: Stanford University Press, 1965),156.

59. For more on Montaigne and ethnography, see William M. Hamlin, "On Continuties between Skepticism and Early Ethnography; Or, Montaigne's Providential Diversity," *Sixteenth-Century Journal* 31:2 (2000): 361–79.

60. Peter Martyr, *De Orbe Novo: the Eight Decades of Peter Martyr D'Anghera*, trans. Francis MacNutt. 2 Volumes (New York: Putnam and Sons, 1912), I: 103–4.

61. See Arthur Barlowe, "The First Voyage to the Country Now Called Virginia" (1584) in Richard Hakluyt, *Voyages and Discoveries*, ed. Jack Beeching (New York: Penguin Books, 1972), 274.

62. English colonialism was largely undermined by its dependence on the indigenous for the bare necessities. For example, Ralph Lane reported that the English almost starved to death because they were dependent on the natives. See "Ralph Lane's Discourse on the First Colony," in Quinn, *Roanoke Voyages*, I, 265–68.

63. Denise Albanese points out that this narrative link of the Picts and Europeans denies "the non-European specificity of the Virginia Indian." See *New Science, New World* (Durham, N.C.: Duke University Press, 1996), 28. See also Jonathan Goldberg's brief analysis of Harriot's historical and sexual tropes in "The History That Will Be," in *Premodern Sexualities*, ed. Louise Fradenburg and Carla Freccero (New York: Routledge, 1996), 3–21.

64. As Kenneth Andrews notes, the English did not simply think the Indians were "irredeemably savage." The documents reveal "mixed thoughts and feelings. Contempt alternates with respect for their mental, physical and moral qualities." Kenneth Andrews, *Trade, Plunder, and Settlement: Maritime Enterprise and the Genesis of the British Empire, 1480–1630* (Cambridge: Cambridge University Press, 1984), 38.

65. Chapman's connections to Marlowe, Harriot, Ralegh, and his interest in the most advanced natural philosophy of his day once made some scholars believe he was part of an atheistic "school of night." Muriel Bradbrook believed that Shakespeare in *Love's Labour's Lost* was poking fun of an actual organized society of free-thinkers, a "School of Night" that included literary as well as scientific exchange. The literary figures she lists are Marlowe, Chapman, Royden, and Warner. Even if the idea of a "school" is now hard to defend for lack of evidence, it is important to consider Harriot's intellectual

circle. See Muriel Bradbrook, *The School of Night: a Study in the Literary Relationships of Sir Walter Ralegh* (Cambridge: Cambridge University Press, 1936).

66. Laura Stevenson shows how popular Elizabethan literature celebrated merchants in an aristocratic language: "The labels Elizabethan authors attached to men of trade, in other words, reveal that they never sought to consolidate the social consciousness of these men by appealing to bourgeois values. Elizabethan praise of bourgeois men was expressed in the rhetoric— and by extension, in the terms of social paradigms—of the aristocracy." See Laura Stevenson, *Praise and Paradox: Merchants and Craftsmen in Elizabethan Popular Literature* (Cambridge: Cambridge University Press, 1984), 6.

67. "To my admired and soule-loved Friend," in Bartlett, ed., *The Poems of George Chapman.*

68. "De Guiana, Carmen Epicum" in Bartlett, ed., *The Poems of George Chapman.*

69. As in Ralegh's *Discoverie of Guiana*, the topos of the land as female body encourages the conquest. See the analysis of this topos by Louis Montrose in "The Work of Gender in the Discourse of Discoverie," *Representations* 33 (1991): 1–41. See also Shannon Miller, *Invested with Meaning* (Philadelphia: University of Pennsylvania Press, 1998).

70. The poems echo the ideas of Richard Hakluyt's dedicatory letter to Ralegh, which discusses Virginia and Queen Elizabeth: "There yet remain for you new lands, ample realms, unknown peoples; they wait yet, I say, to be discovered and subdued, quickly and easily, under the happy auspices of your arms and enterprise, and the sceptre of our most serene Elizabeth, Empress—as even the Spaniard himself admits—of the Ocean." Hakluyt's letter invokes a Homeric, epic desire for the English to establish fame. "Up then, go on as you have begun," he tells Ralegh, "leave to posterity an imperishable monument of your name and fame, such as age will never obliterate." See Richard Hakluyt, "Dedication of Peter Martyr," 367, 368.

71. Chapman's poem may well be alluding to alchemical experiments by Harriot, Ralegh, and the Wizard Earl, which, much to the dismay of whiggish historians of science, continued well into the Jacobean period. The "clear eyes" of the dedicatory poem reminds us of Harriot's work on optics, including his discovery of sunspots and his drawings of craters on the moon. Even though this research has been overshadowed by Galileo, it has left him with a better reputation as a contributor to the "scientific revolution." See Dr. E. Strout, "The very first maps and drawings of the moon," *Journal of the British Astronomical Association* 75 (1965).

72. Captain John Davis. *The Seaman's Secrets* (London, 1595), 2.

73. See, for example, *Nennio, or a Treatise of Nobility,* where the quality of baseness is debated. Virtue and learning as well as blood are used to assess the meaning of "nobility." Giovanni Batista Nenna, *Nennio or A Treatise of Nobility,* trans. William Jones (1595), facsimile ed. (Jerusalem: Israel Universities Press, 1967).

74. Sir Walter Ralegh, *The Discoverie of the Large, Rich, and Beautiful Empire of Guiana* in Richard Hakluyt, *The Principal Navigations,* 12 vols. (Glasgow, J. Maclehose and Sons, 1903–5), x. 406.

75. Daniel Defert theorizes this shift: "No doubt the voyage of discovery should be situated historically between the medieval crusades which it miniaturises and the organization of the laboratory." See "The Collection of the World: Accounts of Voyages From the Sixteenth to the Eighteenth Centuries," *Dialectical Anthropology* 7:1 (1982): 12.

76. William Cronon points out that the English focused almost exclusively on the natural objects that they could make a profit on: "Descriptions framed on such a basis were bound to say as much about the markets of Europe as they did about the ecology of New England." See *Changes in the Land: Indians, Colonists, and the Ecology of New England* (New York: Hill and Wang, 1983), 20.

77. William Shakespeare, *The Tempest*, ed. Stephen Orgel (Oxford: Oxford University Press, 1987).

78. Bacon's science, which advocates the massive collections of facts about nature as part of an inductive process, would find inspiration in collections of wonder—human and natural—brought from the New World.

79. On cabinets of curiosity, see Anthony Allen Shelton, "Cabinets of Transgression: Renaissance Collections and the Incorporation of the New World" in *The Cultures of Collecting*, eds. John Elsner and Roger Cardinal (Cambridge: Harvard University Press, 1994), 177–291. See also Margaret Hodgen, *Early Anthropology in the Sixteenth and Seventeenth Centuries* (Philadelphia: University of Pennsylvania Press, 1964).

Chapter 3. "Religion hides many things from suspicion"

1. Francis Bacon, "An Advertisement touching the Controversies of the Church of England" in Vickers, ed., *Francis Bacon*, 1.

2. "An exhortation, concerning good order and obedience, to rulers and Magistrates," reprinted in Arthur Kinney, ed., *Elizabethan Backgrounds* (Connecticut: Archon Books, 1975).

3. See, for example, Lisa Hopkins, *Marlowe: A Literary Life* (New York: Palgrave, 2000).

4. The passage is from *The Pilgrimage to Parnassus*, a play performed at Cambridge nine years after Marlowe's death. Quoted in David Riggs, "Marlowe's Quarrel with God" in *Marlowe, History, and Sexuality*, ed. Paul Whitfield White (New York: AMS Press, 1998), 15.

5. The charges by Kyd are reprinted in Constance Kuriyama, *Christopher Marlowe: A Renaissance Life* (Ithaca: Cornell University Press, 2002), 228–31.

6. See Constance Kuriyama, *Christopher Marlowe: A Renaissance Life*, 40–43.

7. For an outline of these plots, see Alison Plowden, *The Elizabethan Secret Service* (New York: St. Martin's Press, 1991). On the paranoia of the day, see Lacey Baldwin Smith, *Treason in Tudor England* (London: Jonathan Cape, 1986).

8. For more details on Marlowe's spying, see Charles Nicholl, *The Reckoning* (Chicago: University of Chicago Press, 1992).

9. See Curtis C. Breight, *Surveillance, Militarism and Drama in the Elizabethan Era* (New York: St. Martin's Press, 1996).

10. See Hammer's discussion of those implicated in the murder of Marlowe in "A Reckoning Reframed: the 'Murder' of Christopher Marlowe revisited,"*ELR* 26:2 (1996): 225–42. His essay serves as yet another blow against the theory that Ralegh was part of an organized group (the "school of night") of unorthodox or atheistical thinkers. Part of that theory was based on the notion that Marlowe's murder was planned by Essex and his circle and that Ralegh's circle was opposed to Essex.

11. The confession is reprinted, translated, and analyzed in Roy Kendall, "Richard Baines and Christopher Marlowe's Milieu," *ELR* 24:3 (autumn 1994): 507–52.

12. Paul Kocher made the most assertive claim for the relevance of the Baines document to Marlowe's art, calling it the "master key to the mind of Marlowe." Kocher's exegesis of all the documents on Marlowe and his plays suggests that the Baines testimony does in fact reveal a great deal about Marlowe's oeuvre. See Paul Kocher, *Christopher Marlowe: A Study of his Thought, Learning, and Character* (New York: Russell and Russell, 1962). Roy Kendall has modified Kocher's work, arguing that Baines and Marlowe held similar views and that Baines may well have been a mentor for Marlowe at Cambridge in the 1580s.

13. *The Geneva Bible*, 13:1. All quotations from the Bible in this chapter are from *The Geneva Bible*, facsimile of the 1560 edition (Madison: University of Wisconsin Press, 1969).

14. David Riggs, "Marlowe's Quarrel with God," 24. Riggs, examining the "discursive framework within which a figure like Marlowe could be produced," points out that the "right question is not 'was he or wasn't he' [an atheist] but rather 'Why Marlowe?'"(19).

15. Robert Burton, *The Anatomy of Melancholy* (1621), ed. Holbrook Jackson (1930; rpt. , New York: New York Review of Books, 2001), 328.

16. Luther attacks the Catholic ceremony as an empty ritual: "Let us confine ourselves to the very words by which Christ instituted and completed the sacrament, and commended it to us." See "The Pagan Servitude of the Church," in John Dillenberger, ed., *Martin Luther: Selections from His Writings* (New York: Anchor Press, 1961), 271.

17. John Davies, Epigram 82 in *The Scourge of Folly* (London, 1611).

18. C. G., "The minte of deformities" (London, 1600).

19. Jonathan Goldberg makes the compelling argument that Marlowe's identity "was constituted as an Otherness" and that the Baines' note "locates a place for a homosexual identity in Elizabethan society." Marlowe's "double agency," then, helps us understand the marginal place of the stage and the radical views of religion, power, and politics in such documents and in Marlowe's oeuvre. Jonathan Goldberg, "Sodomy and Society: The Case of Christopher Marlowe," in *Staging the Renaissance*, ed. David Scott Kastan and Peter Stallybrass (New York: Routledge, 1991).

20. Marlowe's bad boy reputation was revived on stage in the 1990s in

New York, when the Target Margin Theater Company's ambitious production of his plays made him look like our rebellious postmodern contemporary. See Celia Wren, "A 400-Year-Old Bad Boy stages a Comeback," *New York Times*, 21 January 2001.

21. Quoted in Burton, *Anatomy of Melancholy*, 329.

22. On the coronation ceremony, see C. G. Bayne, "The Coronation of Queen Elizabeth," in *EHR* 22 (1907): 650–73; quotation is from 662.

23. On the history of the Eucharist, see Miri Rubin, *Corpus Christi* (Cambridge: Cambridge University Press, 1991).

24. *The Geneva Bible*, 11:7–8.

25. See, for example, Johann Weyer's reading of Exodus in George Mora, MD, ed., *De praestigiis daemonum* in*Witches, Devils, and Doctors in the Renaissance: Johann Weyer, De Praestigiis daemonum* (Binghamton, N.Y.: Medieval and Renaissance Texts and Studies, 1991), 82.

26. The term "ambodexter" was coined by Thomas Nashe. Referring to the word "intelligencer" used by Gabriel Harvey to describe Thomas Bodley, Nashe said "The hellish detested Judas name of intelligencer" had been "registered in print for such a flearing false brother or ambodexter." Quoted in Charles Nicholl, *The Reckoning*, 106.

27. See Conyers Read, *Sir Francis Walsingham* (Cambridge: Harvard University Press, 1925), II: 410. Many Elizabethan spies had ambiguous religious affiliations, especially Baines himself.

28. I will be focusing here on religious doubt in *Doctor Faustus*. Readers will also want to engage William Hamlin's recent essay on Pyrrhonist skepticism in the play. See William Hamlin, "Casting Doubt in Marlowe's *Doctor Faustus*," in *SEL* 41:2 (2001).

29. See Keith Thomas, *Religion and the Decline of Magic*, 254–56.

30. George Gifford, *A Discourse of the subtill Practises of Devilles by Witches* (London, 1587), Biir.

31. This is the reading presented by Gerald Strauss in "How to read a Volksbuch: The Faust Book of 1587," in *Faust through Four Centuries* (Tübingen: Max Niemeyer Verlag, 1989), 27–41.

32. Critics have generally been split on whether the play is transgressive and heterodox or moralistic and orthodox. I will be following the tradition that emphasizes the play's challenge to orthodoxy. For a discussion of "transgression," see Jonathan Dollimore, *Radical Tragedy* (Durham, N.C.: Duke University Press, 1993), 109–19. The term "overreacher" became widely used after Harry Levin's classic work on Marlowe. See *The Overreacher: A Study of Christopher Marlowe* (Boston: Beacon Press, 1964).

33. For more on Dee's various magical practices, see Peter French, *John Dee: the World of an Elizabethan Magus* (New York: Dorset Press, 1972), 78. Nicholas H. Clulee and William Sherman have exposed the limitations of the "myth of the magus" proposed by French and Yates. See Clulee, *John Dee's Natural Philosophy* (London: Routledge, 1988) and Sherman, *John Dee* (Amherst: University of Massachusetts Press, 1995). Sherman offers an alternative portrait that reveals Dee's multiple social and professional roles, calling attention to the international mercantile, geographical, political movements that were vital for Dee.

34. In a letter to "the King's most excellent Majestie" in 1604, Dee asked King James to put him on trial for the crime of sorcery. "If by any due, true, and just meanes, the said name of Conjurer, or Caller, or Invocator of Divels, or damned Spirits, can be proved," he pleaded, then he might be stoned to death, buried alive, or burned at the stake. Dee wanted once and for all to be rid of the reputation that had plagued him throughout his life and up to his death in 1608. He was not granted this opportunity and his bad reputation remained with him until the end. Indeed, the label "Conjurer" was spread to others interested in the occult, including, as we have seen, Thomas Harriot. See John Dee, "To the King's most excellent Majestie" (London, 1604).

35. See James Orchard Halliwell, *A Collection of Letters* (London: Historical Society, 1965).

36. John Dee, *General and Rare Memorials Pertaining to the Perfect Arte of Navigation* (London, 1577), facsimile rpt. (New York: Da Capo Press, 1968), "An Advertisement to the Reader." Dee apparently coined the term "British Empire." Bruce Ward Henry argues that the term originated from "a web of relations," which includes John Dee, Abraham Ortelius (the leading cartographer in Europe), and the Welshman Humphrey Llwyd.

37. John Dee, *General and Rare Memorials*, "An Advertisement to the Reader."

38. Dee saw his Christian cabalistic Neoplatonism as a worldwide reforming movement. Desperate to legitimize his magic, Dee thought that globalization would help unify a tolerant Christianity. For more on this movement, See Frances Yates, *The Occult Philosophy in the Elizabethan Age* (London: Routledge, 1979).

39. For more details, see the essays in *Hermeticism in the Renaissance*, eds. Ingrid Merkel and Allen G. Debus (Washington: Folger Books, 1988).

40. Quoted in Peter French, *John Dee: the World of an Elizabethan Magus*, 78.

41. Miri Rubin, *Corpus Christi*, 112.

42. All quotations of the play are from Christopher Marlowe, *Dr. Faustus*, ed. Roma Gill (London: A&C Black, 1989). Gill follows the A text and provides appendices with excerpts from the B text. On the two texts of the play, see Leah Marcus, *Unediting the Renaissance*.

43. For more on the crisis of authority in the Reformation, see Robert Weimann, *Authority and Representation in Early Modern Discourse* (Baltimore: Johns Hopkins University Press, 1996).

44. C. L. Barber has shown that magic might be seen as a substitute for the carnal pleasure of the Eucharist in a society which placed a new emphasis on individual, psychological life and reduced the function of ceremony along with the physical embodiment of religious desire: "In dramatizing Faustus's motives for the pact and his subservience to it, he brings to bear a profound understanding, including bodily understanding, of the predicaments of Protestant theology and of tensions involved in Protestant worship, especially in the service of Holy Communion." C. L. Barber, *Creating Elizabethan Tragedy: the Theater of Marlowe and Kyd* (Chicago: University of Chicago Press, 1988), 88.

45. See Christopher Haigh, ed., *The Reign of Elizabeth I* (Athens: Univeristy of Georgia Press, 1985), 198.

46. Luther, "The Pagan Servitude of the Church," 271.

47. Ibid., 301.

48. Louis Montrose relates the Baines note to the Protestant demystification of Catholic civic spectacle: "As must have been evident to Marlowe and to some of his fellow subjects, including Wotton, the Elizabethan regime made a concerted effort to implement its own ceremonies of mystification, and did so precisely by appropriating and elaborating, in a largely secular context, the ritual and iconic aspects of Catholic worship." See *The Purpose of Playing*, 61.

49. See Rubin, *Corpus Christi*, 243–70.

50. For an Elizabethan description of the procession preceding the coronation ceremony, see "Richard Mulcaster's account of Queen Elizabeth's speech and prayer during her passage through London to Westminster the Day before her coronation," in Marcus et al., eds., *Elizabeth I : Collected Works*, 53–55.

51. Marlowe's plays often present radical shifts from the lofty or exuberant rhetoric of transcendence to the most earthly or base desires. In *Tamburlaine,* for example, we see the striving of "aspiring minds" become in a few short lines the desire for "the sweet fruition of an earthly crown." For many of Marlowe's protagonists, endless sensual appetites, egoism, and fantasies of libertinism are not firmly bounded by natural law or a providential order. For a discussion of these aspects of *Tamburlaine*, see D. J. Palmer, "Marlowe's Naturalism" in *Christopher Marlowe* (Mermaid Critical Commentaries), ed. Brian Morris (New York: Norton, 1968) and Michael Quinn, "The Freedom of Tamburlaine," in *MLQ* 21 (1960): 315–20.

52. Frances Yates, *Giordano Bruno and the Hermetic Tradition* (Chicago: University of Chicago Press, 1964), 45. Frances Yates correctly insists that the play turns magic into witchcraft and places limits on the aspiring Neoplatonic mind. See Frances Yates, *The Occult Philosophy in the Elizabethan Age* (London: Routledge, 1979), 115–27.

53. "Asclepius," in *Hermetica*, ed. Brian Copenhaver (Cambridge: Cambridge University Press, 1992), 69.

54. Yates, *Giordano Bruno*, 116.

55. Pico, who was compelled to insist in an apology that Christ did not use magic, suggests that the link between magic and divinity was treacherous. On the status of miracles in Protestant theology, see D. P. Walker, "The Cessation of Miracles," in *Hermeticism in the Renaissance*, 111–24.

56. Because we do not find comic prose like this designed for a clown in Marlowe's other plays, it is likely that the scenes with the clown, which are more extensive in the B-text, were written with a collaborator. For more on this collaboration, see Roma Gill's introduction to the New Mermaids edition and David Bevington's introduction to *Doctor Faustus and Other Plays* (Oxford: Oxford University Press, 1995).

57. See William Empson, *Faustus and the Censor* (Oxford: Basil Blackwell, 1987).

58. We should also note Marlowe's apparent interest in the heretical religion of Arian, a variation of unitarianism which denied the Holy Trinity and argued that Jesus was human. Marlowe's roomate Thomas Kyd, authorities

discovered, possessed a document praising Arianism in his home, and, when interrogated, insisted that the text belonged to Marlowe.

59. In his dialogue, *The Expulsion of the Triumphant Beast*, Bruno sees the Egyptians as the great practitioners of a natural religion. See Giordano Bruno, *The Expulsion of the Triumphant Beast*, trans. Arthur D. Imerti (Lincoln: University of Nebraska, 1964).

60. Scot, *Discoverie of Witchcraft*, 262.

61. Quoted in Richard Dutton, *Mastering the Revels* (Iowa City: University of Iowa Press, 1991), 77.

62. "The icy water of egoistic calculation," Marx points out in *The Communist Manifesto*, replaces many forms of religious mystification and charismatic authority found in the middle ages. Karl Marx, "The Communist Manifesto" in Robert C. Tucker, ed., *The Karl Marx Reader* (New York: Norton, 1978), 475.

63. All quotations of the play are from *The Jew of Malta*, ed. James R. Siemon (London: A&C Black, 1994).

64. See ibid., 15.

65. For more on the play's anti-Semitism, see Stephen Greenblatt, "Marlowe, Marx, and Anti-Semitism," in *Learning to Curse* (New York: Routledge, 1990).

66. The stereotype of the avaricious Jew can be traced back to Christian hostility toward Jewish moneylenders in the middle ages. See Frank Felsenstein, *Anti-Semitic Stereotypes* (Baltimore: Johns Hopkins University Press, 1995).

67. Sir Walter Ralegh, "The Discoverie of the Large, Rich, and Beautiful Empire of Guiana . . ." *The Principal Navigations, Voyages, Traffiques and Discoveries of the English Nation*, ed. Richard Hakluyt. Vol. 10 (Glasgow: James MacLehose and Sons, 1904), 430.

68. Quoted in L. C. Knights, *Drama and Society in the Age of Jonson* (New York: Norton, 1937), 146.

69. See Norman Jones, *God and the Moneylenders: Usury and Law in Early Modern England* (London: Basil Blackwell, 1989), 55.

70. Thomas Wilson, *A Discourse Upon Usury*, ed. R. H. Tawney (London: G. Bell and Sons, 1925), 361–62.

71. Ibid., 177.

72. Jones, *God and the Moneylenders*, 199–205.

73. It is possible that Marlowe included this figure in part because he shared some of his transgressive ideas. In an admonition from his deathbed, Robert Greene, recognizing one of Marlowe's most subversive ideas, charged him with the following: "what are his rules but meere confused mockeries, able to extirpate in small time, the generation of mankinde. For if Sic volo, sic iubeo, hold in those that are able to command: and if it be lawfull Fas et nefas to doe any thing that is beneficall." According to Greene, Marlowe tried to undermine religion by subsuming morality and natural law under the higher principles of personal power and political policy.

74. Robert Burton, *Anatomy of Melancholy*, 328.

75. For an exploration of English readings of Machiavelli, see Felix Raab, *English Face of Machiavelli* and N. W. Bawcutt, "Machiavelli and Marlowe's

The Jew of Malta" in *Renaissance Drama* (Evanston: Northwestern University Press, 1970), 3–49.

76. Harold Jenkins, editor of the Arden edition of Hamlet, directs us to Matthew 10:29 and Calvin's commentary. In the *Institutes of the Christian Religion*, Calvin writes, "Whence Christ, when he declared that not even a tiny sparrow of little worth falls to earth without the Father's will, immediately applies it in this way. . . ." John Calvin, *Calvin: Institutes of the Christian Religion* (Latin original 1559), trans. Ford Lewis Battles, ed. John T. McNeill (Philadelphia: Westminster Press, 1960), 218–19.

77. Such celebration of the private and personal pleasures of economic gain also resonates with the market ideology developed in later centuries. In *The Passions and the Interests*, Hirschman argues that in the seventeenth century we can find the notion that "interest" (including economic advantage) could be enhanced with the control of other passions such as sexual lust or ambition. See Albert O. Hirschman, *The Passions and the Interests* (Princeton: Princeton University Press, 1977).

78. See L. C. Knights, *Drama and Society in the Age of Jonson*. Building on Knight's work, Don Wayne has added a more nuanced reading of Ben Jonson's plays in relation to the emerging market. See Don E. Wayne, "Drama and Society in the Age of Jonson: Shifting Grounds of Authority and Judgment in Three Major Comedies," *Renaissance Drama* (Evanston, Ill.: Northwestern University Press and The Newberry Library for Renaissance Studies, 1990), 3–29. On the rise of individualism, see Joyce Appleby, *Economic Thought and Ideology in Seventeenth-Century England* (Princeton: Princeton University Press, 1978), Alan Macfarlane, *The Origins of English Individualism* (New York: Cambridge University Press, 1978), and C. B. Macpherson, *The Political Theory of Possessive Individualism* (Oxford: Oxford University Press, 1962).

79. Craig Muldrew makes a strong case that the prevalence of "self-interest" in the early market society has been exaggerated. He points out that "contemporaries did not, in fact, understand marketing through the use of a language which stressed self-interest, but rather one which stressed credit relations, trust, obligation and contracts." Muldrew notes, for example, that informal relationships of credit and trust were essential to early modern life. The market, then, did not necessarily undermine communal relations; in fact, it may have tightened them. See Craig Muldrew, "The ethics of credit and community relations" in *Social History* 18:2 (1993): 163–83.

80. Thomas Wilson, *A Discourse on Usury*, 177.

81. Bob Hodge argues that Ferneze is the "real Machiavellian prince" since "he is a consummate user of conventional pieties to cloak ruthless action on behalf of the state." See "Marlowe, Marx and Machiavelli: Reading into the Past" in *Literature, Language and Society in England*, eds. David Aers et al. (Dublin: Gill and Macmillan, 1981), 7.

82. Karl Marx, "The Communist Manifesto," 476.

83. Sloterdijk makes a distinction between ancient kynicism and modern cynicism: kynicism makes use of the body in a joyful satire of people in power while modern cynicism, which has lost its connection to the embodied cheekiness of Diogenes and his disciples, is less a vehicle of anarchic social

protest than a support for those in power. Peter Sloterdijk, *Critique of Cynical Reason* (Minneapolis: University of Minnesota Press, 1987), 4.

84. Barabas falls into the predicament developed by Slavoj Zizek's elaboration of Sloterdijk: "Cynical distance is just one way—one of many ways—to blind ourselves to the structuring power of ideological fantasy: even if we do not take things seriously, even if we keep an ironical distance, we are still doing them." Slavoj Žižek, *The Sublime Object of Ideology* (London: Verso, 1989), 33.

85. Sextus Empiricus, *Outlines of Scepticism*, 38.

86. Jean-Christophe Agnew, *Worlds Apart* (Cambridge: Cambridge University Press, 1986), 111.

87. Agnew calls the new market "placeless" because it was no longer strictly based on concrete exchange in a given place. Supply and demand in a self-regulating market made the exchange of goods more abstract and less dependent on the use-values of local bartering.

88. William Harrison, *A Description of England* (London, 1577).

89. See Lawrence Stone, "Social Mobility in England, 1500–1700" in *Seventeenth-Century England: Society in an Age of Revolution*, ed. Paul S. Seaver (New York: New Viewpoints, 1976).

Chapter 4. "And that's true too"

1. All quotations of *King Lear* are from *The Arden Shakespeare*: William Shakespeare, *King Lear*, ed. R. A. Foakes (London: Routledge, 1997). I have noted variation in Quarto and Folio where it is significant to the argument of the essay. Most critics and textual scholars agree that there is no authentic or original text of the play available. The reader is compelled to accept something like the ancient skeptic's method of equipollence: the use of the Quarto must be set in balance with the use of the Folio.

2. Thomas Dekker, *The Wonderful Yeare* (London, 1603).

3. Sextus Empiricus, *Outlines on Skepticism*, 51.

4. Stanley Cavell, "The Avoidance of Love," in *Disowning Knowledge* (Cambridge: Cambridge University Press, 1987), 39–123.

5. There is an extensive body of criticism on *Lear* and the "transition" from feudalism to capitalism. One of the finest essays on *Lear* and economic history can be found in Richard Halpern, *The Poetics of Primitive Accumulation*. See also Paul Delany, "King Lear and the Decline of Feudalism," *PMLA* 92 (1977): 429–40; James H. Kavanagh, "Shakespeare in Ideology" in *Alternative Shakespeares*, ed. John Drakakis (London: Methuen, 1985), 144–66; John Turner, "The Tragic Romances of Feudalism" in *Shakespeare: The Play of History* (Iowa City: University of Iowa Press, 1988), 85–150. Turner offers one of the most satisfactory accounts of the "transition": "the true subject of *King Lear* . . . is not an old order succumbing to a new but an old order succumbing to its own internal contradictions" (101).

6. All quotations of *Timon of Athens* are from The Arden Shakespeare: William Shakespeare, *Timon of Athens*, ed. H. J. Oliver (London: Routledge, 1959).

7. Ben Jonson, "To Penshurst," in *Ben Jonson* ed. Ian Donaldson (Oxford: Oxford University Press, 1985), 284. For a study of Ben Jonson and economic change in England, see Don E. Wayne, *Penshurst: The Semiotics of Place and the Poetics of History* (Madison: University of Wisconsin Press, 1984).

8. The debates from the period suggest that blood or birth might be considered only one crucial determination of nobility. In addition to the extensive literature from the period, see J. P. Cooper, *Land, Men, and Beliefs: Studies in Early-Modern History* (London: Hambledon Press, 1985).

9. Gerard de Malynes, *Saint George for England* (London, 1601), 47.

10. Sextus Empiricus, *Outlines on Scepticism*, 26.

11. See also the fascinating analysis of this passage by Karl Marx. Following Shakespeare's lead, Marx says that money "overturns" social bonds and flips the world "upsidedown," but he does not appear to accept the idea that the bonds of society were really "essences in themselves" prior to capitalism. See Karl Marx, *Economic and Philosophical Manuscripts of 1844* in *The Marx-Engels Reader*, ed. Robert C. Tucker 105. See also Hannah Arendt's notion of "expropriation" in *The Human Condition*. She argues that Cartesian doubt (hence modern interiority or subjectivity) was the historical product of the expropriation of land (e.g., the dissolution of the monasteries in England), the "closing-in process" after New World exploration, and the invention of the telescope. Moreover, the radical doubt about sense-perception was the result of the collapse of communal structures and the advent of commercial capitalism. Hannah Arendt, *The Human Condition* (Chicago: University of Chicago Press, 1958).

12. John Florio, *The Essays of Montaigne Done into English* (London: D. Nutt, 1892–93), III: 228.

13. Ibid., II: 364.

14. The classic intellectual history of Renaissance pessimism is Hiram Haydn, *The Counter-Renaissance* (New York: Grove Press, 1950). For a more recent, theoretically informed account, see Jonathan Dollimore, *Radical Tragedy* (Durham, N.C.: Duke University Press, 1993). For more on the play's pessimism, see Rolf Soellner, *Timon of Athens* (Columbus: Ohio State University Press, 1979).

15. Caroline Spurgeon, *Shakespeare's Imagery and What It Tells Us* (Cambridge: At the University Press, 1935), 198.

16. Sir John Davies incorporated the decay of nature idea in his skeptical philosophical poem, *Nosce Teipsum*: "And yet alas, when all our lampes are burned,/Our bodyes wasted, and our spirits spent;/When we have all the learnèd volumes turn'd,/ Which yeeld mens wits both help and ornament:/ What can we know? Or what can we diescerne?" Sir John Davies, *The Complete Works*, ed. Alexander Erosert (1878, rpt. New York: AMS Press, 1967), 46–47.

17. Aristotle, *Politics*, trans. H. Rackham (Cambridge: Harvard University Press, 1932), 51.

18. Lawrence Stone, *Crisis of the Aristocracy 1558–1641*, 87.

19. Francis Bacon, "Of Usury," in Vickers, *Francis Bacon*, 421.

20. On economic change in Tudor and Stuart England, see Barry Coward, *The Stuart Age* (London: Longman, 1994). On *Timon of Athens* and economic

change, see E. C. Pettet, "*Timon of Athens*: The Disruption of Feudal Morality" *R.E.S.* 23:92 (1947) and Kenneth Muir, "*Timon of Athens* and the Cash-Nexus," *Modern Quarterly Miscellany* 1:1 (1947): 57–76.

21. William Elton points out that for Jacobeans, Edmund would represent an Epicurean and hence "atheistic" challenge to Christian beliefs. See William R. Elton's classic *King Lear and the Gods* (Lexington: University Press of Kentucky, 1988).

22. Sir Thomas Smith, *De Republica Anglorum* (1583), ed. Mary Dewar (Cambridge: Cambridge University Press, 1982), 78.

23. Quoted in J. P. Cooper, *Land, Men, and Beliefs*, 55.

24. Christopher Hill, *The Century of Revolution 1603–1714* (Edinburgh: Thomas Nelson and Sons, 1961), 105.

25. On socioeconomic mobility, see Lawrence Stone, *Crisis of the Aristocracy*, 22–23.

26. Weimann's term "platea" describes the "unlocalized 'place'" in opposition to the "locus," the illusionistic scaffold of the great-folk. Certain characters like Edmund or the Fool would be associated with the nonrepresentational mode of the platea-function, granting them an access to the audience not achieved by the symbolic distance of the great-folk. This "unlocalized place" is the site for popular parody or burlesque of figures like the King; it is a site of realism connected to sport or communal mirth and the festivity of the marketplace, street, or village green. Robert Weimann, *Shakespeare and the Popular Tradition* (Baltimore: Johns Hopkins University Press, 1978).

27. On the feudal, economic basis of Lear's madness, see Magreta de Grazia "The ideology of superfluous things: *King Lear* as period piece" in *Subject and Object in Renaissance Culture*, eds. Magreta de Grazia et al. (Cambridge: Cambridge University Press, 1996).

28. See Christopher Hill, *Change and Continuity in 17th-Century England* (New Haven: Yale University Press, 1991), 219–39.

29. "Negation" has had an important position in twentieth-century criticism of *Lear*, particularly in the work of existentialist critics like Jan Kott. Unfortunately, such philosophies of absurdism or nihilism have often failed to place negation in an early modern historical context. Kott makes a strong case that the play is more "grotesque" and "absurd" than it is "cathartic" in the normal sense of tragedy: "The grotesque is a criticism of the absolute in the name of frail human experience. That is why tragedy brings catharsis, while grotesque offers no consolation whatsoever." See Jan Kott, *Shakespeare Our Contemporary*, trans. Boleslaw Taborski (New York: Anchor Books, 1966), 133.

30. A. L. Beier, *Masterless Men*, 4.

31. William Carroll, "'The Base Shall Top Th' Legitimate': The Bedlam Beggar and the Role of Edgar in *King Lear*," *Shakespeare Quarterly* 38 (1987): 432.

32. Harry Berger looks at the "darker" and "darkest" purposes in the ethos of the *Lear* community and recognizes the aggressive aspects of Edgar's behavior. See Harry Berger, "Text against Performance: The Gloucester Family Romance," in *Shakespeare's Rough Magic*, ed. Peter Erickson and Coppélia Kahn (Newark: University of Delaware Press, 1985), 210–29.

33. On this aspect of Edgar's cruelty, see Stanley Cavell, "The Avoidance of Love."

34. Edgar's perspective appears to use the Albertian model of the vanishing point and measurements for the diminished sizes of objects. For a brief Derridean discussion of this scene, see Jonathan Goldberg, "Perspectives: Dover Cliff and Representation," in *Shakespeare and Deconstruction*, eds. Atkins and Bergeron (New York: Peter Lang, 1991). On Jacobean staging and the art of perspective, see Stephen Orgel, "Shakespeare imagines a theater," in *Shakespeare, Man of the Theater*, ed. Kenneth Muir et al. (Newark: University of Delaware Press, 1983).

35. See Paul Slack, *The English Poor Law: 1531–1782* (Cambridge: Cambridge University Press, 1995).

36. The "Apology" is one of the most important sources for *King Lear*. Montaigne's language and themes are deeply interwoven in the play. Nietzsche went so far as to declare that Montaigne was Shakespeare's "model." For a discussion of Florio's Montaigne as a source, see Kenneth Muir's introduction to the second Arden edition of *King Lear*. See also George Coffin Taylor, *Shakspere's Debt to Montaigne* (Cambridge, Mass.: Harvard University Press, 1925).

37. Although Diogenes has not been very popular in recent critical discourse, critics have noted his presence in the past. See Jane Donawerth, "Diogenes the Cynic and Lear's Definition of Man, *King Lear* III.iv.101–109," *ELN* 15 (1977): 10–14. See also the new anthology of essays on the tradition of cynicism, *The Cynics*, ed. R. Bracht Branham and Marie-Odile Goulet-Cazé (Berkeley: University of California Press, 1996).

38. John Florio,*The Essays of Montaigne Done into English*, I:351.

39. See Martin Jay's intellectual history of this metaphor in *Downcast Eyes* (Berkeley: University of California Press, 1993).

40. Sextus Empiricus, *Outlines on Scepticism*, 27.

41. Robert Wood and Robert Bernasconi, eds., *Derrida and Différance* (Evanston, Ill.: Northwestern University Press, 1988), 3.

42. John Florio, *The Essays of Montaigne Done into English*, II: 144.

43. On the theory that specific characters are proleptic of life in a Hobbesian, market society, see John Danby's classic book, *Shakespeare's Doctrine of Nature* (London: Faber and Faber, 1961). The literature on gender roles in *King Lear* is vast. For a subtle, historically informed reading, see Catherine Cox, "'An excellent thing in woman': Virgo and Viragos in *King Lear*," *Modern Philology* 96:2 (1998): 143–57. Like Cox, Claire MacEachern looks carefully at the religious context of the play: see "Figures of Fidelity: Believing in *King Lear*," *Modern Philology* 98:2 (2000): 211–30.

44. See Harvey Cox, *The Feast of Fools* (New York: Harper and Row, 1969) and Mikhail Bakhtin, *Rabelais and His World* (Bloomington: Indiana University Press, 1984).

45. Natalie Davis points out that carnival could provide new ideas for social change, even if it didn't foment revolutionary change. See *Society and Culture in Early Modern France* (Stanford: Stanford University Press, 1975).

46. This prophecy can be found in the Folio but not the Quarto version. Some editors now believe that this an example of revisions made to the

Quarto. See Randal McLeod, "Revision, adaptation, and the fool in *King Lear*" in *The Division of the Kingdoms: Shakespeare's Two Versions of* King Lear, ed. Gary Taylor and Michael Warren (New York: Oxford University Press, 1983).

47. For more on the experimental structure of the Fool's prophecy, see Robert Weimann, *Shakespeare and the Popular Tradition*, 43.

48. In the tragic form of *Lear*, the Fool does not turn the world upside-down as a part of a teleology wherein all is eventually set rightside up. Tragic form calls for a different operation of festive rites than comedy. As critics have shown, the festive structure of comedy allows for accommodation after experimentation, and the reintegration of communal norms. Still, the mad disorder of the play cannot simply be attributed to lessons common in the genre of tragedy. The conclusion of *Gorboduc*, for example, provides a much more certain political and moral message. And we hardly need to be reminded of the frustration numerous generations have felt with the horrific end of *Lear*, which seems to offer no obvious moral guidance, redemption, or hope. Peter Herman has argued, however, that *Gorboduc* also contains skeptical elements as well. See "He Said What?!?': Misdeeming Gorboduc; or, Problematizing Form, Service, and Certainty," *Exemplaria* 13:1 (2001): 287–321.

49. Quoted in Martin Jay, *Downcast Eyes*, 523. The quotation is from "Mémoires d'aveugle: L'autoportrait et autres ruines," catalog of the exhibition at the Louvre's Napoleon Hall, October, 26, 1990–January 21, 1991 (Paris, 1991).

50. Robert Burton, *Anatomy of Melancholy*, 65.

51. John Lyly, *Midas* (London, 1632).

52. For more on skepticism and "value," see Graham Bradshaw, *Shakespeare's Scepticism* (Ithaca: Cornell University Press, 1987).

53. John Calvin, *Calvin's Institutes of the Christian Religion*, 2:93.

CONCLUSION

1. Francis Bacon, "Of Atheism," in Vickers, *Francis Bacon*, 372.

2. See George T. Buckley, *Atheism in the English Renaissance* (New York: Russell and Russell, 1965).

3. See David Wootton, "New Histories of Atheism," in *Atheism from the Reformation to the Enlightenment*, ed. Michael Hunter and David Wootton (Oxford: Clarendon Press, 1992).

4. For example, when James altered diplomatic relations with Spain, England's long-standing enemy, Ralegh maintained a strong anti-Spanish position, a position that angered the newly crowned King.

5. Sir Walter Ralegh, "The Lie," in *Sir Walter Ralegh: Selected Prose and Poetry*, ed. Agnes H. Latham (London: Athlone Press, 1965).

6. Ralegh's religious views are complex and lie beyond the scope of this study. Scholars have had differing views on the nature of Ralegh's skepticism. Ernest Strathmann sees him as a "free-thinker" but also points to the religious orthodoxy of Ralegh's *History of the World*. Christopher Hill and

Stephen Greenblatt take issue with Strathmann's position, however, by giving more emphasis to Ralegh's heterodoxy. See Strathman, *Sir Walter Ralegh: A Study in Elizabethan Skepticism*; Christopher Hill, *Intellectual Origins of the English Revolution*; and Stephen Greenblatt, *Sir Walter Ralegh* (New Haven: Yale University Press, 1973).

7. See Louis Althusser, "Ideology," in *Literary Theory,* ed. Rivkin and Ryan, 294–304.

8. Robert Greene, *Green's Groats-worth of Wit* (London, 1596), E3.

9. Phillip Stubbes, *The Anatomie of Abuses* (New York: Da Capo Press, 1972), preface.

10. It is also significant that Greene compares Marlowe to one of his characters—Tamburlaine—who "dares God out of heaven." Critics (including myself) have found it hard not to see the transgressive Marlowe in his characters.

11. On homosexuality, Alan Bray writes, "It is apparent early on that there is no clear line to be drawn between contemporary attitudes to homosexuality and to debauchery as a whole." Thus homosexuality was often part of a "universal potential for disorder." See Alan Bray, *Homosexuality in Renaissance England* (London: Gay Men's Press, 1982), 31, 26.

12. Thomas Nashe, *Christs Tears Over Jerusalem*, in *Works of Thomas Nashe,* ed. C.B. McKerrow, 114.

13. After tackling Marlowe's atheism, Greene moves on to a different complaint about Shakespeare: "Yes, trust them not: for there is an upstart crow, beautified with our feathers . . ." The word "upstart" may refer to Shakespeare's humble origins and his lack of a university education. In purchasing a coat of arms for his father and becoming a gentleman himself, he demonstrated the fluidity of social order in England.

14. For discussion of Shakespeare's religion, see principally H. Mutschmann and K. Wentersdorf, *Shakespeare and Catholicism* (New York: Sheed and Ward, 1952); John Henry De Groot, *The Shakespeares and "The Old Faith"* (Freeport: Books for Libraries Press, 1968); Peter Milward, *Shakespeare's Religious Background* (Bloomington: Indiana University Press, 1973), and "Religion in Arden," *Shakespeare Survey* 54 (2001), 115–21; Christopher Devlin, *Hamlet's divinity, and other essays* (Carbondale: Southern Illinois University Press, 1964). Recent speculation on the topical basis of *The Phoenix and the Turtle* by Patrick Martin and John Finnes suggests that the mature Shakespeare retained Catholic sympathies. See *TLS* (April 18, 2003): 12–14. See also Jeffrey Knapp, "Jonson, Shakespeare, and the Religion of Players," in *Shakespeare Survey* 54 (2001).

15. The reverend Montague Summers took revenge on Scot for his anti-Catholicism in his introduction to the *The Discoverie of Witchcraft* (rpt. in the Dover edition). Summers's charge seems bizarre, as it defies three hundred years of intellectual transformation. He says that Scot took an "illogical" position on witchcraft and that "for caution's sake" he had covered "his atheism with the thinnest veneer, in fact he wholly and essentially denies the supernatural" (xxx). Another reason for the charge, he says, is Scot's position that "miracles have ceased."

16. Reprinted in G. B. Harrison, ed., *Elizabethan and Jacobean Quartos:*

King James the First Daemonologie and Newes from Scotland (New York: Barnes and Noble, 1966), xi.

17. Thomas Nashe, *Christ's Tears Over Jerusalem*, in *Works of Thomas Nashe*, ed. C. B. McKerrow, 115.

18. Cited in Shirley, *Thomas Harriot: A Biography*, 316.

19. "Sir Walter Raleigh's Sceptick," Sig. B1r.

20. For more on Pyrrhonism, relativism, and ethnography, see Hamlin, "On Continuities between Skepticism and Early Ethnography."

21. The devout poets Sir John Davies and Fulke Greville, who pursued Pyrrhonism, would have demonstrated to Nashe that following aspects of that philosophy did not necessarily destroy one's belief in God. These poets extracted what they wanted out of Pyrrhonism—skepticism toward sense-perception and reason—without accepting the relativist position on religion. For more on Davies and Greville, see Paul H. Kocher, *Science and Religion in Elizabethan England* (San Marino, Ca.: Huntington Library, 1953).

22. Kupperman, *Indians and the English*, 18.

23. Thomas Nashe, *The Unfortunate Traveller,* in *Works of Thomas Nashe,* ed. C. B. McKerrow, 294.

24. Gabriel Harvey, *Three Proper, and Wittie, Familiar Letters* (London, 1580).

Selected Bibliography

Agnew, Jean-Christophe. *Worlds Apart*. Cambridge: Cambridge University Press, 1986.

Agricola, Georg. *De Re Metallica*. Translated by Herbert Hoover. New York: Dover, 1950.

Albanese, Denise. *New Science, New World*. Durham, N.C.: Duke University Press, 1996.

Allen, Don Cameron. *Doubts Boundless Sea*. Baltimore: Johns Hopkins University Press, 1964.

Althusser, Louis. "Ideology and Ideological State Apparatuses." In *Literary Theory: An Anthology*, edited by Julie Rivkin and Michael Ryan. London: Blackwell, 1998.

Andrews, Kenneth. *Trade, Plunder, and Settlement: Maritime Enterprise and the Genesis of the British Empire, 1480–1630*. Cambridge: Cambridge University Press, 1984.

Anglo, Sydney. "Melancholia and Witchcraft: the debate between Wier, Bodin, and Scot." In *Folie et Déraison à la Renaissance*. Edition de L'université de Bruxelles, 1976.

———. "Reginald Scot's *Discoverie of Witchcraft*: Skepticism and Sadduceeism." In *The Damned art: Essays in the Literature of Witchcraft*, edited by Sydney Anglo. London: Routledge and Kagan Paul, 1977.

Appleby, Joyce. *Economic Thought and Ideology in Seventeenth-Century England* Princeton: Princeton University Press, 1978.

Archer, Ian. *The Pursuit of Stability: Social Relations in Elizabethan England*. Cambridge: Cambridge University Press, 1991.

Arendt, Hannah. *The Human Condition*. Chicago: University of Chicago Press, 1958.

Aristotle, *Politics*. Translated by H. Rackham. Cambridge: Harvard University Press, 1932.

Aubrey, John. *Brief Lives*. Edited by Andrew Clark. 2 volumes. Oxford: Clarendon Press, 1898.

Bakhtin, Mikhail. *Rabelais and His World*. Bloomington: Indiana University Press, 1984.

Barber, C. L. *Creating Elizabethan Tragedy: the Theater of Marlowe and Kyd*. Chicago: University of Chicago Press, 1988.

———. *Shakespeare's Festive Comedy*. Princeton: Princeton University Press, 1959.

Barlowe, Arthur. "The First Voyage to the Country Now Called Virginia" (1584). In Richard Hakluyt, *Voyages and Discoveries*. Edited by Jack Beeching. New York: Penguin Books, 1972.

Bartlett, Phyllis Brooks, ed. *The Poems of George Chapman*. New York: Russel and Russel, 1941.

Bawcutt, N. W. "Machiavelli and Marlowe's *The Jew of Malta*." In *Renaissance Drama*. Evanston: Northwestern University Press, 1970.

Bayne, C. G. "The Coronation of Queen Elizabeth." *EHR* 22 (1907): 650–73.

Beier, A. L. *Masterless Men*. London: Methuen, 1985.

Berger, Harry. "Text against Performance: The Gloucester Family Romance." In *Shakespeare's Rough Magic*, edited by Peter Erickson and Coppélia Kahn. Newark: University of Delaware Press, 1985.

Bertram, Benjamin. "New Reflections on the 'Revolutionary' Politics of Ernesto Laclau and Chantal Mouffe." *boundary 2* 22:3 (1995): 81–111.

Bevington, David, ed. *Doctor Faustus and Other Plays*. Oxford: Oxford University Press, 1995.

Biagioli, Mario. *Galileo Courtier*. Chicago: University of Chicago Press, 1993.

Bonnell, Victoria, and Lynn Hunt, eds. *Beyond the Cultural Turn*. Berkeley: University of California Press, 1999.

Boorsch, Susan. *Fireworks! Four Centuries of Pyrotechnics in Prints and Drawings* New York: Metropolitan Museum, 2000.

Booty, John, ed. *The Book of Common Prayer*. Charlottsville: Folger Shakespeare Library, 1976.

Bradbrook, Muriel. *The School of Night: a Study in the Literary Relationships of Sir Walter Ralegh*. Cambridge: Cambridge University Press, 1936.

Bradshaw, Graham. *Shakespeare's Scepticism*. Ithaca: Cornell University Press, 1987.

Branham, R. Bracht, and Marie-Odile Goulet-Cazé, eds. *The Cynics*. Berkeley: University of California Press, 1996.

Bray, Alan. *Homosexuality in Renaissance England*. London: Gay Men's Press, 1982.

Breight, Curtis C. *Surveillance, Militarism and Drama in the Elizabethan Era*. New York: St. Martin's Press, 1996.

Brereton, John. *A Briefe and True Relation of the Discoverie of the North Part of Virginia*. London, 1602.

Briggs, Robin. *Witches and Neighbors*. New York: Penguin, 1996.

Bristol, Michael. *Carnival and Theatre*. New York: Methuen, 1985.

Brodwin, Leonora Leet. "The Domestic Tragedy of Frank Thorney in *The Witch of Edmonton*." *SEL* 7 (1967): 311–28.

Brooke, John Hedley. *Science and Religion: Some Historical Perspectives*. Cambridge: Cambridge University Press, 1991.

Bruno, Giordano. *The Expulsion of the Triumphant Beast*. Translated by Arthur D. Imerti. Lincoln: University of Nebraska, 1964.

Buckley, George T. *Atheism in the English Renaissance*. New York: Russell and Russell, 1965.

Burke, Peter. *Popular Culture in Early Modern Europe*. New York: Harper Torchbooks, 1978.

Burton, Robert. *The Anatomy of Melancholy* (1621). Edited by Holbrook Jackson. New York: New York Review of Books, 2001.

Calvin, John. *Calvin: Institutes of the Christian Religion*. Latin original 1559. Translated by Ford Lewis Battles. Edited by John T. McNeill. Philadelphia: Westminster Press, 1960.

Capp, Bernard. *English Almanacs, 1500–1800*. Ithaca: Cornell University Press, 1979.

Carey, John, ed. *John Donne*. Oxford: Oxford University Press, 1990.

Carroll, William. "'The Base Shall Top Th' Legitimate': The Bedlam Beggar and the Role of Edgar in *King Lear*." *Shakespeare Quarterly* 38 (1987): 426–41.

Cavell, Stanley. *The Claim of Reason: Wittgenstein, Skepticism, Morality, and Tragedy*. Oxford: Oxford University Press, 1979.

———. *Disowning Knowledge*. Cambridge: Cambridge University Press, 1987.

Champion, Larry. "'Factions of Distempered Passions,': The Development of John Ford's Tragic Vision in *The Witch of Edmonton* and *The Lover's Melancholy*." In *"Concord in Discord": The Plays of John Ford, 1586–1986*. Edited by Donald K. Anderson, Jr. New York: AMS Press, 1986.

Clark, Stuart. *Thinking with Demons*. Oxford: Oxford University Press, 1999.

Clucas, Stephen. "Thomas Harriot and the Field of Knowledge in the English Renaissance." Oxford Harriot Lecture, 1994.

Clulee, Nicholas H. *John Dee's Natural Philosophy*. London: Routledge, 1988.

Cooper, J. P. *Land, Men, and Beliefs: Studies in Early-Modern History*. London: Hambledon Press, 1985.

Copenhaver, Brian, ed. *Hermetica*. Cambridge: Cambridge University Press, 1992.

Cormack, Leslie. *Charting an Empire*. Chicago: University of Chicago Press, 1997.

Corrigan, Philip and Derek Sayer. *The Great Arch: English State Formation as Cultural Revolution*. Oxford: Basil Blackwell, 1985.

Coudert, Allison P. "The Myth of the Improved Status of Protestant Women: The Case of the Witchcraze." In *The Politics of Gender in Early Modern Europe*. Edited by Jean R. Brink et. al. Kirksville: Sixteenth Century Journal Publishers, 1989.

Coward, Barry. *The Stuart Age*. London: Longman, 1994.

Cox, Catherine. "'An excellent thing in woman': Virgo and Viragos in *King Lear*," *Modern Philology* 96:2 (1998): 143–57.

Cox, Harvey. *The Feast of Fools*. New York: Harper and Row, 1969.

Cressy, David. *Bonfires and Bells*. Berkeley: University of California Press, 1989.

Cronon, William. *Changes in the Land: Indians, Colonists, and the Ecology of New England*. New York: Hill and Wang, 1983.

Danby, John. *Shakespeare's Doctrine of Nature*. London: Faber and Faber, 1961.

Daniel, Samuel. *Musophilus; containing a general defense of all learning*. West Lafayette: Purdue University Studies, 1965.

Davies, John. *The Scourge of Folly*. London, 1611.

Davis, Captain John. *The Seaman's Secrets*. London, 1595.

Davis, Natalie. *Society and Culture in Early Modern France*. Stanford: Stanford University Press, 1975.

Dawson, Anthony B. "Witchcraft/Bigamy: Cultural Conflict in *The Witch of Edmonton*" in *Renaissance Drama* 20 (1989).

De Grazia, Magreta, "The Ideology of Superfluous Things." In *Subject and Object in Renaissance Culture*. Edited by Magreta de Grazia et al. Cambridge: Cambridge University Press, 1996.

De Groot, John Henry. *The Shakespeares and "The Old Faith."* Freeport: Books for Libraries Press, 1968.

De Montaigne, Michel. *The Complete Essays of Montaigne*. Translated by Donald Frame. Stanford, Calif.: Stanford University Press, 1965.

Dee, John. *General and Rare Memorials Pertaining to the Perfect Arte of Navigation*. London, 1577. Facsimile Reprint. New York: Da Capo Press, 1968.

———. "To the King's most excellent Majestie." London, 1604.

Defert, Daniel. "The Collection of the World: Accounts of Voyages From the Sixteenth to the Eighteenth Centuries." *Dialectical Anthropology* 7:1 (1982).

Dekker, Thomas. *The Wonderful Yeare*. London, 1603.

Dekker, Thomas, John Ford, and William Rowley. *The Witch of Edmonton*. Edited by Peter Corbin and Douglas Sedge. Manchester: Manchester University Press, 1999.

Delany, Paul. "King Lear and the Decline of Feudalism." *PMLA* 92 (1977): 429–40.

Delumeau, Jean. *Catholicism Between Luther and Voltaire*. Translated by Jeremy Moiser. London: Westminster Press, 1977.

Derrida, Jacques. *Writing and Difference*. Translated by Alan Bass. Chicago: University of Chicago Press, 1978.

Devlin, Christopher. *Hamlet's divinity, and other essays*. Carbondale: Southern Illinois University Press, 1964.

Dillenberger, John, ed. *Martin Luther: Selections from His Writings*. New York: Anchor Press, 1961.

Dolan, Frances. *Dangerous Familiars*. Ithaca: Cornell University Press, 1994.

———. Introduction to *The Taming of the Shrew*, by William Shakespeare. Boston: Bedford Books, 1992.

Dollimore, Jonathan. *Radical Tragedy*. Durham, N.C.: Duke University Press, 1993.

Donaldson, Ian, ed. *Ben Jonson*. Oxford: Oxford University Press, 1985.

Donawerth, Jane. "Diogenes the Cynic and Lear's Definition of Man, *King Lear* III.iv.101–109." *ELN* 15 (1977).

Douglas, Mary. "The social preconditions of radical scepticism." In *Power, Action and Belief*. Edited by John Law. London: Routledge, 1986.

Duffy, Eamon. *The Stripping of the Altars: Traditional Religion in England 1400–1580*. New Haven: Yale University Press, 1992.

Dutton, Richard. *Mastering the Revels*. Iowa City: University of Iowa Press, 1991.

Easlea, Brian. *Witch-Hunting, Magic, and the New Philosophy: An Introduction to the Debates of the Scientific Revolution, 1450–1750*. Sussex: Harvester Press, 1980.

Ehrenreich, Barbara and Deirdre English. *For Her Own Good: 50 Years of the Expert's Advice to Women*. New York: Vintage Books, 1978.

Elmer, Peter. "Toward a Politics of Witchcraft in Early Modern England." In *Languages of Witchcraft*. Edited by Stuart Clark. New York: St. Martin's Press, 2001.

Elton, William R. *King Lear and the Gods*. Lexington: University Press of Kentucky, 1988.

Empiricus, Sextus. *Outlines of Scepticism*. Edited by Julia Annas and Jonathan Barnes Cambridge: Cambridge University Press, 1994.

Empson, William. *Faustus and the Censor*. Oxford: Basil Blackwell, 1987.

Engel, Lars. *Shakespearean Pragmatism*. Chicago: University of Chicago Press, 1993.

"An Exhortation against the Fear of Death," in *Certain Sermons or Homilies*. London, 1676.

Felsenstein, Frank. *Anti-Semitic Stereotypes*. Baltimore: Johns Hopkins University Press, 1995.

Fletcher, Anthony and John Stevenson. *Order and Disorder in Early Modern England* Cambridge: Cambridge University Press, 1985.

Florio, John. *The Essays of Montaigne Done into English*. London: D. Nutt, 1892–93.

Fradenburg, Louise, and Carla Freccero, eds. *Premodern Sexualities*. New York: Routledge, 1996.

French, Peter. *John Dee: the World of an Elizabethan Magus*. New York: Dorset Press, 1972.

G., C. "The minte of deformities." London, 1611.

Garber, Marjorie. "Out of Joint." In *The Body in Parts: Fantasies of Corporeality in Early Modern Europe*. Edited by David Hillman and Carla Mazzio. New York: Routledge, 1997.

Gatti, Hillary. "The Natural Philosophy of Thomas Harriot." Oxford: Lecture at Oriel College, 1993.

———. *The Renaissance Drama of Knowledge*. London: Routledge, 1989.

The Geneva Bible (1560). Facsimile reprint. Madison: University of Wisconsin Press, 1969.

Gibson, Marion. *Early Modern Witches*. London: Routledge, 2000.

Gifford, George. *A Dialogue Concerning Witches and Witchcraftes*. London, 1583.

———. *A Discourse of the subtill Practises of Devilles by Witches*. London, 1587.

Gilbert, Sir Humphrey. "Queen Elizabeth's Academy." London: Early English Text Society, 1869.

Goldberg, Jonathan. "Perspectives: Dover Cliff and Representation." In *Shakespeare and Deconstruction*, edited by Atkins and Bergeron. New York: Peter Lang, 1991.

———. "Sodomy and Society: The Case of Christopher Marlowe." In *Staging the Renaissance*. Edited by David Scott Kastan and Peter Stallybrass. New York: Routledge, 1991.

Goodcole, Henry. "The Wonderful Discoverie of Elizabeth Sawyer a Witch . . ." London, 1621.

Greenblatt, Stephen. *Hamlet in Purgatory*. Princeton: Princeton University Press, 2001.

———. *Learning to Curse*. New York: Routledge, 1990.

———. *Renaissance Self-Fashioning*. Berkeley: University of California Press, 1980.

———. *Shakespearean Negotiations*. Berkeley: University of California Press, 1988.

———. *Sir Walter Ralegh*. New Haven: Yale University Press, 1973.

Greene, Robert. *Green's Groats-worth of Wit*. London, 1596.

Grinnel, Richard. "Naming and Social Disintegration in *The Witch of Edmonton*." *Essays in Theatre/Études théatrales* 16:2 (1998).

Hadfield, Andrew. "Writing the 'New World': More 'Invisible Bullets'" *Literature and History* 2, second series (1991): 3–19.

Haigh, Christopher, ed. *The Reign of Elizabeth I*. Athens: University of Georgia Press, 1985.

Halliwell, James Orchard. *A Collection of Letters*. London: Historical Society, 1965.

Halpern, Richard. *The Poetics of Primitive Accumulation*. Ithaca: Cornell University Press, 1991.

Hamlin, William H. "Casting Doubt in Marlowe's *Doctor Faustus*." *SEL* 41:2 (2001).

———. "On Continuities between Skepticism and Early Ethnography; Or, Montaigne's Providential Diversity." *Sixteenth-Century Journal* 31:2 (2000):361–79.

———. *The Image of America in Montaigne, Spenser, and Shakespeare: Renaissance Ethnography and Literary Reflection*. New York: St. Martin's Press, 1995.

———. "A Lost Translation Found? An Edition of The Sceptick (c.1590)." *ELR* 31:1 (2001): 34–51.

———. "Skepticism in Shakespeare's England." *The Shakespearean International Yearbook* 2 (1999): 290–304.

Hammer, Paul. "A Reckoning Reframed: the 'Murder' of Christopher Marlowe Revisited."*ELR* 26:2 (1996).

Hamor, Ralph. *A True Discourse of the Present Estate of Virginia*. London, 1615.

Harley, David. "Historians as Demonologists: The Myth of the Midwife-Witch." *Social History of Medicine* 3 (1990): 1–26.

Harriot, Thomas. *A Briefe and True Report of the New Found Land of Virginia*. Facsimile of De Bry's 1590 edition. New York: Dover, 1972.

Harris, Timothy, ed. *Popular Culture in England*. New York: St. Martin's Press, 1995.

Harrison, G. B. ed. *Elizabethan and Jacobean Quartos: King James the First Daemonologie and Newes from Scotland*. New York: Barnes and Noble, 1966.

Harrison, William. *A Description of England*. London, 1577.

———, ed. *Willobie His Avisa*. New York: Barnes and Noble, 1966.

Harvey, Gabriel. *Three Proper, and Wittie, Familiar Letters*. London, 1580.

Haydn, Hiram. *The Counter-Renaissance*. New York: Grove Press, 1950.

Herman, Peter. "He Said What?!?': Misdeeming Gorboduc; or, Problematizing Form, Service, and Certainty." *Exemplaria* 13:1 (2001): 287–321.

Hill, Christopher. *The Century of Revolution 1603–1714*. Edinburgh: Thomas Nelson and Sons, 1961.

———. *Change and Continuity in 17th-Century England*. New Haven: Yale University Press, 1991.

———. *Intellectual Origins of the English Revolution*. Oxford: Clarendon Press, 1980.

Hirschman, Albert O. *The Passions and the Interests*. Princeton: Princeton University Press, 1977.

Hodge, Bob. "Marlowe, Marx and Machiavelli: Reading into the Past." In *Literature, Language and Society in England*, edited by David Aers et al. Dublin: Gill and Macmillan, 1981.

Hodgen, Margaret. *Early Anthropology in the Sixteenth and Seventeenth Centuries* Philadelphia: University of Pennsylvania Press, 1964.

Hopkins, Lisa. *Marlowe: A Literary Life*. New York: Palgrave, 2000.

Howard, Jean. *The Stage and Social Struggle in Early Modern England*. London: Routledge, 1994.

Hunt, Lynn, ed. *The New Cultural History*. Berkeley: University of California Press, 1989.

Hunter, Michael and David Wootton. *Atheism from the Reformation to the Enlightenment*. Oxford: Clarendon Press, 1992.

Jacquot, Jean. "Harriot, Hill, Warner and the New Philosophy." In *Thomas*

Harriot: Renaissance Scientist. Edited by John W. Shirley. Oxford: Clarendon Press, 1974.

Jardine, Lisa. "Ladies' Trials: Women and the Law in Three Plays of John Ford." *Cahiers Elisabéthains* 56 (1999):

Jay, Martin. *Downcast Eyes*. Berkeley: University of California Press, 1993.

Jones, Norman. *God and the Moneylenders: Usury and Law in Early Modern England* London: Basil Blackwell, 1989.

Kahn, Victoria. *Rhetoric, Prudence, and Skepticism in the Renaissance*. Ithaca: Cornell University Press, 1985.

Kavanagh, James H. "Shakespeare in Ideology." In *Alternative Shakespeares*. Edited by John Drakakis. London: Methuen, 1985.

Kelly, J. Thomas. *Thorns on the Tudor Rose*. Jackson: University of Mississippi Press, 1977.

Kendall, Roy. "Richard Baines and Christopher Marlowe's Milieu." *ELR* 24:3 (autumn 1994): 507–52.

Kinney, Arthur, ed. *Elizabethan Backgrounds*. Connecticut: Archon Books, 1975.

———, ed. *Hamlet: New Critical Essays*. New York: Routledge, 2002.

Klein, Joan Larsen, ed. *Daughters, Wives, and Widows: Writings by Men about Women and Marriage in England, 1500–1640*. Urbana: University of Illinois Press, 1992.

Knapp, Jeffrey. *An Empire Nowhere*. Berkeley: University of California Press, 1992.

———. "Jonson, Shakespeare, and the Religion of Players." *Shakespeare Survey* 54 (2001).

Knights, L. C. *Drama and Society in the Age of Jonson*. New York: Norton, 1937.

Kocher, Paul. *Christopher Marlowe: A Study of his Thought, Learning, and Character*. New York: Russell and Russell, 1962.

———. *Science and Religion in Elizabethan England*. San Marino, Calif.: Huntington Library, 1953.

Kott, Jan. *Shakespeare Our Contemporary*. Translated by Boleslaw Taborski. New York: Anchor Books, 1966.

Kramer, Heinrich and James Sprenger. *The Malleus Maleficarum* (1485). Translated by Montague Summers. New York: Dover, 1971.

Kupperman, Karen Ordahl, *Indians & English: Facing Off in Early America*. Ithaca: Cornell University Press, 2000.

Kuriyama, Constance. *Christopher Marlowe: A Renaissance Life*. Ithaca: Cornell University Press, 2002.

Lacan, Jacques. "The Mirror Stage as Formative of the Function of the I as Revealed in Psychoanlaytic Experience." In *Literary Theory: An Anthology*. Edited by Julie Rivkin and Michael Ryan. London: Blackwell, 1998.

Lacapra, Dominick. *Rethinking Intellectual History*. Ithaca: Cornell University Press, 1983.

Laclau, Ernesto. *New Reflections on the Revolution of Our Time.* London: Verso, 1990.

Laclau, Ernesto and Chantal Mouffe. *Hegemony and Socialist Strategy.* London: Verso, 1985.

Laertius, Diogenes. *Lives of Eminent Philosophers.*Volume 2. Translated by R. D. Hicks, Loeb Classical Library. Cambridge: Harvard University Press, 1925.

Landesman, Charles. *Skepticism: the Central Issues.* Oxford: Blackwell, 2002.

Laneham, Robert. *A Letter Describing the Entertainment of the Queen at Kenilworth* (1575), reprinted in *A Midsummer Night's Dream* by William Shakespeare. Edited by Gail Kern Paster and Skiles Howard. Boston: Bedford, 1999.

Larner, Christina. *Witchcraft and Religion: The Politics of Popular Belief.* New York: Basil Blackwell, 1984.

Laroque, Francois. *Shakespeare's Festive World.* Translated by Janet Lloyd. Cambridge:Cambridge University Press, 1991.

Latham, Agnes H., ed. *Sir Walter Ralegh: Selected Prose and Poetry.* London: Athlone Press, 1965.

Levin, Harry. *The Overreacher: A Study of Christopher Marlowe.* Boston: Beacon Press, 1964.

Lyly, John. *Midas.* London, 1632.

MacEachern, Claire. "Figures of Fidelity: Believing in *King Lear.*" *Modern Philology* 98:2 (2000): 211–30.

MacFarland, Alan. *Witchcraft in Tudor and Stuart England.* London: Routledge and Kegan Paul, 1970.

Macfarlane, Alan. *The Origins of English Individualism.* New York: Cambridge University Press, 1978.

Machiavelli, Niccolo. *The Prince and the Discourses.* New York: Modern Library, 1950.

Macpherson, C. B. *The Political Theory of Possessive Individualism.* Oxford: Oxford University Press, 1962.

Malynes, Gerard de, *Saint George for England.* London, 1601.

Marcus, Leah. *Unediting the Renaissance.* London: Routledge, 1996.

Marcus, Leah, et al. *Elizabeth I: Collected Works.* Chicago: University of Chicago Press, 2000.

Marlowe, Christopher. *The Complete Plays.* Edited by J. B. Steane. London: Penguin, 1969.

———. *Dr. Faustus.* Edited by Roma Gill. London: A&C Black, 1989.

———. *The Jew of Malta.* Edited by James R. Siemon. London: A&C Black, 1994.

Martyr, Peter. *De Orbe Novo: the Eight Decades of Peter Martyr D'Anghera.* Translated by Francis MacNutt. 2 Volumes. New York: Putnam and Sons, 1912.

Maus, Katherine. "Proof and Consequences: Inwardness and its Exposure in the English Renaissance." In *Materialist Shakespeare*, edited by Ivo Kamps. London: Verso, 1995.

McAlindon, Tom. "Testing the New Historicism: 'Invisible Bullets' Reconsidered." *SP* 92:4 (fall 1995): 411–38.

McClusky, Katherine. *Dekker and Heywood*. New York: St. Martin's Press, 1994.

McEachern, Claire and Deborah Shugar. *Religion and Culture in Renaissance England*. Cambridge: Cambridge University Press, 1997.

McKerrow, Ronald, ed. *The Works of Thomas Nashe*. 4 Volumes. New York: Barnes and Noble, 1966.

McLeod, Randal. "Revision, adaptation, and the fool in *King Lear*." In *The Division of the Kingdoms: Shakespeare's Two Versions of King Lear*, edited by Gary Taylor and Michael Warren. New York: Oxford University Press, 1983.

McLusky, Kathleen. *Renaissance Dramatists*. New York: Harvester Wheatsheaf, 1989.

Merkel, Ingrid and Allen G. Debus, eds. *Hermeticism in the Renaissance*. Washington: Folger Books, 1988.

Miller, Shannon. *Invested with Meaning*. Philadelphia: University of Pennsylvania Press, 1998.

Milward, Peter. "Religion in Arden." *Shakespeare Survey* 54 (2001), 115–21.

———. *Shakespeare's Religious Background*. Bloomington: Indiana University Press, 1973.

Montrose, Louis. *The Purpose of Playing*. Chicago: University of Chicago Press, 1996.

———. "The Work of Gender in the Discourse of Discoverie." *Representations* 33 (1991): 1–41.

Mora, George, MD, ed. *De praestigiis daemonum* in*Witches, Devils, and Doctors in the Renaissance: Johann Weyer, De Praestigiis daemonum*. Binghamton, N.Y.: Medieval and Renaissance Texts and Studies, 1991.

Moretti, Franco. *Signs Taken for Wonders*. London: Verso, 1983.

Muchembled, Robert. "Satanic Myths and Cultural Reality." In *Early Modern European Witchcraft*, edited by Bengt Ankarloo and Gustav Henningsen. Oxford: Clarendon Press, 1990.

Muir, Kenneth. "*Timon of Athens* and the Cash-Nexus," *Modern Quarterly Miscellany* 1:1 (1947): 57–76.

Muldrew, Craig. "The ethics of credit and community relations." *Social History* 18:2 (1993): 163–83.

Mutschmann, H., and K. Wentersdorf. *Shakespeare and Catholicism*. New York: Sheed and Ward, 1952.

Neill, Michael. *Issues of Death*. Oxford: Clarendon Press, 1993.

Nenna, Giovanni Batista. *Nennio or A Treatise of Nobility*. Translated by William Jones (1595). Facsimile Edition. Jerusalem: Israel Universities Press, 1967. New Viewpoints, 1976.

Nicholl, Charles. *The Reckoning*. Chicago: University of Chicago Press, 1992.

Nussbaum, Martha. *The Therapy of Desire*. Princeton: Princeton University Press, 1994.

———. "Valuing Values: A Case for Reasoned Commitment." *Yale Journal of Law & the Humanities* 6:197–217.

Orgel, Stephen. "Shakespeare imagines a theater." In *Shakespeare, Man of the Theater*. Edited by Kenneth Muir, et al. Newark: University of Delaware Press, 1983.

Palmer, D. J. "Marlowe's Naturalism." In *Christopher Marlowe: Mermaid Critical Commentaries*. Edited by Brian Morris. New York: Norton, 1968.

Pascal, Blaise. *Pensées*. Translated by Honor Levi. Oxford: Oxford University Press, 1995.

Patterson, Annabel. *Shakespeare and the Popular Voice*. Oxford: Basil Blackwell, 1989.

Peetz, William. "The Problem of the Fetish I." *R.E.S.* 9 (1983).

Pettet, E. C. "*Timon of Athens*: The Disruption of Feudal Morality." *R.E.S.* 23:92 (1947).

Plowden, Alison. *The Elizabethan Secret Service*. New York: St. Martin's Press, 1991.

Popkin, Richard. *The History of Skepticism*. Berkeley: University of California Press, 1979.

Popkin, Richard and Avrum Stroll, *Skeptical Philosophy for Everyone*. Amherst, Mass.: Prometheus Books, 2002.

Purkiss, Diane. *The Witch in History*. New York: Routledge, 1996.

Quinn, D. B. *The Roanoke Voyages*. 2 volumes. London: Hakluyt Society, 1955.

Quinn, David B. and John W. Shirley, "A Contemporary List of Harriot References," *Renaissance Quarterly* 22:1 (1969): 9–27.

Quinn, Michael. "The Freedom of Tamburlaine." *MLQ* 21 (1960): 315–20.

Raab, Felix. *The English Face of Machiavelli*. London: Routledge, 1964.

Read, Conyers. *Sir Francis Walsingham*. Cambridge: Harvard University Press, 1925.

Ralegh, Sir Walter. *The Discoverie of the Large, Rich, and Beautiful Empire of Guiana*. In *The Principal Navigations*, edited by Richard Hakluyt. 12 volumes. Glasgow, J. Maclehose and Sons, 1903–5.

———. "Sir Walter Raleigh's Sceptick." London: W. Bentley, 1651.

Richter, Jean Paul, ed. *The Notebooks of Leonardo Da Vinci*. 2 volumes. New York: Dover Publications, 1970.

Riggs, David. "Marlowe's Quarrel with God." In *Marlowe, History, and Sexuality*. Edited by Paul Whitfield White. New York: AMS Press, 1998.

Rosen, Barbara, ed.*Witchcraft in England: 1558–1618*. Amherst: University of Massachusetts Press, 1969.

Rosen, Edward. "Harriot's Science: The Intellectual Background." In *Thomas Harriot, Renaissance Scientist*. Edited by John Shirley. Oxford: Clarendon Press, 1974.

Rosier, James. *A True Relation of the most prosperous voyage made this present yeere 1605*. London, 1605.

Rubin, Miri. *Corpus Christi*. Cambridge, Mass.: Cambridge University Press, 1991.

Scot, Reginald. "Discourse on Devils and Spirits." In *The Discoverie of Witchcraft*. Edited by Brinsely Nicholson. New Jersey: Roman and Littlefield, 1973.

———. *The Discoverie of Witchcraft* (1584). Edited by Rev. Montague Summers. New York: Dover Books, 1972.

Shakespeare, William. *The Complete Works*. Edited by Stanley Wells, et al. Oxford: Clarendon, 1988.

———. *Hamlet*. Edited by Harold Jenkins. London: Routledge, 1982.

———. *Henry IV Part 1*. Edited by David Bevington. Oxford: Oxford University Press, 1987.

———. *King Lear*. Edited by R. A. Foakes. London: Routledge, 1997.

———. *The Tempest*. Edited by Stephen Orgel. Oxford: Oxford University Press, 1987.

———. *Timon of Athens*. Edited by H. J. Oliver. London: Routledge,1959.

Sheehan, Bernard. *Savagism and Civility*. Cambridge, Mass.: Cambridge University Press, 1980.

Shelton, Anthony Allen. "Cabinets of Transgression: Renaissance Collections and the Incorporation of the New World." In *The Cultures of Collecting*. Edited by John Elsner and Roger Cardinal. Cambridge: Harvard University Press, 1994.

Sherman, William. *John Dee*. Amherst: University of Massachusetts Press, 1995.

Shirley, John W., *Thomas Harriot: A Biography*. Oxford: Clarendon Press, 1983.

———, ed. *Thomas Harriot: Renaissance Scientist*. Oxford: Clarendon Press, 1974.

Shugar, Deborah. *Habits of Thought in the English Renaissance*. Berkeley: University of California Press, 1990.

Sinfield, Alan. *Faultlines*. Berkeley: University of California Press, 1992.

Slack, Paul. *The English Poor Law, 1531–1782*. Cambridge: Cambridge University Press, 1995.

Sloterdijk, Peter. *Critique of Cynical Reason*. Minneapolis: University of Minnesota Press, 1987.

Smith, Bruce R., "Mouthpieces: Native American Voices in Thomas Harriot's True and Brief Report (sic) of . . . Virginia, Gaspar Pérez de Villagra's Historia de la Nuevo México, and John Smith's General History of Virginia." *New Literary History* 32:3 (2001): 501–17.

Smith, Lacey Baldwin. *Treason in Tudor England*. London: Jonathan Cape, 1986.

Smith, Sir Thomas. *De Republica Anglorum* (1583). Edited by Mary Dewar. Cambridge: Cambridge University Press, 1982.

Soellner, Rolf. *Timon of Athens*. Columbus: Ohio State University Press, 1979.

Sokol, B. J. "The Problem of Assessing Thomas Harriot's *A briefe and true report* of his Discoveries in North America." *Annals of Science* 51 (1994): 1–16.

Solomon, Julie. "'To Know, To Fly, To Conjure': Situating Baconian Science at the Juncture of Early Modern Modes of Reading." *Renaissance Quarterly* 44:3 (1991):

Sposky, Ellen. *Satisfying Skepticism*. Aldershot: Ashgate, 2001.

Spurgeon, Caroline. *Shakespeare's Imagery and What It Tells Us*. Cambridge: At the University Press, 1935.

Stevenson, Laura. *Praise and Paradox: Merchants and Craftsmen in Elizabethan Popular Literature*. Cambridge: Cambridge University Press, 1984.

Stone, Lawrence. *The Causes of the English Revolution 1529–1642*. New York: Harper and Row, 1972.

———. *The Family, Sex, and Marriage*. New York: Harper Torchbooks, 1977.

Strathmann, Ernest. "John Dee as Ralegh's 'Conjuror.'" *Huntington Library Quarterly* 10 (1947): 365–72.

———. *Sir Walter Ralegh. A Study in Elizabethan Skepticism*. New York: Octagon Books, 1951.

———. "Social Mobility in England, 1500–1700." In *Seventeenth-Century England: Society in the Age of Revolution*. Edited by Paul Seaver. New York: New Viewpoints, 1976.

Strauss, Gerald. "How to read a Volksbuch: The Faust Book of 1587." In *Faust through Four Centuries*. Tübingen: Max Niemeyer Verlag, 1989.

Strout, Dr. E. "The very first maps and drawings of the moon." *Journal of the British Astronomical Association* 75 (1965).

Stubbes, Phillip. *The Anatomie of Abuses* (1583). Facsimile edition. New York: Da Capo Press, 1972.

Suster, Gerald, ed. *John Dee: Essential Readings*. Wellington: Crucible, 1986.

Taylor, George Coffin. *Shakspere's Debt to Montaigne*. Cambridge, Mass.: Harvard University Press, 1925.

Thomas, Keith. *Religion and the Decline of Magic*. New York: Charles Scribner's Sons, 1971.

Toulmin, Stephen. *Cosmopolis*. Chicago: University of Chicago Press, 1990.

Tucker, Robert C., ed. *The Karl Marx Reader*. New York: Norton, 1978.

Turner, John. "The Tragic Romances of Feudalism." In *Shakespeare: The Play of History*. Iowa City: University of Iowa Press, 1988.

Urkowitz, Steven. Shakespeare's Revision of *King Lear*. Princeton: Princeton University Press, 1980.

Veeser, H. Aram, ed. *The New Historicism*. New York: Routledge, 1989.

Vickers, Brian, ed. *Francis Bacon*. Oxford: Oxford University Press, 1996.

———, ed. *Occult & Scientific Mentalities in the Renaissance*. Cambridge: Cambridge University Press, 1984.

Wayne, Don E. "Drama and Society in the Age of Jonson: Shifting Grounds of Authority and Judgment in Three Major Comedies." *Renaissance Drama*. Evanston, Ill.: Northwestern University Press and The Newberry Library for Renaissance Studies, 1990.

———. *Penshurst: The Semiotics of Place and the Poetics of History*. Madison: University of Wisconsin Press, 1984.

Weimann, Robert. *Authority and Representation in Early Modern Discourse*. Baltimore: Johns Hopkins University Press, 1996.

———. *Author's Pen and Actor's Voice: Playing and Writing in Shakespeare's Theatre*. Cambridge: Cambridge University Press, 2000.

———. *Shakespeare and the Popular Tradition*. Baltimore: Johns Hopkins University Press, 1978.

West, Robert. *Reginald Scot and Renaissance Writings on Witchcraft*. Boston: Twayne, 1984.

Whitaker, Alexander. *Good News from Virginia*. London, 1612.

Wilson, Stephen. *The Magical Universe: Everyday Ritual and Magic in Pre-Modern Europe*. London: Hambledon and London, 2000.

Wilson, Thomas. *A Discourse Upon Usury*. Edited by R. H. Tawney. London: G. Bell and Sons, 1925.

Wittgenstein, *Philosophical Investigations*. Translated by G. E. M. Anscombe. New York: MacMillan, 1953.

Wood, David, and Robert Bernasconi, eds. *Derrida and Différance* (Evanston, Ill.: Northwestern University Press, 1988.

Wooton, David, "Reginald Scot, Abraham Fleming/ the Family of Love." In *Languages of Witchcraft*, edited by Stuart Clark. New York: St. Martin's Press, 2001.

Wren, Celia. "A 400-Year-Old Bad Boy Stages a Comeback," *New York Times*, 21 January 2001.

Wrightson, Keith. *English Society 1580–1680*. London: Hutchinson, 1982.

Yates, Frances. *Giordano Bruno and the Hermetic Tradition*. Chicago: University of Chicago Press, 1964.

———. *Theatre of the World*. Chicago: University of Chicago Press, 1969.

———. *The Occult Philosophy in the Elizabethan Age*. London: Routledge, 1979.

Zetterberg, J. Peter. "The Mistaking of 'the Mathematicks' for Magic in Tudor and Stuart England." *Sixteenth Century Journal* XI, No.1 (1980):83–97.

Zizek, Slavoj. *The Sublime Object of Ideology*. London: Verso, 1989.

INDEX

219